Praise for *The Making of Barack Obama* . . .

"With its timely and engaging focus on the rhetorical performances of Barack Obama, this collection makes a significant contribution to the study of contemporary public rhetoric and political discourse. The contributors analyze a variety of political speeches—on topics ranging from racial politics, to the U.S. military's use of torture, to conflict in the Middle East—and critically examine the rhetorical strategies employed by Obama to negotiate diverse national and international audiences, to navigate political and material constraints, and to construct and reinvent his personal and political identity. The book invites a deeper exploration into Obama's use of persuasion, and with its analysis of how his performances before multiple and composite audiences are both flawless and flawed, enriches our understanding of how rhetorical performances function as sites for intervention and political agency and how rhetorical actions both enable and limit social change."

—*Mary Jo Reiff, Associate Professor of English*
University of Kansas

"From the inspiring slogans and speeches of his campaign to the eloquent successes and failures of his presidency, Barack Obama has been extravagantly praised and sarcastically criticized for the distinctive power of his rhetoric. The essays in this collection persuasively analyze that rhetoric in all its specific tactics and general strategies, in its idealist yearnings and its pragmatic compromises, in its ambitious strivings and its political obstacles."

—*Steven Mailloux, President's Professor of Rhetoric,*
Loyola Marymount University

"By confronting topics often avoided in politically correct discourse—including religious identity, racial belonging and the cultural politics of difference—THE MAKING OF BARACK OBAMA doesn't hesitate to engage divisive and difficult issues; producing some of the most challenging, insightful and provocative perspectives to date."

—*Rhea Lathan, Assistant Professor of English,*
Florida State University

THE MAKING
OF BARACK OBAMA

The Politics of Persuasion

Edited by
Matthew Abraham and Erec Smith

For Judy!
To my politically astute Aunt!
Love, Matthew

Parlor Press
Anderson, South Carolina
www.parlorpress.com

Parlor Press LLC, Anderson, South Carolina, USA

SAN: 254-8879

Library of Congress Cataloging-in-Publication Data

The making of Barack Obama : the politics of persuasion / edited by Matthew
Abraham and Erec Smith.
    pages cm
  Includes bibliographical references and index.
    ISBN 978-1-60235-467-8 (pbk. : alk. paper) -- ISBN 978-1-60235-468-5
(hardcover : alk. paper) -- ISBN 978-1-60235-469-2 (adobe ebook) -- ISBN 978-
1-60235-470-8 (epub) -- ISBN 978-1-60235-471-5 (kindle) -- ISBN 978-1-60235-
472-2 (ibook)
  1. Obama, Barack--Oratory. 2. Obama, Barack--Language. 3. Rhetoric--Political
aspects--United States--History--21st century. 4. Communication in politics--United
States--History--21st century. 5. United States--Politics and government--2009- I.
Abraham, Matthew, 1972-
  E908.3.M35 2013
  973.932092--dc23

                        2013031674

Front cover image: President Barack Obama and Jon Favreau, head speechwriter,
edit a speech on health care in the Oval Office, Sept. 9, 2009, in preparation for
the president's address to a joint session of Congress. (Official White House Photo
by Pete Souza). Back cover image: The President delivers remarks on Afghanistan
before cadets at West Point (Dec. 1, 2009). (Official White House photo by Pete
Souza)

Cover design by David Blakesley
Printed on acid-free paper.

1 2 3 4 5

Parlor Press, LLC is an independent publisher of scholarly and trade titles in print and
multimedia formats. This book is available in paper, hardcover, and Adobe eBook
formats from Parlor Press on the World Wide Web at http://www.parlorpress.com or
through online and brick-and-mortar bookstores. For submission information or to
find out about Parlor Press publications, write to Parlor Press, 3015 Brackenberry
Drive, Anderson, SC 29621, or e-mail editor@parlorpress.com.

CONTENTS

Acknowledgments

The editors wish to acknowledge the expert help of Professor Richard Marback in preparing the manuscript for publication. Rick did a good bit of the heavy lifting for the collection, without which the project could not have been brought to completion. The editors also wish to thank Professor David Blakesley at Parlor Press for his early interest in this project, as well as his commitment to seeing the manuscript come into print. We would also like to thank Amy Hubbard in DePaul University's Department of Writing, Rhetoric, and Discourse, who provided invaluable support in copyediting the collection. We are also indebted to the anonymous reviewer whose suggestions for revision proved to be invaluable. Finally, Matthew wishes to acknowledge the generous support of a 2012 DePaul University Liberal Arts and Social Sciences summer research grant, as it gave the him some necessary release time to place the final touches on the collection.

THE MAKING
OF BARACK OBAMA

Editors' Introduction

Matthew Abraham and Erec Smith

Barack Obama's rise to political superstardom—from his beginnings as a state representative, to his time as an Illinois junior senator, to his capturing the Democratic nomination for president in 2008, and to his eventual election to the presidency—represents a testament to the power of persuasion, just as much as it is a testament to the power of political identification and solidarity. In an attempt to examine Obama's uncanny power to persuade American citizens to locate commonalities across polarizing lines of political identification, this collection analyzes several of Obama's speeches through various lenses, working through the significance of Obama's embodiment as the first African American president of the United States. Obama's re-election to a second term on November 7, 2012 affirmed Obama's rhetorical brilliance and the responsiveness of his campaign to our historical moment.

Everyone remembers how Obama surmounted numerous challenges to the viability of his presidential candidacy in the 2008 election, demonstrating time and again how gifted he is in crafting the spoken word within difficult rhetorical situations. From his 2004 speech at the Democratic National Convention, to his handling of the Jeremiah Wright controversy in a March 2008 speech in Philadelphia, to his June 2009 "New Beginning" speech in Cairo, Obama has repeatedly proven that he can deliver a deft and extremely persuasive message within difficult circumstances, and in front of complex audiences. *The Making of Barack Obama: The Politics of Persuasion* examines the implications of Obama's persuasive capabilities, as these are grounded in Obama's subject position. Obama seems to have mastered Burkean concepts such as identification and consubstantiality, as well as Perelman and Olbrecht-Tyteca's conception of adherence, perhaps without knowing (or even needing to know) anything about these rhetorical theorists and their ground-breaking contributions. In this sense, Obama is a rhetorician. Even though he does not possess a rhetorician's theoretical grounding, his rhetorical and diplomatic skills have been described as "natural," "instinctual," and "innate."

As a bi-racial man of Kenyan descent, Obama strikes an interesting pose in comparison to past U.S. presidents. Undoubtedly, Obama capitalized on this shared contrast during the 2008 and 2012 elections. His presidency signals to the world that the U.S. has perhaps moved past its divisive history of racial segregation by embracing Martin Luther King's dream, proving that African Americans can be judged not by the color of their skin, but instead by the content of their character. The prospect that Obama represents the fulfillment of all the civil rights movement promised energizes young Americans as they seek to move beyond the crippling cynicism of Generation X. Despite this promise and potential for improved race relations, questions surrounded Obama as an African American presidential candidate because he was not part of the civil rights generation. In addition, some question his place in, and commitment to, the black community because of his father's Kenyan ancestry and his white mother.[1]

Contributors to this edited collection analyze a range of Obama's rhetorical performances, between 2008 and 2012, examining the specific techniques Obama employed to navigate difficult political terrain. From tackling controversial topics, such as how racial politics plays out and is represented in the public sphere, to addressing the U.S. military's use of torture at Guantanamo Bay and the political dynamics of Israeli-Palestinian conflicts, Obama has not hesitated to engage burning, divisive, and difficult issues. Obama's ability to use rhetoric in engaging and responding to these issues remains unmatched. Just when it seems a specifically divisive issue has been exhausted, or repeatedly returns to ubiquitous commonplaces, Obama gives us new and inventive ways to understand the stakes of remaining divided. Obama's capacity to re-envision a particular cultural predicament in insightful and productive ways solidifies his effectiveness as a master of rhetorical discourse.

What Is Rhetoric?

The term *rhetoric* has fallen into disrepute among many Americans as a result of misunderstanding and misrepresentation. Those who consider rhetoric as a tool of the ignoble use the term as a synonym for deception and verbal subterfuge; this may be for good reasons. More than a few historical figures have used keen communicative skills to do more harm than good, and some of the most sinister historical figures are thought to have committed hideous crimes using the skill of rhetoric. However, rhetoric's ability to supplement the sinister goals of some should not eclipse its ability to support the good intentions of others. Whereas Hitler and Mussolini used their words to inflame nationalistic passions, Gandhi and Martin Luther King Jr. used their rhetorical skills for the liberation of oppressed populations and for the advancement of civil rights. Irrespective of a speaker's intentions, one cannot deny that rhetoric is a powerful and beneficial tool.

The question still stands: What is rhetoric, exactly? How can or should it be defined? Plato referred to rhetoric as a knack—a clever way of doing something that may or may not be easy to teach—and, in his more mature years, as an ability to discern the nature of one's soul in order to translate knowledge accordingly. He considered the former a pernicious, "bad" rhetoric, and the latter "good" rhetoric.[2] "Bad" rhetoric, also known as *sophistry*, or, at best, mere flattery, is a tool that has the danger of being usurped by ethically questionable characters; we may find logical fallacies and several omissions in such characters' speeches. "Good" rhetoric, on the other hand, is used by a person who speaks according to what he or she discerns are the capabilities within the audience's "soul." Good rhetoric seeks to do more teaching than persuading, even if teaching is a kind of persuasion.

Aristotle does not present rhetoric as a two-sided entity, but as a neutral tool to be taken up as one sees fit. In *Rhetoric*, Aristotle defines rhetoric as "the faculty of observing in any given case the available means of persuasion."[3] The good, the bad, and the ugliest of orators can use rhetoric to get a point across, regardless of the intention of the message. Whether one wants to inform, teach, or persuade, skill in rhetoric is necessary.

Rhetorical prowess is a necessary skill for those pursuing respected public occupations. As implied earlier, politics is the most common forum for public rhetoric in contemporary America. The concept of the politician as "the great communicator" is still alive, but the standards for what we may consider "great" may have waned a bit. In fact, we may have reached a point where rhetoric is so mistrusted that an apparent lack of rhetorical skill denotes authenticity. That is, simplicity in speech equals strength in character. Another field strongly associated with rhetoric—law—can tell us much about the mistrust of elaborate communication. Lawyers, often charged to sway a jury or trip up the opposing council's witnesses, are often shunned, if not feared, for their less-than-virtuous uses of rhetoric.

By identifying law and politics as distinctly rhetorical occupations, we seek to provide an apt segue to the subject of this collection, President Barack Obama, who happens to be a lawyer-turned-politician. One may suspect that President Obama has a keen knowledge of rhetoric, and this suspicion may be confirmed by listening to some of his speeches. Many agree that Barack

Obama is one of the most articulate presidents this country has seen in a long while, suggesting a rhetorical prowess and, at the very least, acceptance of Aristotle's conception of rhetoric as a neutral tool. However, exploring the Platonic categories of rhetoric—"bad" rhetoric as well as "good" rhetoric—also pertains to the essays in this collection. Therefore, revisiting what we mean by "good" and "bad" in light of Obama's political speeches is in order.

Of course, people already have their opinions about Obama's speeches, but moving away from what may be called "common sense" to actual analysis of his speeches and their occasions may shed some light on Obama's rhetoric. Whether Obama's speeches are "bad" or "good" depend on what we discern as his ultimate purposes when campaigning for the presidency. Of course, his main purpose during the years of his campaign and early presidency were to get elected and bring Congress and the American people to his side, but how did he go about doing this? Did he employ a "good" rhetoric?

Good rhetoric, designed to truly inform one's audience, may give us a clue as to how Obama achieved success. As an ideal, good rhetoric is addressed by Elvin Lim in his 2008 book, *The Anti-Intellectual Presidency: The Decline of Presidential Rhetoric from George Washington to George W. Bush.* Lim writes that anti-intellectualism—an oversimplification of language to promote accessibility—motivates politicians toward rhetorically reductive speech that may do more harm than good. According to Lim, we can reform presidential rhetoric by conceptualizing leadership as pedagogy:

> Democratic leaders face a peculiar tension in their rhetorical appeals to the public. They need both to seek the public's permission, as well as to guide it. The former goal requires that leaders faithfully represent the relevant facts of the political issue under consideration in a manner that facilitates an informed decision; the latter goal requires a degree of rhetorical manipulation to direct citizens toward a preferred conclusion. The anti-intellectual president leans immoderately on the latter end of this dilemma, making him more similar to a Mussolini than to a Roosevelt. I suggest, then, that what separate Mussolini from Roosevelt are the different models of leadership they represent. While Mussolini was a demagogue who stoked the people's prejudices and passions toward his particular ends, Roosevelt was a pedagogue who, while having a political agenda, as we would expect of all politicians, also tried to educate the audience in the hope that citizens would come down on his side. We

> prefer the latter to the former because we want presidents
> to be statesmen not propagandists, teachers not salesmen.[4]

One could say that Obama's initial success was based on a pedagogical image, as opposed to the anti-intellectual subject positions of other politicians. Of course, various factors supported Obama's victory, but to distinguish the role of rhetoric in Obama's campaign, Lim's "leadership as pedagogy" paradigm may make sense. If this is an accurate assessment of Obama's subject position as a speaker, what exactly was Obama "teaching"?

Some of the essays in this collection suggest that Obama's main goal in his campaign—and in the early stages of his administration—was to promote his biographical story as part of the American Dream. One should be careful not to confuse Obama's promotion of his biography with his promotion of the American Dream. The latter tactic, used by all politicians to some degree, is meant to present one's self as a viable candidate by endorsing a national narrative. Of course, Obama did not refrain from this tactic. However, his inevitable self-promotion may be seen as a byproduct of educating the public about his background: informing the public about who he is, how he came to become what he is, and what that means about American society in general. Obama intentionally connected the American Dream to his own story, positioning his life metonymically in relation to the American Dream. As a singularity within the larger American story, Obama attempted to demonstrate that his travails and victories were emblematic of America's travails and victories.

Why Obama?

One may wonder why we focus so heavily on Obama's rhetorical savvy during his first term as president. After all, past presidents have been known for their well-crafted speeches and powerful political prose. Furthermore, other presidents have crafted persuasive speeches that seemed at odds with their actions in moral and political realms. Given past precedent, why our interest in Obama's rhetoric? The answer to this question is found in Obama's character, which is itself also a rhetorical construction. In fact, Obama's rhetorical construction of his own character enabled all his other constructions. Obama embodied America as a melting pot, as eclectic, and as diverse. He also embodied our hopes as a nation of competence and intelligence. He was African American and a personified anesthetic for racial tension and the guilt felt by many in the wake of desegregation. His ethnicity also serves as an icon of the success of progressive politics, as an apparent sign of such politics implementing a welcome change from the prior administration's failures, and applauded by American and international factions.[5] No other president in recent history could construct himself as the personification of American and global hopes and needs like Barack Obama. As political theorist Paul Street observes, Obama was "the right candidate in the right place at the right time."[6] No president in recent history, if at all, has had such a germane and historically potent subject position. Thomas Sugrue, in *Not Even Past: Barack Obama and the Burden of Race*, makes this point well:

> Obama's power—as a candidate—and as a president—has been his reappropriation for liberals of a unifying *language* of Americanism, one that, like all exercises in nation building, transforms history into the stuff of legend and poetry. From the cacophony of the recent past, from its messiness and tumult, Obama extracts a powerful, reassuring message of progress, a story as compelling as Ronald Reagan's evocation of a "city on the hill" or Abraham Lincoln's reinterpretation of the founding creed of equality in Gettysburg Address, both true and mythological at the same time. Thus Barack Obama's quest for identity, and the distinctive history of the black freedom struggle, of urban struggle, of urban politics, of civil rights and black power, became the American story. What Obama called "my story" became "our story."[7]

The rhetorical contexts within which Obama sought to intervene provided opportunities for him to enhance his image at different points throughout his campaign and early presidency, as one may see upon reading this collection. However, the general rhetorical situation surrounding Obama gave him the opportunity to reap the benefits of good rhetoric and the flattery of *sophistic* rhetoric: He used his words to not only educate audiences, but took advantage of that flattery to construct himself as an embodiment, and a synonym, for the American citizenry.

RHETORIC, OBAMA, AND YOU

It is a commonplace of democratic theory that democracies require committed participants. Of course, strong democracies require strong participation.[8] However, what happens when citizens are not committed to the democracies within which they live, believing that their participation is either meaningless or subject to manipulation within a broken system? In such a context, citizens begin to tune out even the most well-intentioned words of their representatives because they have bought into Plato's conception of bad rhetoric, where words have no substance or are produced with no intention of offering either moral or ethical improvement to the listener. In his *Saving Persuasion*, Bryan Garsten reminds us of the pitfalls for the contemporary polis (city) in which this sort of thinking takes hold. Garsten notes:

> In ancient Athens and Rome, in medieval schools and Renaissance cities, in early modern Europe and nineteenth-century America, both scholars and statesmen taught their students that a well-functioning republican polity required citizens who could articulate arguments on either side of a controversy, link those arguments to the particular opinions and prejudices of their fellow citizens, and thereby facilitate the arguing and deliberating that constituted a healthy political life.[9]

With Garsten's historical reminder in view, we should ask ourselves, "What can politicians and concerned rhetoricians do to ward off the kind of crippling cynicism that attends the collapse of trust, as the very fabric of the constitutional system itself comes into question?" Indeed, what role can rhetoric play in reviving the citizenry's faith in democracy at a historical moment plagued with doubt about the prospect of reviving an active role for the American democratic project?

Enter Barack Obama, whose successful 2008 presidential campaign and 2012 re-election were supposed to reinvigorate America's hope in, and prospects for, achieving democracy and meaningful social change. At the time of his campaigns, Obama stood for the yet-to-be tapped potential of America. Obama also represented the repudiation of the disastrous agenda of the Bush administration.

Now that over four years have passed since Obama's first election as president, the hard realities associated with the collapse of the economy and the stretching of resources in various theatres of war, a once supportive electorate has become more skeptical of Obama. He has not been the panacea for all that ails the country everyone thought he would be. Indeed, many critics of Obama believe he is a pawn of powerbrokers within the Beltway and on Wall Street. Perhaps Obama now represents the disillusionment of our waning idealism, the recognition that the promises of his campaign will not be fulfilled. While we are perhaps not quite willing to ascribe the success of his 2008 and 2012 campaigns to hype and the effectiveness of slogans, even his supporters have doubts about whether the famous "Yes, we Can" chant might have to be revised to: "Well, we tried, but we can't." Naturally, we don't want to believe that Obama is the savior who could not deliver.

Marilyn Cooper argues in her recent *College Composition and Communication* article, "Rhetorical Agency as Emergent and Enacted," that Obama showed us the prospect for the exercise of agency in his 2008 "More Perfect Union" speech, a speech that saved his candidacy and began a difficult dialogue on race, as Obama skillfully navigated the treacherous discursive terrain of U.S. race relations.[10] In this speech, Obama showed us how rhetoric works, its capacity to shape our perception of reality, and the prospect of self-invention and recreation. As David Remnick notes in his *The Bridge: The Life and Rise of Barack Obama*, in explaining Obama's appeal to young people on the South Side of Chicago where he got his start as a community organizer, "Obama seemed to offer a new kind of politics or, at least, a marriage of conventional liberal-policy positions to a temperament that relied on reconciliation rather than grievance."[11]

The attractiveness of Obama's policy positions are just as much rhetorical constructions as they are material ones. Obama often employs what Wayne Booth calls a "Listening Rhetoric." As Booth argues in his *The Rhetoric of Rhetoric*:

> When LR [Listening Rhetoric] is pushed to its fullest possibilities, opponents in any controversy listen to each other not only to persuade better, but also find common ground behind the conflict. They pursue the shared assumptions (beliefs, faiths, warrants, commonplaces) that both sides depend on as they pursue their attacks and disagreements.[12]

Sugrue also notes that "Obama's power as an orator is his ability to seamlessly bring together—as he did at the 2004 convention, at Selma, and throughout his campaign for the presidency—his personal story with a narrative of national redemption."[13] He adds: "During his journey through the polarized racial world of late twentieth century America, Obama discovered his calling. It was to overcome the acrimonious history of racial polarization, whether that of Black power or the culture wars, acting on the understanding that such polarization was anathema to national unity."[14]

Obama's major tactic was not to present himself as a viable candidate, but to create identifications between his candidacy and the American public, a public comprised of upstanding and virtuous citizens. The public desperately needed to believe this about itself. Perhaps Obama's triumph in gaining the presidency of the United States resulted not so much from how he made us feel good about *him*, but instead from how Obama succeeded in making us feel good about ourselves. Or, at the very least, he implied that if we elected him, he would eventually make us feel good about the American democratic project. Obama may have catered to the national narcissism of the time, "teaching" us how great we are supposed to be; to vote for Obama was to cast a vote of confidence for ourselves and the American Dream. He would, in fact, integrate us into a proud and fulfilling whole.

This collection primarily explores how Obama went about doing this before and after being inaugurated as president of the United States of America. It focuses on speeches as "rhetorical moments," before national and international audiences on subjects ranging from race relations to torture, where Obama tried to sell himself by selling the image of a model America. Before accusations were lodged against Obama insisting that he was just another politician in the pockets of corporations, and before Obama's actions—or inactions—spoke louder than his well-crafted words, Obama moved to rhetorically construct himself as a model American. These moves played themselves out in various ways, but they all provided the same lesson: rhetoric— the ability to recognize the various means of persuasion at one's disposal— constitutes the key component in Obama's repertoire.

OBAMA'S RHETORIC AT HOME AND ABROAD

This collection is divided into two main parts devoted to "Obama's Rhetoric at Home" and "Obama's Rhetoric Abroad." In the opening essay of Part One, entitled "The Rhetorical Constraints Limiting President Obama's Domestic Policy Advocacy," Robert Rowland uses criticism from Obama's commentators as a starting point to explore the political and systemic constraints that President Obama faced in attempting to sell his domestic agenda. As Rowland notes, such constraints include the public's lack of knowledge and interest in complex domestic policies, the failure of the media to cover policies in detail, and the need for sixty votes to enact any policy in the United States Senate.

Rowland examines the relevant political constraints, including an incredible rise in partisanship that created a situation in which the president's opponents made it their top priority to defeat any policy initiatives proposed by the administration, including policies that conservatives had long supported. The combination of systemic and political constraints created a uniquely difficult rhetorical environment for President Obama. Rowland demonstrates that, despite this environment, the president was much more successful than his critics recognized in using domestic policy rhetoric to support his agenda.

In the second essay of Part One, Courtney Jue Sloey explores the rhetorical nature of Obama's "Yes We Can" campaign slogan. This slogan was a unifying agent that created and perpetuated a necessary common identity between Obama and potential voters. This slogan speaks to the theme of Obama as a personification of the American Dream.

In the third essay in this section, "Appointments and Disappointments: A Rhetorical Analysis of the Relationship Between President Obama, Catholics, and Their Church," John Jasso and Anthony Wachs take a look at Obama's attempts, during the initial months of his presidency, to smoothly incorporate representatives of Catholicism into a substantially pro-choice administration. In being the personification of American ideals, Obama worked to find common ground between Catholic and non-Catholic sensibilities. Unfortunately, Obama's attempts were not always successful, as Jasso and Wachs demonstrate.

In the fourth essay, "Barack Obama, Islam, and the Discourses of American Racial Belonging," Steve Salaita addresses the tension between American and Islamic cultures and how Obama, whose cultural identity was questioned throughout his campaign and during the initial months of his presidency, dealt with this tension. Salaita examines how "post-racial" celebrations of Obama gave way to classically racialist (race-based, but not necessarily vindictive) conversations about identity and belonging in the United States. This is to say that Obama's attempts to alleviate the tension through inclusive rhetoric may have backfired, causing the further exclusion of Arab and Islamic culture.

In the final essay of Part One, Erec Smith addresses Obama's approach to race and racism among American blacks and whites. In "The New Cultural Politics of Obama: Race, Politics, and Unity in Obama's 'A More Perfect Union,'" Smith claims that the Jeremiah Wright incident that almost ruined Obama's campaign gave the future president chances to rhetorically construct himself as the embodiment of America and the American Dream, alleviate racial anxiety that may have caused whites to second-guess their support of Obama, and place the onus of racial healing on the American people themselves. Thus, by supporting Obama, Americans could support racial tolerance and relinquish culpability in general.

In "Obama's West Point Address: The Symbolic Construction of Policy and Authority," Michael Kleine rhetorically analyzes Obama's West Point address to show that it succeeded in constructing Obama as a virtuous orator who utilized Plato's "true rhetoric," even if it did not succeed in swaying his intended audiences in any particular direction. Ultimately, Obama's West Point speech gave him the proper "ethos" to speak as commander in chief of the American military.

In the first essay of Part Two, "Obama's Rhetoric Abroad," Richard Marback, in "A Few Bad Apples: Barack Obama's Response to the Bush Administration Policy on Torture," claims that Obama's lack of persuasive success has less to do with his rhetorical skill and more to do with a tricky and challenging rhetorical situation unique to his presidency. As with Kleine's essay, the rhetorical situation is highlighted as an occasion for Obama to address the torture of supposed terrorists by Americans.

René De Los Santos's essay, "The Specter of Nuestra America: Barack Obama, Latin America, and the 2009 Summit of the Americas" explores Obama's relationship with Latin America—at least the potential for a relationship. De los Santos interprets Obama's address as a rhetorical construction of the president's character based on the specific rhetorical context: Castro's absence as a political figure and his presence as a morally ambiguous ideal. Obama's speech is tempered and shaped by the combination of his sought image, the image of Castro, and the needs and expectations of the Summit.

In his "Obama's Cairo Speech: Beyond the Rhetoric and Politics of 'Good Muslim, Bad Muslim,'" Matthew Abraham explores how Obama appeals to the Arab world for a "new beginning" in the wake of the War on Terror while drawing on the distinction between good Muslims and bad Muslims employed by past U.S. presidents. Abraham asks us to look beyond the speech's appealing veneer and to interrogate how Obama employs a previously invoked rhetoric of "Good Muslim, Bad Muslim" in his call for partnership and cooperation with the Arab world.

In his Afterword, David Frank, Dean of the Honors College and Professor of Rhetoric at the University of Oregon, explores the collection's potential to contribute to a greater understanding of the making of Barak Obama. A glossary of terms, keyed to the important concepts and terms used by contributors, rounds out *The Making of Barack Obama: The Politics of Persuasion*.

NOTES

1. Shelby Steele, in his book, *A Bound Man: Why We Are Excited About Obama and Why He Can't Win* (London: Free Press, 2008) predicted that Obama would be unable to capture the presidency because of the perpetual tight rope he would be forced to walk as an African American raised predominantly by a white mother and by white grandparents (81-95). According to Steele, this tight rope required Obama to wear the "mask" of a "challenger" to appease whites who were eager and willing to embrace an African American candidate who would not hold their race against them, and in turn, who would also not hold Obama's race against him (97-105). At the same time, according to Steele, Obama would be unable to pass authenticity tests the African American community would impose on him; specifically, he would be a "challenger" in the tradition of Jessie Jackson, Sr. and Al Sharpton (107-127).

2. Rhetoric as "knack" can be found in Plato's *Gorgias*. Rhetoric, or the ability to speak in response to one's audience, is described in his dialogue, *Phaedrus*, written sixteen years later. Both works, and short but informative summaries of each, can be found in Patricia Bizzell and Bruce Herzberg's *The Rhetorical Tradition: Readings from Classical Times to* the Present (New York: Bedford/St. Martin's, 2000)

3. See Kennedy, George A., trans. *Aristotle On Rhetoric: A Theory of Civic Discourse.* (New York and Oxford: Oxford U P, 1991), 35.

4. Elvin Lim, *The Anti-Intellectual Presidency: The Decline of Presidential Rhetoric from George Washington to George W. Bush* (Oxford: Oxford Univ. Press, 2008), 118.

5. See chapter five of Paul Street's *Barack Obama and the Future of American Politics* (Boulder, CO: Paradigm Publishers, 2009).

6. Street, *Barack Obama,* 169.

7. Sugrue, *Not Even Past* (Princeton, NJ: Princeton Univ. Press, 2010), 54 (emphasis added).

8. See Benjamin Barber's *Strong Democracy: Participatory Politics for a New Age* (Berkeley: Univ. of California Press, 1984) and his *A Passion for Democracy: American Essays* (NJ: Princeton Univ. Press, 1998)

9. Garsten, *Saving Persuasion: A Defense of Rhetoric and Judgment* (Cambridge, MA: Harvard Univ. Press, 2006), 3.

10. Cooper, "Rhetorical Agency as Emergent and Enacted," *College Composition and Communication* 62, no. 3 (February 2011): 420–49.

11. Remnick, *The Bridge: The Life and Rise of Barack Obama* (New York: Knopf Publishing, 2010), 294.

12. Booth, *The Rhetoric of Rhetoric* (Malden: Blackwell Publishing, 2004), 10.

13. Sugrue, *Not Even Past,* 53.

14. Ibid., 54.

Part One: Obama's Rhetoric at Home

1 THE RHETORICAL CONSTRAINTS LIMITING PRESIDENT OBAMA'S DOMESTIC POLICY ADVOCACY

Robert C. Rowland

President Obama is universally recognized for his rhetorical skill, and his gift for rhetoric is viewed as one of the hallmarks of the 2008 presidential campaign. Any number of commentators could be cited who identify his eloquence as one of the primary explanations of his success in the campaign. Ryan Lizza called him an "inspirational figure—more so even than the candidate John F. Kennedy"; and Matt Bai labeled him "a brilliant orator," and condensed the 2008 campaign to a battle between "the old soldier and the young orator"; Chuck Todd and Sheldon Gawiser concluded that "The key to his campaign were his speeches."[1] Many commentators made similar comments.[2] Conservative commentators, including William Safire and William Kristol, also recognized his rhetorical skill in the 2008 campaign, although they sometimes criticized Obama for his rhetorical success—a criticism that reflected a wish that their candidate had a similar gift for rhetoric.[3] The influence of his rhetoric was so great in 2008 that it was compared to that of John Kennedy, Franklin D. Roosevelt, Martin Luther King, Jr., and Abraham Lincoln, based on its capacity to inspire the nation.[4]

Since becoming president, however, evaluations of his rhetoric have become more mixed. I note later that a number of his speeches as president, especially about foreign policy or those presented on ceremonial occasions, have received strong praise. The conventional wisdom is that this rhetorical success does not extend to his rhetoric on domestic policy. A number of commentators argue that the president failed to adequately present a coherent domestic agenda. In this view, the failure has been one of explanation and of boldness. For example, Elizabeth Drew argues that Obama allowed "the Republicans to define the agenda and even the terminology."[5] Leonard Pitts claimed "President Obama, unlike candidate Obama, has yet to articulate a goal that excites and unites."[6] Thomas Friedman has criticized Obama for "failing to put a credible, specific economic plan on the table—at the scale of our problem."[7] His criticism is based on the conclusion that "people are . . . hungry for a big plan from the president to fix the economy, one that will bite and challenge both parties," a plan "about making America great again."[8] Friedman also has argued that the president should call for "a 'grand bargain' with Republicans focused on a near-term infrastructure stimulus tied with a Simpson-Bowles long-term fiscal rebalancing" to show the people "a sensible plan to fix the economy—*which is what people want most from the president.*"[9] In Friedman's view, Obama's rhetorical failures come down to a failure to use the "bully pulpit" to argue for a grand vision of how to both rebuild the nation and to confront the debt crisis.[10]

In contrast, others take almost precisely the opposite position, arguing that the president who wowed us in 2008 has suddenly become dull. In this view, Obama may have presented a bold vision, but he did so in a way that excited no one. Andrew Hacker argues that President Obama demonstrates a "*didactic* disposition: wordy discourse not connected with clear plans for action," and concluded that "the charisma so attractive during his election has failed along with his failure to stimulate the economy."[11] Maureen Dowd observed that rather than charisma, Obama enacted a "cool, aloof style" that reflected an "inability to read America's panic and its thirst for a strong leader."[12] Dowd boils down her argument that Obama needed more passion in the context of the health care debate by arguing that he should be "Less Spocky, More Rocky," and claims, three years later: "The president who started off with dazzle now seems incapable of stimulating either the economy or the voters."[13] Similarly, Paul Krugman criticizes the president, arguing that voters don't understand his accomplishments because "the Obama team has consistently failed to highlight Republican obstruction, perhaps out of a fear of seeming weak."[14] Ross Douthat, a conservative, states that "In 2008, Barack Obama seemed to have almost FDR-like gifts," but that "the presidency, unexpectedly, has exposed his limits as a communicator. Now when Obama demonizes, it seems clumsy; when he tries to persuade, it falls on deaf ears. Unlike Reagan and Clinton, the two masters, he seems unable to either bully or inspire."[15] Writing in the *Washington Post*, Aaron Blake highlights Obama's rhetorical failure by noting the many different slogans he has used as president. Blake concludes that "Obama's slogans have been suffering from the product they are selling."[16]

In one way, these criticisms are quite accurate. There is no question that the president has not been nearly as successful in persuading people to accept his domestic policy agenda as he was in persuading them to embrace his campaign themes—notably hope and change. This failure to move national audience obscures the more fundamental truth that President Obama's rhetorical failures reveal far more about the constraints on domestic policy rhetoric than they do about any weaknesses in his rhetorical practices. Obama has not lost his ability to explain complex arguments, link those arguments to fundamental values and the American Dream, and demonstrate an understanding of how his policies impact real Americans. If anything, he has become more skillful in enacting these strategies as he has grown accustomed to the role of president. Rather, his failure to consistently move the national audience reflects basic constraints on the American rhetorical republic, constraints that make it very hard to confront fundamental domestic problems.

In what follows, I first consider two criticisms of the president's rhetorical practice: that he failed to lead and that he lost his capacity to inspire. After demonstrating the falsity of these perspectives, I turn to the rhetorical constraints facing the president and show how these factors largely explain those policy areas where the president failed to move the nation. I then use a brief case study of the evolution of the health care debate to show how the rhetorical constraints facing the president largely explain the difficulties the president has had in shifting public opinion to support his ground-breaking health care initiative.

A FAILURE TO LEAD

The argument that the president has failed to lead takes two primary forms. Some argue that the president has failed to develop a coherent agenda. Others make a slightly different version of this argument, claiming that the president failed to develop an agenda that confronts the big problems facing the nation. The second form of the failure to lead argument is developed in some detail by Thomas Friedman, and is focused on the need for policies that both spur growth in the short term and present a credible plan to reduce the national debt in the long term.

The oddity of the failure to lead argument is that the president has consistently and precisely laid out big plans to both produce growth and to deal with debt that many proponents of this position desire. Admittedly, his rhetoric has not always resonated, but that lack of resonance isn't from a lack of trying. As he assumed office, President Obama made it clear that he intended to focus not only on the economic crisis that confronted the nation, but also on dealing with long-term problems that threatened to undermine the American Dream.

Shortly after assuming office, the new president laid out the agenda for his first term in a speech at Georgetown.[17] Obama's focus in the speech is on both short-term problems brought on by the financial collapse, producing what became known as the Great Recession, and on long-term problems that have afflicted the nation for decades. In the conclusion of the speech, he makes the point that focusing only on the short term can be disastrous over time: "For too long too many in Washington put off hard decisions for some other day. There's been a tendency to spend a lot of time scoring political points instead of rolling up sleeves to solve real problems" (72). By "rolling up sleeves" and focusing on creating a "new foundation" (44), the nation could create "an American future that is far different than our troubled economic past. It's an America teeming with new industry and commerce, humming with new energy and discoveries that light the world once more—a place where anyone from anywhere with a good idea or the will to work can live the dream they've heard so much about" (76).

According to Obama, the way to produce that better America was to not only focus on short-term problems, but to build a new foundation consisting of:

> five pillars that will grow our economy and make this new century another American century: Number one, new rules for Wall Street that will reward drive and innovation, not reckless risk taking—number two, new investments in education that will make our workforce more skilled and competitive—number three, new investments in renewable energy and technology that will create new jobs and new industries—number four, new investments in health care that will cut costs for families and businesses; and number five, new savings in our federal budget that will bring down the debt for future generations. (45)

Obama then laid out his agenda in each of these areas.

The president focuses special attention on refuting potential objections to his proposals, demonstrating that he is committed to real deficit reduction involving cuts to entitlement programs. Obama's effort to explain the rationale behind his policy is evident throughout the speech, including the first forty paragraphs that focus on short-term responses to the recession itself, such as TARP, the stimulus, and the auto industry bailout. For example, he explains in some detail why it makes perfect sense for a family or a business to cut back on expenses during a recession, but why it would be disastrous if the government did so:

> To begin with, economists on both the left and the right agree that the last thing a government should do in the middle of a recession is to cut back on spending. You see, when this recession began, many families sat around the kitchen table and tried to figure out where they could cut back. And so have many businesses. And this is a completely reasonable and understandable reaction. But if everybody—if everybody—if every family in America, if every business in America cuts back all at once, then no one is spending any money, which means there are no customers, which means there are more layoffs, which means the economy gets even worse. That's why the government has to step in and temporarily boost spending in order to stimulate demand. That's exactly what we are doing right now. (19)

Later, he explains why achieving real deficit reduction in the long term requires cuts in entitlement, saying "let's not kid ourselves and suggest that we can solve this problem by trimming a few earmarks or cutting the budget for the National Endowment for the Arts" (68). He then adds, "So if we want to get serious about fiscal discipline . . . we will also have to get serious about entitlement reform" (68).

At Georgetown, the president attempted to justify the steps his administration has taken to deal with the financial collapse and the Great Recession. Citing a parable from the New Testament about building a house on rock rather than on shifting sands (43), he argues for the importance of the five pillars of his new foundation. As with the rhetorical campaign for health care reform, the president makes a strong effort to explain the rationale behind his policy proposals.[18] The president clearly believes it important to take the time to explain why the overall policy goals of his administration are important, and how the policy reforms would work. Equally clear is that he knows that getting the message across would be difficult. It is noteworthy that in the introduction of the speech, he tells the audience that "This is going to be prose and not poetry."[19]

The idea that a new foundation for the economy needed to be created through reform and investment is one that Obama has championed for some time. Although hope and change were the broad themes of the 2008 campaign, along with a call to create a new politics based in reason and bipartisanship, in his discussion of specific issues, then Senator Obama often spoke of rebuilding the nation and restoring the American Dream.[20] In fact, these themes pre-date the 2008 campaign, and are evident as early as 2006, in *The Audacity of Hope*. The book tour for *Audacity* played an important role in convincing the first-term Senator to seek the presidency.[21] In the book, he writes about the importance of reforming education, providing greater support for research and development, shifting toward renewable energy, and enacting health care reform to provide access to health care and because reform is essential in reducing health care inflation. These broad policy areas are discussed in relation to threats to "the social compact FDR helped construct," threats he traces to Republican opposition to regulation and social investment.[22] Obama boils down these threats with the phrase "Ownership Society." On both fairness and fiscal grounds, he calls for tax reform and for raising rates on the rich. Thus, the agenda that Obama labels the "New Foundation" at Georgetown had been a core part of his program before he announced his run for the presidency.

The Obama administration also clearly attempted to encapsulate its economic agenda with the phrase "New Foundation," a phrase used in at least fifteen speeches.[23] While the new president developed a bold and coherent economic agenda at Georgetown—an agenda that, according to David M. Kennedy, is "very comprehensive" and much more developed than that of FDR in 1933[24]—there is no question that the agenda and the phrase "New Foundation" failed to resonate. In the aftermath of the address, commentators critiqued the address and the slogan "New Foundation" as forgettable, nothing new in terms of policy, and not feasible.[25] Presidential historian Robert Dalleck said of the phrase: "I'm not sure what it means" adding that "foundation doesn't strike me as a word people will comfortably take to."[26] Unsurprisingly, the conservative response was overwhelmingly negative. Newt Gingrich calls "the foundation" of Obama's approach "the leaden, immovable force of big bureaucracy" and "the most radical, government-expanding agenda in American history."[27] It is clear that the agenda was comprehensive and bold, but it was not one that served the same rallying function as the "New Deal" had for Roosevelt—except possibly for conservatives who opposed every aspect of the agenda. I discuss later why the New Foundation and other domestic policy rhetoric failed to resonate, but the key point at this stage is that the criticism of Obama in failing to lay out a substantive agenda addressing big issues is clearly false.

Precisely the same point can be made about Obama's supposed failure to lay out a case for a grand bargain consisting of short-term stimulus and long-term reductions in the deficit. Initially, it is important to recognize that Obama did discuss the deficit in a major address at George Washington University on April 13, 2011.[28] The president situated his argument for a "balanced approach to achieve $4 trillion in deficit reduction over twelve years"

(44) in a discussion of the individualistic and communitarian variants of the American Dream:[29]

> More than citizens of any other country, we are rugged individualists, a self-reliant people with a healthy skepticism of too much government.
>
> But there's always been another thread running through our history—a belief that we're all connected, and that there are some things we can only do together as a nation. We believe, in the words of our first Republican President, Abraham Lincoln, that through government, we should do together what we cannot do as well for ourselves. (7-8)

Obama references the responsibility of the community to all its members, arguing that "each one of us deserves some basic measure of security and dignity" (10). In the remainder of the address, Obama does not so much argue for stimulus because, at that time, it appeared the economy might be gaining momentum. Instead, he argues against cuts to discretionary spending and entitlements proposed by Republicans in the House.

At the same time, the president makes it very clear that along with greater revenue from closing tax loopholes and letting the Bush tax cuts for the wealthy expire, there must be real cuts in entitlements that will require "sacrifices" (43). The president is quite candid about the need for sacrifice. He notes that "most Americans tend to dislike government spending in the abstract, but like the stuff that it buys," adding that "nobody wants to pay higher taxes" (26-27). Sacrifice is required because "Around two-thirds of our budget—two thirds—is spent on Medicare, Medicaid, Social Security and national security" (28). The president then lays out his agenda for the cuts, including $750 billion in cuts over a dozen years to domestic spending, $400 billion in cuts to defense in addition to cuts already made, reductions in health care spending he hoped to make via reforms in the health care law, and $500 billion in Medicare and Medicaid savings (45–53). To those who doubted that what he labels as "reforms" would actually work, he promises the following:

> But just to hold Washington—and to hold me—accountable and make sure that the debt burden continues to decline my plan includes a debt fail-safe. If by 2014, our debt is not projected to fall as a share of the economy—if we haven't hit our targets, if Congress has failed to act—then my plan will require us to come together and make up the additional savings with more spending cuts and more spending reduc-

tions in the tax code. That should be an incentive for us to
act boldly now, instead of kicking our problems down the
road. (59)

At the conclusion of the speech, he recognizes that negotiation for a final
agreement on a "grand bargain" would be needed. He says, "I don't expect
the details in any final agreement to look exactly like the approach I laid out
today. This is a democracy; that's not how things work. I'm eager to hear
other ideas from all ends of the political spectrum" (76). He then adds that
although "my critique of the House Republican approach has been strong,
Americans deserve and will demand that we all make an effort to bridge our
differences and find common ground" (76).

With these words, he spoke to Republican leaders, including the author
of the House budget and Republican Paul Ryan (who was in the audience),
telling them that he could match their sharp words with equally sharp words,
but also making clear that he is ready to bargain in good faith.

Ryan was offended by the president's words.[30] Given the sharp criticisms that Republicans made of the president, some of which labeled him
un-American, Ryan's response is odd. The president made it clear that he
understood that a final deal requires compromise and sacrifice from both
sides. Reactions from long-term budget hawks indicate that they at least understood the message. Pete Peterson, who had focused on the issue for many
years, notes: "President Obama's proposed framework is a big step toward the
compromise we need to achieve fiscal sustainability. The President has made
it clear that he supports a comprehensive plan for long-term deficit reduction,
and his framework provides another credible approach to tackling the key
drivers of our long-term debt."[31]

President Obama continued demonstrating willingness to compromise
in his negotiations with the Speaker of the House, John Boehner, about a
grand bargain. In those negotiations, he makes it quite clear that he favors
a large package that would raise revenues, but also cut backs on entitlement
spending.[32] It is true as Friedman and others argued that the president failed
to identify specific budget cuts or to embrace the proposal of a group recom-
mending deficit reductions, such as the National Commission on Fiscal Responsibility and Reform (usually referred to as the Simpson-Bowles commission).[33] Why didn't he embrace a specific program? The obvious answer, implied quite clearly in the speech, is that he knew that any such grand bargain
required compromise from both sides. If he embraced a specific proposal,
absent an agreement from the other side, two problems would arise. First, the
other side would be able to demonize the specifics of the proposal. Second,
they would then argue that the president had already agreed to the domestic

cuts, and that since there was agreement, the cuts should be enacted immediately. The grand bargain could only work if both sides made concessions, and that can occur only if each side is willing to give up something to protect a core value. That requires bargaining, not an upfront rhetorical offer.

It seems quite clear that criticisms of President Obama for failing to present a clear rhetorical vision about the economy and deficit reduction are misguided. Before the 2008 election, he enunciated a program of investment, reform, tax increases on the rich, and painful cuts in entitlements. If he had such a clear program, why was he so unsuccessful in convincing voters and commentators alike about the power of the program? I turn to that question in the next section, when I consider whether, as Maureen Dowd argues so colorfully in comparing the president to Mr. Spoch, if he had lost the capacity to inspire.

A FAILURE TO INSPIRE

What of the alternate theory of President Obama's rhetorical failing that he had lost his capacity to inspire? Initially, it seems odd that a candidate so acclaimed for his rhetoric would suddenly lose the capacity to use it effectively. A number of the president's speeches have been strongly praised by various commentators for their inspiring content. Those speeches include his address on Afghanistan at West Point, the Nobel Prize Address, the memorial speech for the victims of the Tucson shooting, and the Address to Congress on Health Care.[34] Each of these speeches was highly praised by knowledgeable observers, and, in some cases, there was an immediate bounce in the polls. Yet, there is also no question that the president had difficulty maintaining momentum produced by any successful individual speech.

A related theory is that while the president can be inspiring on occasion, he does not take the time to explain his policy proposals in detail. In this view, momentum produced by major addresses dissipates because of his failure to explain how the policy will assist ordinary people. The difficulty here is that the president has not failed to explain his position. The best example concerns health care reform, where he not only makes a major speech to the nation, but also presents any number of speeches at town hall meetings and other contexts to defend the proposal. In addition, the White House makes this case in a number of different contexts. It is true that his case-making didn't always work, but it is fundamentally untrue to argue that he didn't try.

In the remainder of this essay, I argue that on one point, critics of President Obama are exactly right. In many cases, his rhetoric on domestic policy is not very effective in moving public opinion. However, I argue that this failure reveals more about the constraints on rhetoric, especially complex domestic policy issues, than it does about poor rhetorical choices made by the president.

Constraints on the Capacity of Domestic Policy Rhetoric to Shape the Agenda

Well-known presidential scholar George Edwards argues quite strongly that presidents have little capacity to shape public opinion. Contrary to conventional wisdom, Edwards claims "even able communicators like Ronald Reagan and Bill Clinton could not move the public much on their own," and, rather than shape public opinion, Edwards claims that "presidents are facilitators who reflect, and may intensify, widely held views."[35] Edwards's views are controversial in large part because they undercut the conventional wisdom that the "bully pulpit" is one of the key powers wielded by any president.

There are clear weaknesses in the perspective developed by Edwards that rhetoric has very limited power to shape public opinion, even when wielded by a skillful president. It is obvious that this does not apply in the contexts of campaigns, ceremonies, and occasions of foreign policy. For example, there is simply no question that Senator Obama's "race speech" played an influential role in shaping public opinion at a key moment in the 2008 primary season.[36] It is equally obvious that at least some presidents have the capacity to shape the broader public agenda and influence how the public defines the world. David Zarefsky focuses on the power of such definitional rhetoric.[37] Clearly, there are presidents who are masters of this form of rhetoric. Reagan is the obvious post-war example of a president who, over time, used rhetoric to redefine the political universe for many Americans. There is a reason that commentators and academics now routinely refer to the "Age of Reagan."[38] The reason is that Reagan used speeches and other rhetorical occasions to shift debates about the role of government toward limited government intervention and toward a greater role of the marketplace. The phrase from his First Inaugural address, "In this present crisis, government is not the solution to our problems; government is the problem," has been particularly influential, and is now emblematic not only of his presidency, but of conservatism as a movement.[39] The influence of this phrase has been noted by liberal academics, including Alan Wolfe, who claim that Reagan was essentially "engaged in a direct dialogue with [Franklin] Roosevelt" when he argued that government was the problem, not the solution, to the economic crisis facing the nation in 1981.[40] Apparently, President Obama recognized the importance of this worldview. Writing in the *New York Times* about his inaugural address, Peter Baker observed that President Obama "seemed to take issue with

Ronald Reagan, who declared when he took office in 1981 that 'government is not the solution to our problem; government is the problem.'"[41] Reagan's example demonstrates that presidential rhetoric can be enormously powerful, especially in the long term, by shaping how people understand the political world.

Yet, in terms of garden variety domestic policy rhetoric, Edwards has a point. Edwards argues persuasively that even President Reagan was unable to move public opinion very much on domestic issues related to spending and taxes. As I noted later, President Obama succeeded, to a limited degree, in shaping public opinion about health care reform. These short-term failures (though the long term may be quite different), however, can be tied not to a weakness in rhetoric, but to strong rhetorical constraints that even the most skillful president faces in calling for domestic policy changes. In what follows, I explain how domestic policy rhetoric faces systemic and political constraints, both of which make it difficult to shift opinion.

SYSTEMIC AND POLITICAL CONSTRAINTS ON DOMESTIC POLICY RHETORIC

Presidents and other political leaders must adapt to the situation facing them when advocating any public policy. Some of the constraints they face relate to the particulars of the policy in dispute, interest groups involved, and other issue-related barriers. Other constraints, however, are tied to systemic issues in American politics, issues relating to citizen engagement, difficulties in dealing with complex policies, and so forth. Another set of constraints relates to the broad, domestic political environment facing the politician. Of course, in advocating for his agenda, President Obama faced particular constraints related to each of the policies he supported. Those constraints, in some cases, were quite daunting; however, in relation to his total domestic agenda, he also faced very severe systemic and (especially) political constraints. In the next two sections, I identify those constraints and explain how they limited the president's ability to move public opinion in the short term.

SYSTEMIC CONSTRAINTS

The rhetorical effectiveness of presidents and other political leaders is constrained by a number of factors inherent to the American political system. The first systemic constraint on domestic policy rhetoric is lack of voter knowledge. Domestic policy issues—from housing and health care, to taxation and transportation—involve complex policy disputes. The unfortunate truth is that voters rarely have adequate background knowledge to pick between competing claims on these issues. Research presents a grim picture of how much the average citizen knows about public policy, and even about very basic aspects of the American political system. For example, the Pew Research Center found in a 2010 survey that only 43% of the public understood that the Republican Party controlled the House of Representatives, but not the Senate, and almost one sixth of the nation (15%) thought that Republicans controlled the Senate, but not the House.[42] Still more worrisome, the public doesn't understand even basic facts about how Congress operates. For example, only 26% of the Pew sample understood that it took sixty votes to overcome a filibuster in the Senate.[43]

The public is even less knowledgeable about very basic public policy issues. A Pew survey in 2011 found, "many Americans have a hard time answering detailed questions about U.S. government spending. Roughly three-in-ten (29%) correctly say that the federal government spends more on Medicare than on scientific research, education or on interest on the national debt. Slightly more (36%) say that interest on the debt is the greater government expenditure."[44] Clearly, such low percentages on very basic knowledge about spending reflect a general lack of knowledge about policy. Another example of the public's lack of knowledge is the finding from a Pew survey taken roughly a week after the Supreme Court decision upholding the health care law, a decision that was "the month's most closely followed story," that only "55% of the public knows that the Supreme Court upheld most of the health care law's provisions."[45] The finding that only slightly more than half of the people knew of the outcome of the most important and most followed Supreme Court decision in many years is suggestive of the general lack of knowledge about public policy. Political commentators often castigate politicians for failing to explain the details of their policy proposals. The unfortunate truth is that very few Americans have the knowledge or even the interest needed to respond to or even understand those specific proposals. The lack of public knowledge about policy and the democratic process strongly constrains presidents as they strive to move public opinion.

A second systemic constraint relates to the complexity of domestic policy advocacy. Domestic policy rhetoric is by its very nature complex, and from the viewpoint of many voters, both dull and sometimes incomprehensible. Paul Krugman makes this point cogently, observing "voters aren't policy wonks who pore over Tax Policy Center analyses."[46] In this situation, lack of public understanding, combined with ideological rigidity, has created a situation in which, as Leonard Pitts argues, "facts seem overmatched by falsehood, too slow to catch them, too weak to stop them," concluding that contemporary American politics is dominated by "the increasingly obvious impotence of fact"[47] Facts have so little power because, from the perspective of the public, the details of public policy are quite dull. Consequently, most of the public makes little effort to search out those facts.

A related constraint concerns the way that the media deals with complex policy debates. Given the public's lack of knowledge about and interest in detailed policy disputes, it is quite understandable that the media is far more interested in the horse race of politics than in the details of any given policy dispute. According to Matthew Nisbet, the overwhelming percentage of political coverage is focused on aspects of the campaign race rather than issue analysis. He notes, "Lost in the media spectacle is any careful coverage of issues and policy proposals, or serious discussion of candidate background," also cites a Pew and Harvard survey of the 2008 campaign coverage that found only "15% . . . focused on the candidates' ideas and policy proposals and just 1% of stories . . . examined the candidates' records or past public performance."[48] Krugman's observation that "most voters get their news from short snippets on TV, which almost never contain[s] substantive policy analysis" is unfortunately quite accurate.[49]

Related to the lack of focus on policy in media coverage is a general wariness among major news organizations about taking clear positions about policy disputes, even when the facts are clearly on one side. In particular, the media is very cautious about labeling even obviously false claims as such, for fear of appearing partisan. Thus, the new media environment makes it difficult to effectively refute even the most ridiculous charge. Thomas Mann and Norman Ornstein write, "In the new age and the new culture, the negative and false charges are made rapidly and are hard to counter or erase. They also make rational discourse in campaigns and in Congress more difficult and vastly more expensive."[50]

Moreover, the goal of appearing balanced produces analyses that "simply repeat the he-said-she-said of political speeches."[51] One difficulty with simply presenting both sides is that "A balanced treatment of an unbalanced phenomenon is a distortion of reality."[52] On issues like global warming, where there is a scientific consensus, balanced reporting on facts is unbalanced, suggesting to readers that there is an active controversy, when in fact there is a consensus among experts in the field. In this context, it is understandable that even the most knowledgeable voter has difficulty judging between the competing views of partisans on many domestic issues.

POLITICAL CONSTRAINTS

In addition to the systemic constraints facing all presidents, President Obama faced a number of daunting political constraints in defending his domestic agenda. Ironically, the first of those constraints came from his rhetorical successes in 2008, creating quite unreasonable expectations about what he could accomplish. During the campaign, a few commentators recognize that the reaction the senator produced with his rhetoric of hope and change spelled difficulty for him once he had become president. Andrew Kohut of the Pew Research Center notes, "The reception he's getting is unlike anything we've seen in decades," and adds, "It's a very high set of expectations to live up to."[53] Peter Baker observes that Obama "set the expectations so high among different constituency groups."[54] The difficulty, as John Meachem observes, was that "Liberals who have thrilled to Obama could grow disenchanted with him if he fails to deliver a progressive Valhalla by, say, Valentine's Day."[55] Of course, Meachem was exactly right, but disenchantment with the president was inevitable given the unreasonable expectations created by his 2008 campaign.

In addition, a post-partisan theme both was prominent in Obama's rhetoric and made him appealing to many Independents and Republicans who forced him to reach out to the other side to confront many important issues. Obama discussed the post-partisan theme at many points during the campaign, but perhaps nowhere as eloquently as on the night of his defeat in the New Hampshire primary, saying that "we are not as divided as our politics suggest, that we are one people, we are one nation."[56] Given his use of this theme as far back as the 2004 Democratic National Convention speech, once he became president, he had to try and forge consensus by reaching out to Republicans in Congress. Obama was correct that the nation as a whole was not as divided as it sometimes appeared. There is strong support for pragmatic policies on a host of issues, regardless of ideology. For example, polling after Obama became president consistently supported Federal aid to states so that key public workers, including teachers, firemen, and police would not be laid off. There was strong public support for infrastructure development and a host of other policies the president favored. While the new president was correct about the public as a whole, he was dead wrong about committed partisans within the leaderships of the parties.[57]

The ideologies of committed partisans were in almost total conflict, in part because of "the shock dealt by the Great Recession to the political order," a shock that Eduardo Porter said was "hard to overstate."[58] While, in the past, there was room for compromise based on a pragmatic mixing of ideological perspectives, this was no longer true, mostly because of the unwillingness of conservatives to support almost any kind of government action (except in foreign and defense policy) and any additional government spending. Consequently, "the president's plans to stimulate the economy with tax cuts and spending programs have invariably crashed against solid Republican opposition in Congress."[59]

A second constraint the president faced was that it is easier to demonize a specific policy than it is to explain that policy. The unfortunate truth, as Mann and Ornstein note, is that "a vicious and unrelenting negative ad campaign can work."[60] Perhaps the best example of this pattern relates to the $500 billion cut in Medicare used to pay for part of the cost of the Affordable Care Act. This cut was premised on the fact that, currently, Medicare subsidizes a great deal of uncompensated care for hospitals. With a large expansion of the number of Americans with insurance, however, there would be much less uncompensated care. It is for this reason that the hospitals agreed to the cuts. Moreover, another large portion of this cut came from eliminating subsidized, private Medicare accounts that cost considerably more than traditional Medicare. Conservatives supported these programs with the argument that the private sector would be more efficient, and therefore cut costs. In fact, the private sector was not more efficient, and the accounts were sold based on additional services provided to populations of seniors that were healthier than average. It was a money-making program for insurance companies, but not a program that strengthened Medicare. Democrats wanted to cut the private Medicare accounts because, in their view, the program cost too much and hadn't worked. In addition, it is important to recognize that the $500 billion cut was a cut to the budget—not to basic benefits. Thus, Medicare recipients could not be harmed by this cut, except for those receiving extra services, like health club memberships, as part of the private Medicate (Medicare Advantage) plans.

However, in the 2010 mid-term campaign, Republicans relentlessly attacked the health care law for cutting Medicare by $500 billion. They did this despite the fact that their own proposals would cut Medicare by a similar amount, and turn Medicare into a subsidized benefit program that cut benefits or forced people to pay a much larger share of their own expenses.[61] Thus, the charge was fundamentally untrue and also completely disingenuous, since the very people making the charge favored a much more radical version of the cuts they decried. There is also no question that the attack worked to a large degree. This illustrates the point that it is much easier to demonize a program than it is to explain how a complex policy worked, and to answer objections to it. Sarah Palin's charge that the health care law created death panels illustrates this point.

A third political constraint that strongly limits domestic policy rhetoric is that the public rarely supports policies that call for genuine sacrifice. Polling about the budget deficit illustrates this problem. The Pew Research Center reported on a number of polls, finding conflicting results about the magnitude of the government debt problem and the appropriate actions to confront it. On the one hand, a strong majority (70%) "said the federal budget deficit is a serious problem that must be addressed now," and 65% "said the best way to reduce the federal budget deficit is to cut major programs and increase taxes," with "Majorities of Republicans, Democrats and independents" favoring such an approach.[62] On the other hand, when specific cuts or tax increases were proposed, the public strongly opposed them. Pew concluded that members of the public overwhelmingly "reject any specific ideas for reducing the deficit," with 60% and 70% opposition to raising the gas tax, cutting federal aid to education or transportation, taxing health insurance benefits, raising the retirement age, and so forth.[63] The only specifics to attract majority support were "freezing the salaries of federal workers and raising the Social Security contribution cap for high earners."[64] In other words, the public strongly favors deficit reduction, and is aware that cuts must be made and that taxes raised, but do not favor any specific program, unless it primarily impacts someone else. One suspects strongly that federal workers and high income seniors weren't thrilled with the idea of cutting pay or raising taxes on them.

The unwillingness of the public to support policies requiring sacrifice means that it will be enormously difficult to sell domestic policy reforms unless there are essentially no costs to such reforms. This situation helps clarify why President Obama has not embraced a detailed deficit reduction program. Given the fact that such a program would inevitably require sacrifice, to endorse a particular plan in advance of negotiating agreement on the program would likely prevent it from being adopted. On this topic, Mann and Ornstein made the point that high-minded rhetoric demanded by commentators like Thomas Friedman is unlikely to resonate widely. They note, "There is simply no reliable evidence to support the belief that voters would flock to a straight-talking, centrist, independent, or third-party candidate articulating the favored policies."[65] They added that, in fact, "Obama favored most of the policies embraced by those longing for a 'grand bargain.'"[66] Obama supported the policies, but was wise to not be too specific. The "eat your spinach" approach to domestic rhetoric rarely works for anyone except spinach farmers.

The fourth political constraint the president faced was an extraordinary rise in partisanship. Of course, partisan disagreement has characterized American rhetoric since the founding of the republic. With that said, the incredible anger expressed by opponents of President Obama, and the consistent opposition to his program (even where it contains policies that were previously supported by conservatives), is a new and very troubling development. One way to make this point is to observe that the president did not receive a traditional honeymoon period. Instead, he faced total opposition at the very beginning. Senate Minority Leader Mitch McConnell was quite candid about his goals to not focus on ideology or even pragmatic policies that might help the nation out of the Great Recession. Instead, he said, "The single most important thing we want to achieve is for President Obama to be a one-term president."[67] The opposition was so unified that, on signature achievements such as the stimulus and the health care bill, Republican support came only from the state of Maine and Republican Senator Arlen Specter, who found himself so alone as a Republican moderate that he changed parties to become a Democrat. The case of the stimulus is particularly interesting. Some members of the administration, notably Christine Roemer, recognized that the proposed stimulus bill might not be large enough to quickly pull the nation out of a severe recession, but the partisan environment made it impossible to achieve anything more, precisely because there were exactly three Republicans in the Senate willing to work with the president on a stimulus package—even after the administration made major compromises in relation to the size of the legislation and the inclusion of more tax incentives—rather than on direct spending that Obama preferred.[68] As a result, "Mr. Obama's accomplishments would come almost solely from the Democratic majorities in Congress."[69]

The environment of partisanship was unprecedented. Michael Kinsley observes that from the beginning of his term, Obama confronted "an opposition of really spectacular intransigence and downright meanness."[70] Mann and Ornstein describe the political situation: "President Obama's postpartisan pitch fell flat, and the Tea Party movement pulled the GOP further to its ideological pole. Republicans greeted the new president with a unified strategy of opposing, obstructing, discrediting, and nullifying every one of his important initiatives."[71] This created an increasingly polarized atmosphere where issues on which both parties previously had been willing to compromise suddenly became a political death match. Perhaps the best example is the deficit ceiling debate, leading to the downgrading of the nation's credit rating. Previously, the debt ceiling had been raised many times under administrations of both parties. On occasion, the party not occupying the presidency used the vote to highlight their opposition to the policies of the acting president, but there never was any serious doubt that the debt ceiling would be raised.[72] To not do so would risk the good credit of the United States. In the spring and summer of 2011, Obama faced a very different situation, in which many Tea Party Republicans were willing to push the nation to the brink, and perhaps over, that brink of default. Mann and Ornstein describe the debacle as "an appalling spectacle of hostage taking."[73] Noam Scheiber observed, "In 2011 . . . the Republicans were in the grips of true fiscal fanaticism while the economy was distressingly fragile."[74] This "fiscal fanaticism," was first evident in statements indicating a willingness to shut down the government, and later, in an unwillingness to raise the debt ceiling. For good reason, the situation "terrified the White House."[75] Moreover, despite the fact that Democrats were willing to compromise, and the president sought a grand bargain that would cut $4 trillion from the long term deficit, requiring real cuts in entitlement, "A problem precipitated by one party's deliberate intransigence caused damage to all the actors in the process, suggesting that any real accountability for bad behavior would be elusive."[76]

The opposition was so committed to opposing Obama that according to Paul Krugman, they carried out a sort of "post-truth politics" in which their positions were based in opposing Obama, rather than assessing the real problems confronting the nation.[77] As a consequence, Obama's critics often described "the president as a suspect character, someone who doesn't share American values."[78] Mark Lilla comments that "Apocalypticism trickled down, not up, and is now what binds Republican Party elites to their hardcore base. They all agree that the country must be 'taken back' from the usurpers by any means necessary, and are willing to support any candidate, no matter how unworldly or unqualified or fanatical, who shares their picture of the crisis of our time."[79] Because of the worldview that Obama was a "usurper," many of the president's opponents "don't feel compelled to explain how even a reduced government should meet the challenges of the new global economy, how our educational system should respond to them, what the geopolitical implications might be, or anything of the sort," resulting in the "decline of reality-based conservatives."[80] Race undoubtedly played some role in the zeal with which his opponents attacked centrist policies that, in many cases, Republicans had previously supported. Frank Bruni's comment that race "poisons some of his opponents, pumping them full of toxic zeal beyond the partisan norm," is exactly right.[81]

As I noted, the president faced unrelenting opposition to programs that many Republicans had previously supported.[82] While the charge is often made that President Obama is a leftist, a socialist, or even a communist, a review of the intellectual history of many of his proposals illustrates how off-base this conclusion is. Considering three of the most contentious areas is quite revealing: health care, global warming, and immigration. Conservatives decried the individual mandate, the core of the health care proposal, as a government take-over and an unconstitutional restriction on individual rights. However, the individual mandate was originally developed by Stuart M. Butler of the very conservative Heritage Foundation, and was embraced by many conservatives as both superior to a government-oriented system appropriate for establishing the personal responsibility of all Americans to purchase health care insurance.[83] A similar story applies to cap and trade, the administration's preferred approach for dealing with global warming. Cap and trade was originally the market-oriented conservative approach to pollution. Chris Good notes, "Supporting a cap-and-trade approach to greenhouse gas regulation is basically taboo in the GOP these days, but most of the top-tier Republican presidential contenders have backed it in the past."[84]. Comprehensive immigration reform was supported not only by Ronald Reagan, who signed an immigration reform law in the 1980s, but also by John McCain and George W. Bush.[85] It is startling given the intellectual roots of the major initiatives proposed by President Obama that on all his major domestic initiatives he received support in the form of exactly three Republican votes in the Senate—all on the stimulus.

Moreover, Obama was no radical on other policies. Timothy Egan notes "you have to go back to Dwight Eisenhower's administration, more than 50 years ago, to find a rate of federal spending growth lower than that of the Obama administration."[86] Despite the fact that Obama is anything but a big spender (at least after the stimulus), and that the intellectual roots of many of his proposals lay on the right, not the left, President Obama faced unrelenting opposition. Mitch McConnell made it quite clear that rather than serving the nation, the most important Republican priority was making sure that the president failed. One sign of both how united and strident the opposition was to Obama can be found in the campaign rhetoric of Governor Mitt Romney, who attacked the president for supporting "the most anti-investment, anti-business, anti-jobs series of policies in modern American history."[87] There certainly were grounds to criticize the Obama administration, especially on unemployment, but Romney's over-the-top language reveals more about the ideological status of his Republican opponent than it does about the president's rhetoric or policies. Perhaps the most basic problem is what Mann and Ornstein refer to as the fact that "near religious anti-tax cant continues to rule" the Republican Party.[88]

The partisan environment I have described was driven in part by the fact that very few House districts were competitive. Rather, almost all districts heavily favored one party or the other. In this situation, primary campaigns mattered more than the general election; Democrats in Congress worried about a primary challenge from the left, and Republicans worried about a primary challenge from the right. The effect was particularly dramatic on the ideological makeup of Republicans in Congress. Mann and Ornstein, scholars at the conservative American Enterprise Institute and the liberal Brookings Institute, respectively, write that:

> the fact, however awkward it may be for the traditional
> press and nonpartisan analysts to acknowledge, one of the
> two major parties, the Republican Party, has become an

insurgent outlier—ideologically extreme; contemptuous of the inherited social and economic policy regime; scornful of compromise; unpersuaded by conventional understanding of facts, evidence, and science; and dismissive of the legitimacy of its political opposition. When one party moves this far from the center of American politics, it is extremely difficult to enact policies responsive to the country's most pressing challenges.[89]

They later cite "veteran Republican congressional staffer, Mike Lofgren," who, upon retiring from government, wrote: "It should have been evident to clear-eyed observers that the Republican Party is becoming less and less like a traditional political party in a representative democracy and becoming more like an apocalyptic cult."[90]

A combination of the rise of partisanship and the fact that few seats in the House were competitive created a situation in which public opinion of the nation as a whole mattered much less than in the past. The debate about the debt ceiling and President Obama's proposed job package in the summer and fall of 2011 is instructive. The president largely won this debate, with large majorities supporting his views nationally. Public opinion sharply favored Obama's approach to continue Federal spending to confront the recession, while supporting a balance of long-term spending cuts and tax increases on the rich. A *New York Times*/CBS poll in mid-October, 2011 found that 65% labeled it a "good idea" for the Federal Government to give aid to states to avoid layoffs of teachers, police, and firefighters, while 80% favored increased investment in infrastructure, and 65% favored raising taxes on those with incomes over one million dollars.[91] In April 2012, by a 56% to 37% majority, the public favored spending more on education and infrastructure and raising taxes on the wealthy, versus cutting spending and taxes. The same poll found that 57% of Americans thought the wealthy paid less than their fair share of Federal taxes. Moreover, Pew found that a two-thirds majority also supported allowing the Bush tax cuts to expire for those with incomes over $250,000. On the deficit, a Pew survey found that 62% favored "a balanced approach to deficit reduction—both cuts in major programs and tax increases," a finding that "has been consistent over the past year."[92] Pew found that a mere 17 percent favored a deficit plan focusing "mostly on program reductions."[93] The public was firmly on Obama's side, but this did not matter because of the ideological orthodoxy required in the conservative movement, an orthodoxy reinforced by the threat of a primary challenge from the right. In this case, it would seem that his rhetoric worked in shaping public opinion. Yet, his success mattered little because ideologues refused to compromise, and there was little political pressure on most incumbents in the House because of the nature of their districts.

The fifth political constraint on Obama's domestic policy rhetoric was the flood of special interest money made possible by the Citizens United decision, creating a situation in which "American elections are awash in money."[94] The campaign finance law gave outside influence to enormously wealthy individuals who essentially opposed any government regulation.[95] Opposition to Obama's program from the energy industry and the financial sector was particularly important. Given policy consensus on the need to confront global warming and to enact meaningful reforms of the financial sector, such opposition was inevitable. Citizens United and other campaign finance rulings allowed for unlimited contributions from donors with extremely deep pockets. Given the power of negative advertising, Citizens United made problems facing the president still more difficult to solve.

Sixth, it is important to recognize that the economy itself constrained the president. There is no question that a bad or a good economy can overwhelm other issues in shaping public opinion about the agenda of any president. Notably, the "Great Communicator," (President Ronald Reagan) wasn't so great until the economy started to revive in 1983.[96] The economy is influential in shaping public opinion because it is crucial to the well-being of every family, from the middle-class to the very poor. If the economy had come back more quickly, Obama would have had a much easier time making his case on a host of issues. Crucially, the oft-heard complaint that the president should have focused only on the economy mischaracterizes the rhetorical situation the president faced. In relation to the stimulus, the president worked very hard to get Congress to pass a bill as large as it was. After that bill was passed, it was very difficult to persuade Congress to enact additional support. This became quite clear in the summer and fall of 2011, when the president made a case for his jobs package. As noted, he persuaded the American people, but not Congress, of the importance of more spending. Given this economic and political situation, it made sense that after passing the stimulus, Obama pivoted from the economy to focus on long-term issues. He had strong Democratic support in the House and the Senate, although, in both cases, the Democratic caucus was much more divided than the Republican caucus. In addition, it was clearly correct that energy and global warming, education, financial reform, the budget deficit, and especially health care were the core issues facing the nation.

The final political constraint the president faced was an incredibly fragile banking sector. Crucially, all presidents need someone to blame when things don't go well. In Obama's case, the obvious scapegoat to blame for the economic ills facing the nation was the financial sector, especially big banks, who had taken terrible risks that ultimately resulted in the crisis of late summer and fall of 2008. Here, however, there was a problem. Especially in the first two years of his presidency, Obama dared not demonize the bankers because of the potential effects that such criticism could have on public perceptions of the stability of the financial sector. Given the weakness of the banks—manifested in the need for stress tests to reassure people that there was no danger of a bank run—a sustained attack on the people who had brought on the crisis because of their irresponsible greed risked harming market confidence. Scheiber notes that "the president's options were limited" in what he could say about the banking sector, and referenced the views of Treasury Secretary Tim Geithner that there was a danger of "destroy[ing] institutions you were trying to save."[97] This created a situation in which the very people who had produced the economic crisis, and who had been bailed out by the Federal Government, had to be treated gently for fear of causing another banking crisis. Obama clearly recognized this point. He notes in a July 22, 2011 Town Hall:

> That's always a balance for a president. On the one hand, you want to project confidence and optimism. And remember, in that first year, people weren't sure whether the banking system was going to melt down, and whether we were going to go into a Great Depression. And so it was important for me to let the American people know we're going to be all right, we're going to be able to get through this.
>
> On the other hand, I think maybe people's expectations were that somehow we were going to be able to solve this in a year. And we knew pretty soon after I took office that this was going to last for a while.[98]

Obama knew that the crisis was deep, but he also understood that demonizing the banks for their very real sins risked worsening the problem. This created a situation in which the president could be attacked for being soft on the bankers, but also could be blamed by the financial industry for supporting regulation in the form of the Dodd-Frank law that eventually passed Congress. In terms of political constraints on his domestic policy rhetoric, the combination of extraordinarily difficult economic conditions and a banking sector that was both largely responsible for those conditions and so fragile that attacks on behavior risked worsening the situation, created an extremely daunting rhetorical environment for the president.

The foregoing analysis of systemic and political constraints facing President Obama largely explains why his rhetoric on a host of domestic issues often failed to greatly move public opinion. It is notable that on the deficit and on taxes, his rhetoric actually worked in influencing public opinion, but his rhetoric still did not matter in Congress. Ronald Reagan famously pressed Congress to enact his economic program by appealing to the people. Obama attempted the same strategy, and was quite successful in gaining public support. He was much more successful than Edwards's research suggests is the norm for even a skillful presidential persuader, such as Reagan. However, the political environment has changed since 1981. In 1981, general public opinion mattered much more than it did in the summer of 2011.

All presidents face systemic constraints and some forms of partisan opposition identified earlier. This explains why it is difficult for any president, even in the best of times, to decisively shift public opinion on domestic issues. It is important to recognize, however, that Obama did not assume the presidency in the best of times. He faced a uniquely difficult rhetorical environment for several reasons. First, he faced something unprecedented: united partisan opposition from his first day in office. Much of this opposition was based not merely in policy disagreement, but in the view that he was in some sense a "usurper," and therefore an illegitimate president. Frequent statements by conservative activists of the need to "take back" their country reflected this viewpoint. Reagan was able to bridge the partisan divide to some extent by appealing to "Reagan Democrats." There were plenty of "Obama Republicans" in the country, but not in the Congress. Second, Obama faced an opposition willing to use the filibuster even on minor issues—another unprecedented development. Mann and Ornstein note that "the pervasive use of the filibuster [that Obama faced] had never before happened in the history of the Senate," adding that Republicans "erect[ed] a filibuster bar for nearly everything."[99] Absent the filibuster, he would have enacted his entire domestic agenda in the first two years, an agenda that was supported by the majority of Americans, but blocked because of the filibuster. Finally, the bad economic situation the president inherited; the weakness of the banks, combined with their opposition to regulation; and the Citizens United decision made the overall political climate quite unfriendly. Reagan faced a very difficult rhetorical situation in 1981 and 1982, but not nearly as difficult as Obama faced on assuming office.

The key point is that it is important to evaluate the success of Obama's domestic rhetoric in relation to the constraints that he faced, and those constraints were enormous. It also should be remembered that the president succeeded in passing major programs on health care, financial regulation, and other priorities. These accomplishments were achieved because the president mobilized support within the Democratic Party as well as among the national audience. Contrary to the views of commentators cited earlier, the president was successful at least in mobilizing support among Democrats and Democratic-leaning independents.

This is not to say that the president bears no responsibility for rhetorical failures. In retrospect, it is clear he should have pushed harder for a larger stimulus and shifted away from post-partisan themes more quickly. It was also a major error not to negotiate an extension of the debt ceiling, with the deal extending tax cuts, after the 2010 midterm elections. However, these judgments are much clearer in retrospect than they were at the time. Overall, given the enormous political and systemic constraints facing him, it is his rhetorical successes, rather than failures, that are truly astonishing. This point is most obvious in a brief review of how the president sold health care reform.

HEALTH CARE REFORM

I noted earlier that Obama worked very hard to develop a health care proposal that could appeal to a bipartisan audience. He also spent enormous energy first explaining and then defending the proposal. And as I noted, his speech to Congress and the nation was highly praised for its lucidity and emotional resonance. Despite these facts, his advocacy of health care reform is usually viewed as a failure because there has been such consistent public opposition to the health care law. For example, Abby Goodnough concludes that "most evidence suggests it [the Obama administration] has lost miserably in the court of public opinion."[100] Once again, the explanation for this finding was that the Obama Administration had "been halfhearted in its sales pitch from the beginning."[101] Characteristically, Maureen Dowd put it more strongly, accusing the president of "failure from the start to sell his plan or even explain it," something she labeled as "bizarre and self-destructive."[102]

In fact, Obama tried very hard selling his health care plan. He spoke again and again about it in town hall events and major speeches before Congress passed the plan and spoke repeatedly about it after its passage. A review of the White House website reveals numerous speeches and other events selling the plan.[102] In actuality, Obama's health care advocacy illustrates both the constraints on domestic policy rhetoric and the fact that it remains a powerful, if limited, weapon.

The various constraints I describe are all obvious in the evolution of the public debate about health care. For example, there is no question that the public's general lack of knowledge and difficulty dealing with complexity influenced the debate. Despite the president's best efforts, many people continued to believe that the bill established death panels, that it included a Federal takes over that of the health care industry, and that a large number of people would pay a health care tax. This led Jim Rutenberg and Gardiner Harris to observe in the summer of 2009 in *The New York Times* that "The roiling debate over health care this summer has included a host of accusations from opponents of the plan that have been so specious that many in the mainstream news media have flatly labeled them false."[103] The accusations may have been false, but they were widely believed. Three years later, little had changed. Paul Krugman noted that "the most striking thing about the campaign against reform was its dishonesty. Remember 'death panels'? Remember how reform's opponents would, in the same breath, accuse Mr. Obama of promoting big government and denounce him for cutting Medicare."[104]

The debate illustrates political constraints as well. The president faced unrelenting opposition to what was, for over a decade, the default conservative approach to health care reform. He was called a socialist for embracing a program quite similar to ones that George H.W. Bush and Bob Dole supported. Moreover, the fact that it is easier to attack a specific proposal than either explain that proposal or answer objections to it was obvious at any number of points in the debate. I've already focused on how critics spoke of cuts in Medicare—those that, in fact, did not cut benefits—in order to demonize the law. Many other examples could be cited. In addition, the influence of money on public debate is nowhere more obvious than in relation to health care. The words "job killing" has been used in countless attack commercials to describe the law, despite the absence of evidence that it would in fact have such an effect.[105] It also seems quite likely that public opinion about the law was influenced by the economic climate. If the economy had grown more rapidly, all aspects of the president's agenda would likely have been more popular.

Even with those constraints, it is too strong to claim that the president's rhetoric did not have an impact. Initially, it is important to recognize that Obama was successful in mobilizing Democrats to support the law in the crucial period immediately prior to Congressional passage, achieving something that every Democratic president since Harry Truman had attempted but failed to achieve. In addition, while public opinion surveys indicated that many opposed the law, polling also indicated that almost all provisions of the law were quite popular. There was strong support for most of the components of the law, with the notable exceptions of the individual mandate.[106] Based on these findings, *The New Republic* concluded that while "People may not like the Affordable Care Act, per se . . . they like nearly all of its component parts, in some cases by huge margins."[107]

Moreover, close analysis of the polls indicates that the public was much more split than a mere look at the topline poll number indicates. In the period immediately prior to the Supreme Court ruling, 43% of the people approved of the law, while 48% disapproved. Even so, a 48% to 44% majority would be unhappy if the law were overturned. The survey also found that a strong majority of Democrats, and a small majority of independents, favored the individual mandate.[108] Additionally, "about a fifth of those who oppose it [the health care law] say it did not go far enough, essentially frustrated liberals."[109] Charles M. Blow explains the importance of this finding, observing that a *New York Times*/CBS News Poll found that "37% of Americans believed the law went too far, while 27% said not far enough and 25% said about right."[110] He then notes, "When you cross-reference the numbers, just over two-thirds of the people who wanted the law struck down thought it went too far. That's only 27% of those polled," concluding the "The 'too much government' crowd is just grasping at straws."[111] Other surveys indicated more support for the law, especially among knowledgeable voters, than the headlines might have indicated. For example, Pew research indicates "Among those who tracked news about the health care decision very closely, 50% approve of the decision, while 45% disapprove," and those who did not follow the decision closely were just 24% approve and 37% disapprove.[112] This finding suggests that there was much stronger support for the law among those who were most aware of the details of the legislation. It also seems likely that support may grow over time, given the vast number of people who didn't understand that the law provided subsidies to help in purchasing coverage, or falsely believed that the law was a takeover of the health care system that would drastically reduce choice. One reason so many people believe these falsehoods is that those opposed to the law spent $235 million on advertising, while supporters of the law spent only $69 million. Elizabeth Wilner, a vice president of the Campaign Media Analysis group, concludes that the balance of advertising "explains, in a nutshell, why polling shows attitudes about the law to be at best mixed."[113]

Clearly, President Obama faced an uphill battle in selling health care. He certainly was not successful in every instance in justifying or explaining the law. At the same time, the polling data cited earlier indicates that claims of failure are far too strong. In fact, given the constraints he faced, it is astonishing that the president was as successful as he was in influencing public opinion in favor of The Affordable Care Act.

CONCLUSION

In the introduction of this essay, I cited the surprising conclusion of commentators that the man universally labeled as the most eloquent political leader since Reagan had lost his capacity to inspire. The foregoing analysis of domestic policy rhetoric makes it clear that the president has not lost his rhetorical skill; in fact, the surprise—given the systemic, political, and economic constraints facing President Obama—is not that his rhetoric often failed to move public opinion decisively, but that he succeeded as much as he did. It should be recalled that in addition to the stimulus and health care reform, the president succeeded in passing regulations of the financial sector, a major education initiative through grant programs in the stimulus, a waiver program that encouraged educational reform as part of No Child Left Behind, and began rule-making on global warming. There certainly were failures, notably on immigration and achieving a grand bargain on the deficit, but overall, the president was quite successful in not only enacting his agenda, but in using rhetoric to do so.

The judgment that the president has not lost his rhetorical skill, but that his successes are limited by a daunting political environment, is supported by the outcome of the 2012 presidential campaign. Crucially, the systemic constraints and, to some extent, the political constraints facing the president, were less difficult in the campaign than in selling his domestic agenda. In the campaign, Obama faced an opponent who could be attacked for taking extremely conservative ideologically inconsistent positions. Therefore, the president had the ability to strongly attack, and even demonize, his opponent using his rhetorical arsenal, creating a more level rhetorical playing field than he faced in supporting his domestic agenda. Moreover, the president's fundraising prowess made the Citizens United decision a non-factor. Since campaigns are not about legislation, the threat of a filibuster no longer constrained his rhetoric. By fall 2012, the economy in general, and the banking sector in particular, were stronger than they had been in 2009 and 2010. Moreover, the fact that campaigns are fought about broad themes means that the complexity of public policy and citizen's lack of knowledge no longer were major factors limiting his rhetoric. In the campaign environment, the president had far more rhetorical options than he possessed in supporting his domestic agenda. In this environment, it is not surprising that President Obama was more successful than in selling his domestic agenda. Mario Cuomo famously observed that candidates "campaign in poetry," but "govern in prose."[114] Clearly, given the political environment, poetry is easier.

The analysis of factors constraining President Obama's rhetorical options is revealing not only for what it tells us about how Obama sold his domestic program, but also for what it reveals about the status of American politics and of political debate in the metaphorical public square. Several conclusions are obvious. First, the system is heavily weighted against policy reform that threatens existing power brokers. Entrenched opponents fought Obama on all of his reform efforts of government regulation at all level. Second, key actors on the American political scene often fail to fulfill the functions that

their particular role is designed to fulfill in a democratic society. It is obvious, for example, that millions and millions of citizens do not view it as
their responsibility to be aware of the debate on major questions of public
policy, or even to understand very basic questions about the government and
political process. In fact, public knowledge of policy is so low that there are
relatively few truly informed citizens. In addition, the media has not done a
good job educating the public about such issues. Some media groups focus
on the horse race aspect of politics, while others take a partisan tone and advocate for one side or another. President Obama tried to overcome both of
these problems by clearly explaining his proposals on numerous occasions.
When he took this approach, commentators on the left and right called him
dull, a criticism that perhaps reveals more about their approach to commentary than it does about the rhetoric of the president. While the president did
not fully succeed in educating the public, it is obvious that he worked much
harder at explaining his positions in a way that ordinary citizens could understand than did other key actors in the American public sphere.

Will Obama's words have the same kind of long-term influence so evident
in the rhetorical legacy of President Reagan? That question will not be an-
swered for a generation, though tantalizing evidence suggests that, like Reagan, Obama has a coherent vision of the nation, a vision rooted in his own
variant of American Exceptionalism and the American Dream. Like Reagan,
he comes after a period dominated by a competing ideology, and he also has
a vision of a better America that provides opportunity for all Americans.
It should be remembered that Reagan's vision of the nation as an inclusive
one, where all have a chance to succeed, was shaped by his experience in the
depression, and his strong support for the agenda of Franklin Roosevelt. He
later argued that the liberal agenda had been pushed too far, but always believed that the American Dream should be open to all who had the values
and work-ethic to achieve it. Obama's vision is similar to that of Reagan, but
is shaped by the view that pendulum had shifted too far toward individualism and away from a vision of a community that provides opportunities for
all. Obama, like Reagan, has a coherent ideological vision tied to a variant
of the American Dream. Presidents with such a rhetorical agenda include
Reagan, both Roosevelts, and Abraham Lincoln. The potential influence of
Obama's rhetoric should be obvious in the list of his predecessors who enacted similar, coherent ideological/mythic worldviews.

Notes

1. Ryan Lizza, "Battle Plans: How Obama Won," *New Yorker*, November 17,
2008, http://www.newyorker.com/reporting/2008/1/17/081117fa_fact_liz; Matt

Bai, "The Edge of Mystery," *New York Times Magazine*, January 18, 2009, 44 and "Promises to Keep," *New York Times Magazine*, July 13, 2008, 12; Chuck Todd and Sheldon Gawiser, *How Barack Obama Won: A State-by-State Guide to the Historic 2008 Presidential Election* (New York: Vintage Books, 2009), 11.

2. See, for instance, Alec MacGillis, "Finding Political Strength in the Power of Words: Oratory Has Helped Drive Obama's Career—and Critics' Questions," *Washington Post*, February 26, 2008, A1; Katharine Q. Seelye, "History as a Guide for an Inaugural Address that Frames the Moment," *New York Times*, January 18, 2009, A18; Karen Tumulty, "Health Care: Can Obama Find a Cure?" *Time*, August 10, 2009, 26; Joe Klein, "Inspiration vs. Substance," *Time*, February 18, 2008, 18; Thomas L. Friedman, "Radical in the White House," *New York Times*, January 21, 2009, A23; Peter Baker, "Obama Takes Oath, and Nation In Crisis Embraces The Moment," *New York Times*, January 21, 2009, P3; Jodi Kantor, "For a New Political Age, A Self-Made Man," *New York Times*, August 28, 2008, A21; Michael Chabon, "Obama & the Conquest of Denver," *New York Review of Books*, October, 9, 2008, 48; David Broder, "Ability to Inspire May be Obama's Greatest Gift," *Lawrence Journal-World*, November 2, 2008, 9B; Peter Appelbombe, "Is Eloquence Overrated?" *New York Times*, January 13, 2008, WK3; Michiko Kakutani, "From Books, New President Found Voice," *New York Times*, January 19, 2009, A1; Bob Herbert, "More than Charisma," *New York Times*, January 24, 2009, A19; *Kansas City Star*, "Barack Obama for President," October 18, 2008, B6; Evan Thomas, *A Long Time Coming*. New York: Public Affairs, 2009, 183.

3. William Safire, "The Audacity of Hype," *New York Times*, August 31, 2008, WK12; William Kristol, "Be Afraid, Please," *New York Times*, July 28, 2008, A21.

4. Ron Fournier, "Obama as Comforter in Chief," *Kansas City Star*, April 30, 2009, A2; Matthew Dallek, "The Comparisons Between Barack Obama and Abraham Lincoln," *U.S. News & World Report*, November 20, 2008, http://www.newsbank.com.

5. Elizabeth Drew, "What Were They Thinking? *New York Review of Books*, August 18, 2011, 14. After the speeches at Osawatomie and the State of the Union were built around themes developed in Kansas, the attitudes of Democrats in Congress shifted substantially toward supporting the president. See also Jonathan Weisman, "House Democrats Welcome Obama's Confrontational Tone Toward G.O.P." *New York Times*, January 7, 2012, A16.

6. Leonard Pitts, Jr., "Greatness Achieved, Not Declared," *Lawrence Journal-World*, July 5, 2012, 8A.

7. Thomas L. Friedman, "Wasting Warren Buffett," *New York Times*, June 20, 2012, A27.

8. Thomas L. Friedman, "Taking One for the Country," *New York Times*, July 1, 2012, SR 11.

9. Thomas L. Friedman, "What the Locusts Ate," *New York Times*, June 6, 2012, A23.

10. Thomas L. Friedman, "Obama Should Seize the High Ground," *New York Times*, May 27, 2012, SR 11.

11. Andrew Hacker, "The Next Election: The Surprising Reality," *New York Review of Books*, August 18, 2011, 79-80.

12. Maureen Dowd, "Showtime at the Apollo," *New York Times*, January 22, 2012, SR 13, and "Dreaming of a Superhero," *New York Times*, June 3, 2012, SR13.

13. Maureen Dowd, "Less Spocky, More Rocky," *The New York Times*, September 9, 2009, A25.

14. Paul Krugman, "The Republican Economy," *New York Times*, June 4, 2012, A21.

15. Ross Douthat, "A Good Candidate Is Hard to Find," *New York Times*, January22, 2012, SR14.

16. Aaron Blake, "President Obama: A man of any slogans," *Washington Post*, July 10, 2012, http://www.washigntonpost.com/blogs/the-fix/post/president-obama-a.

17. Barack Obama, "Remarks by the President on the Economy," April 14, 2009, http://whitehouse.gov/the_press_office/Remarks-by-the-President-on-the-Economy-at. Future references are made within the text by paragraph number.

18. See also Robert C. Rowland, "Barack Obama and the Revitalization of Public Reason," *Rhetoric and Public Affairs*, 14 (2011): 693-725. Obama's address produced positive reactions from commentators. These reactions are summarized in the essay.

19. Barack Obama, "Remarks by the President on the Economy," April 14, 2009, http://whitehouse.gov/the_press_office/Remarks-by-the-President-on-the-Economy-at. Here, President Obama alludes to Senator Hillary Clinton's comment during the 2008 primaries that presidents govern in prose, not poetry. The original phrase came from Mario Cuomo, and Clinton quoted it as part of a criticism of Senator Obama for having great eloquence, but not an adequate record to be president. See Dan Balz and Haynes Johnson, *The Battle for America 2008: The Story of an Extraordinary Election* (New York: Viking, 2009), 136.

20. See. Rowland, "The Fierce Urgency of Now," 203-21.

21. See Julie Bosman, "Obama's New Book Is Surprise Best Seller," *New York Times*, November 9, 2006, B1, B6.

22. Barack Obama, *The Audacity of Hope: Thoughts on Reclaiming the American Dream* (New York: Crown, 2006). Obama's discussion of these themes is found in Chapter 5, "Opportunity," pp. 137-94. The specific policies and commentary cited are on pp. 161-63, 167-71, 177-78, 184-85, 188, 192-93.

23. Kennedy is quoted in Dan Balz, "From the Start, Putting a Bold Stamp on the White House," *Washington Post*, April 29, 2009, A6.

24. Peter Baker, "New Deal. Great Society. New Foundation?" *New York Times*, May 16, 2009, A8.

25. See Charles Krauthammer, "The Sting, In Four Parts," *Washington Post*, April 17, 2009, A19; Charles Moore, "Obama's house of prosperity may yet be a castle in the air; He feels like the right man to be President, but has he come at the right time, asks Charles Moore in Washington," *The Daily Telegraph*, April 18, 2009, 22; David Brooks, "Big-Spending Conservative," *The New York Times*, April 21, 2009, A25.

26. Dallek is quoted in Baker, "New Deal. Great Society. New Foundation?," A8 (see n. 23).

27. Newt Gingrich, "Obama's Radical Agenda," *USA Today*, April 29, 2009, 8A.

28. Barack Obama, "Remarks by the President on Fiscal Policy," April 13, 2011, http://www.whitehouse.gov/the-press-office/2011/04/13/remarks-presi. Future references are made in the text by paragraph number.

29. For an analysis of how Obama taps into both variants of the American Dream, see Robert C. Rowland and John M. Jones, "Recasting the American Dream and American Politics: Barack Obama's Keynote Address to the 2004 Democratic National Convention," *Quarterly Journal of Speech*, 93, (2007): 425–48.

30. Ryan apparently was upset by the president's strong attacks on his budget proposal. One commentator said he was "really hurt and insulted." See Peter Catapano, "An Uncivil Civil War," April 15, 2011, http://opinionator.blogs.nytimes.com/2011/04/15/an-uncivil-war/.

31. Peterson is quoted in Michael D. Shear, "Reaction to Obama Deficit Reduction Speech Swift—and Partisan," *The Caucus*, April 13, 2011, http://thecaucus.blogs.nytimes.com/2011/04/13/reaction-to-obama-deficit-reduction-speech-swift-and-partisan/.

32. The president's willingness to accept a grand bargain with significant cuts in entitlements, including possibly raising the age at which people receive Medicare, is made clear in Thomas E. Mann and Norman J. Ornstein, *It's Even Worse Than It Looks: How the American Constitutional System Collided With the New Politics of Extremism* (New York: Basic Books, 2012), 15–25.

33. See the National Commission on Fiscal Responsibility and Reform, http://www.fiscalcommission.gov/.

34. The Tucson speech was received so well that even conservatives praised it. See Dan Amira, "Obama's Tucson Speech Wins Rare Praise from Conservatives," January 21, 2011, http://nymag.com/daily/intel/2011/01/obama_tucson_speech_reactions.html The same point applies to the Nobel Prize speech. See Eamon Javers, "Conservative praise for Nobel speech," December 10, 2009, http://www.politico.com/news/stories/1209/30448.html. The *New York Times* editorialized about the Afghanistan speech at West Point, that "President Obama showed considerable political courage by addressing that pessimism and despair head-on." See "The Afghanistan Speech," *New York Times*, December 1, 2009, http://www.nytimes.com/2009/12/02/opinion/02wed1.html?pagewanted=all. Earlier, I cited commentary praising the health care speech, pp. 42-56.

35. George C. Edwards II, *On Deaf Ears: The Limits of the Bully Pulpit* (New Haven: Yale University Press, 2003), 74. Also see George Edwards III, "Presidential Rhetoric: What Differences Does It Make?" in *Beyond the Rhetorical Presidency*, ed. Martin J. Medhurst (College Station: Texas A & M Univ. Press, 1996), 199–217.

36. The public response to the speech is discussed in Robert C. Rowland and John M. Jones, "One Dream: Barack Obama, Race, and the American Dream," *Rhetoric and Public Affairs*, 14 (2011): 125–54.

37. David Zarefsky responded to Edwards by focusing on the capacity of presidents and other skilled leaders to shape public worldviews. See David Zarefsky, "Presidential Rhetoric and the Power of Definition," *Presidential Studies Quarterly* 34 (2004): 607–19.

38. It is notable that two recent books use this title, although the authors are a distinguished liberal academic and a Fellow, respectively, at the conservative think tank, the American Enterprise Institute. See Sean Willentz, *The Age of Reagan: A History 1974–2008* (New York: Harper Collins, 2008); Steven F. Haward, *The Age of Reagan: The Conservative Couunterrevolution 1980–1989* (New York: Crown Forum, 2009).

39. See Ronald Reagan, Inaugural Address, http://www.reagan.utexas.edu/archives/speeches/1981/12081a.htm, January 20th (1981), paragraph 9.

40. Alan Wolfe, *The Future of Liberalism* (New York: Knopf, 2009), 239.

41. Peter Baker, "A Milestone in History," *The New York Times*, 21 January 2009, P3.

42. Pew Research Center, "Public Knowledge: Senate Legislative Process a Mystery to Many," January 28, 2010, http://pewresearch.org/pubs/1478/political-iq-quiz-knowledge-filibuster-debt-colbert-steele.

43. Pew Research Center, "Well Known: Clinton and Gadhafi; Little Known: Who Controls Congress," March 31, 2011, http://www.people-press.org/2011/03/31/well-known-clinton-and-gadhafi-little-known-who-controls-congress/.

44. Pew Research Center, "Division, Uncertainty over Court's Health Care Ruling," July 2, 2012, http://www.people-press.org/2012/07/02/division-uncertainty-over-courts-health-care-ruling/

45. Pew Research Center, "Division, Uncertainty over Court's Health Care Ruling," July 2, 2012, http://www.people-press.org/2012/07/02/division-uncertainty-over-courts-health-care-ruling/

46. Paul Krugman, "Policy and the Personal," *New York Times*, July 16, 2012, A17.

47. Leonard Pitts, Jr. "U.S. Politics Dealing in Fear, Not Facts," *Lawrence Journal-World*, July 1, 2012, 9A.

48. Matthew C. Nisbet, "Horse Race Coverage & the Political Spectacle," December 31, 2007, http://scienceblogs.com/framing-science/2007/12/31/horse-race-coverage-the-politi/.

49. Krugman, "Policy and the Personal," A17.

50. Mann and Ornstein, *It's Even Worse Than It Looks*, 66.

51. Krugman, "Policy and the Personal," A17.

52. Mann and Ornstein, *It's Even Worse Than It Looks*, 194.

53. Kohut is cited in Lawrence Jill, "Poll: Hopes Soaring for Obama Administration," *USA Today*, November 11, 2008, A1.

54. Peter Baker, "Whose President Is He Anyway?" *The New York Times*, November 16, 2008, WK 7.

55. John Meachem, "Prologue," in Evan Thomas, *"A Long Time Coming": The Inspiring, Combative 2008 Campaign and the Historic Election of Barack Obama* (New York: Public Affairs, 2009), xiii.

56. Barack Obama, "Remarks of Senator Barack Obama: New Hampshire Primary," January 8, 2008, http://www.barackobama.com/2008/01/08/remarks_of_senator_barack_oba_82.php.

57. Ryan Lizza makes this argument in "The Obama Memos," *New Yorker*, January 30, 2012, 36-49.

58. Eduardo Porter, "Obama's Fate Rests in Part on Europe," *New York Times*, June 6, 2012, B1.

59. Ibid.

60. Mann and Ornstein, *It's Even Worse Than It Looks*, 78.

61. For an informative discussion of the case, see Jackie Calmes, "Delicate Pivot as G.O.P. Blasts Rivals on Medicare," *New York Times*, July 7, 2012, A9.

62. Pew Research Center, "The Deficit Debate: Where the Public Stands," April 12, 2011, http://pewresearch.org/pubs/1964/public-views-deficit-debate-eve-ob.

63. Ibid.

64. Ibid.

65. Mann and Ornstein, *It's Even Worse Than It Looks*, 113.

66. Ibid, 114.

67. David M. Herszenhorn, "Hold On to Your Seat: McConnell Wants Obama Out," *The Caucus*, October 26, 2010, http://thecaucus.blogs.nytimes.com/2010/10/26/hold-on-to-your-seat-mcconnell-wants-obama-out/; See also Carl Hulse and Adam Nagourney, "Senate G.O.P. Leader Finds Weapon in Unity," March 16, 2010, http://www.nytimes.com/2010/03/17/us/politics/17mcconnell.html?pagewanted=all.

68. See Noam Scheiber, *The Escape Artists: How Obama's Team Fumbled the Recovery* (New York: Simon and Schuster, 2011), 24–111.Scheiber argues that the Obama administration should have fought for a larger figure, but his description of the significant political compromises made to get the three votes in the Senate illustrates how little room Obama had to maneuver..

69. John Harwood, "Reality and Re-election Sharpen Obama's Zig-Zags," *New York Times*, December 10, 2011, A6.

70. Michael Kinsley, "Bipolar America," *New York Times Book Review*, January 8, 2012, 12.

71. Mann and Ornstein, *It's Even Worse Than It Look*, xi.

72. Ibid, 6–7.

73. Ibid, xii.

74. Noam Scheiber, "Obama's Worst Year: The Inside Story of his Brush with Political Disaster," *The New Republic*, March 15, 2012, 15.

75. Scheiber, *The Escape Artists*, 275.

76. Mann and Ornstein, *It's Even Worse Than It Looks*, 27.

77. Paul Krugman, "The Post-Truth Campaign," *New York Times*, December 23, 2011, A27.

78. Ibid.

79. Lilla, "Republicans for Revolution,"14.

80. Ibid, 16.

81. Frank Bruni, "The Emotional Tug of Obama," *New York Times*, May 27, 2012, SR3.

82. See Mann and Ornstein, *It's Even Worse Than It Looks*, 187.

83. The first version of this proposal was presented in 1989. See Stuart M. Butler, Assuring Affordable Health Care for All Americans (Heritage Foundation, October 2, 1989) and *A Policy Maker's Guide to The Health Care Crisis: Part II: The Heritage Consumer Choice Health Plan* (Heritage Foundation, March 5, 1992); David Leonhardt, "Real Choice? It's Off Limits in Health Bills," *The New York Times*, August 26, 2009, A15; Paul Krugman, "Missing Richard Nixon," *The New York Times*, August 31, 2009, A17.

84. Chris Good, "Almost Every 2012 Republican Has a Cap-and-Trade Problem," *The Atlantic*, May 13, 2011, http://www.theatlantic.com/politics/archive/2011/05/almost-every-2012-republican-has-a-cap-and-trade-problem/238776/.

85. Daniel Gozalez and Rebekah Sanders, "Comprehensive immigration reform elusive," *USA Today*, July 1, 2012, http://www.usatoday.com/USCP/PNI/Front%20Page/2012–07–01-PNI0701met-SB1070-reformPNIBrd_ST_U.htm and "A Reagan Legacy: Amnesty for Illegal Immigrants," NPR, July 4, 2010, http://www.npr.org/templates/story/story.php?storyId=128303672.

86. Timothy Egan, "The Clown and the Cop," *New York Times*, June 17, 2012, SR11.

87. Romney is quoted in Helene Cooper, "Adding a Fresh Metaphor to a Familiar Campaign Message," *New York Times*, June 14, 2012, A20.

88. Mann and Ornstein, *It's Even Worse Than It Looks*, 29.

89. Ibid, xiv.

90. Ibid, 54.

91. A link to the poll can be found in "Jeff Zeleny and Megan Thee-Brenan, "New Poll Finds a Deep Distrust of Government," NYTimes.com, October 25, 2011, http://www.nytimes.com/2011/10/26/us/politics/poll-finds-anxiety-on-the-economy-fuels-volatility-in-the-2012-race.html?_r=0.

92. Pew Research Center, "More Blame Wars than Domestic Spending of Tax Cuts for Nation's Debt," June 7, 2011, http://pewresearch.org/pubs/2017/poll-what-created-thenational-debt-wars-spending-tax-cut.

93. Pew Research Center, "Obama Job Approval Improves, GOP Contest Remains Fluid," November 17, 2011, http://www.people-press.org/2011/11/17/obama-job-approval-edges-up-gop-contest-remains-fluid/.

94. Mann and Ornstein, *It's Even Worse Than It Looks*, 67.

95. Ibid, 70-76.

96. See Lou Cannon, *President Reagan: The Role of a Lifetime* (New York: Simon and Schuster, 1991), 514.

97. Scheiber, *The Escape Artists*, 112, 128.

98. Barack Obama, "Remarks by the President at University of Maryland Town Hall," July 22, 2011, http://www.whitehouse.gov/the-press-office/2011/07/22/rmarks-president-university-maryla.

99. Mann and Ornstein, *It's Even Worse Than It Looks*, 88. .

100. Abby Goodnough, "Opinion of Health Care Law Reflects Ad Spending," *New York Times*, June 21, 2012, A14.

101. Abby Goodnough, "Too Quiet, Again, on Health Care," *New York Times*, July 4, 2012, A18.

102. Maureen Dowd, "Men In Black," *New York Times*, April 4, 2012, A19.

102. I review the effort to sell the health care reform proposal in some detail in Rowland, "Barack Obama and the Revitalization of Public Reason," 693-725.

103. Jim Rutenberg and Gardiner Harris, "Conservatives See Need for Serious Health Debate," *The New York Times*, September 3, 2009, A19.

104. Paul Krugman, "The Real Winners," *New York Times*, June 29, 2012, A21.

105. See Goodnough, A14, A18.

106. Henry J. Kaiser Family Foundation, "Kaiser Health Tracking Poll," January 2010, 5. Public support also remained strong for a public option. Even at the nadir of support for reform in late fall of 2009, a CBS/*New York Times* poll found that support for a "public option." PollingReport.Com, http://pollingreport.com/health.htm.

107. "Healthy Respect," *The New Republic*, October 28, 2010, 1.

108. Pew Research Center, "Obama Health Care Law: Where Does the Public Stand?" June 15, 2012, http://www.people-press.org/2012/06/15/obama-health-care-law-where-does-the-public-stand/

109. Peter Baker, "Justices Mostly Satisfied, but Health Overhaul Is Still No Hit With Public," *New York Times*, June 30, 2012, A12.

110. Charles M. Blow, "Obama, for the Win!", *New York Times*, June 30, 2012, A21. Also see *The New York Times*/CBS News Poll, April 13-17, 2012.

111. Ibid.

112. Pew Research Center, "Division, Uncertainty over Court's Health Care Ruling."

113. Wilner is quoted, and the statistics are cited in Goodnough, A14, A18.

114. Matt Bai, "Mario Cuomo Still Believes," *New York Times Magazine*, April 7, 2011, http://www.nytimes.com/2011/04/10/magazine/mag-10Cuomo-t.html?pagewanted=all.

2 "Yes, We Can!": Identification and the Invitation to Collective Identity in Barack Obama's Campaign Rhetoric

Courtney Jue

In Barack Obama's first formal announcement declaring his intention to run for the presidency, he began the first sentence of his speech in the first person, using the word "we."[1] Throughout the campaign, he continued to primarily address policies, issues concerning the campaign, and the future of the nation by using the first person "we." At the outset, this may seem a trivial observation; yet, when paired with the assertion that "without a common identity, individuals cannot form a collective agent" (or driving force), the power of this small pronoun is even more pronounced.[2] The first-person pronoun "we" provides the identity necessary for the driving force that characterizes the movement of Obama's 2008 presidential election. This pronoun provided a subject position for Obama to describe his own aspirations because he was, in fact, talking about himself. Yet Obama presented his proposals with the assumption that he and his audience spoke and acted as one. Obama centered his campaign upon the conviction that it was not Barack Obama who was running for the presidency, but the American people as a whole.

"Yes We Can" Slogan as an Example of Constitutive Rhetoric

This article examines Obama's rhetorical process in successfully constructing *constitutive identities*—identities constructed through appeals to a collective's

52

sense of who it is—during the presidential campaign of 2008. I argue that in the first presidential election, Obama triumphed, in large part, because of his success in reifying, reinvigorating, and most importantly, identifying with the American people. This analysis draws upon the original speech announcing Obama's intent to run for president, the Democratic Convention Speech, and Obama's Presidential Acceptance Speech to examine how Obama drew upon the rhetorical resources of that time to appeal to his audience. I also mention a few points from Obama's 2010 State of the Union Address as a follow-up analysis of this same theme found in his post-campaign rhetoric.

"Si, se puede" is a slogan popularized by the United Farm Workers under the leadership of Cesar Chavez. This slogan translates literally as "Yes, we can," or "Yes, it can be done."[3] The slogan was adopted by Obama most notably in his New Hampshire Concession Speech, and, from that night forward, the slogan became a defining feature of the campaign. The slogan solidified its celebrated status through the creation of the widespread music video, "Yes We Can," produced by will.i.am, a member of the musical group, The Black Eyed Peas. The video was launched in 2008 on Dipdive.com and Youtube.com, and later received an Emmy award for "Best New Approaches in Daytime Entertainment."[4] In 2010, Dipdive.com showed almost twenty-nine million views of this video, and Youtube received almost twenty-one million. This video strengthened and reinforced the slogan as a national phenomenon, catapulting Obama from his status as a singular political figure into a national celebrity. Will.i.am delivered the song, with music artist John Legend, at the 2008 Democratic National Convention.[5]

How does the first person "we" function within the slogan, the song, and Obama's speeches? Speaking in first person, specifically utilizing "we" as the primary point of view, calls the audience's attention to their involvement in the proposed language and ideas of the speaker. Maurice Charland, following Althusser, refers to this process as *interpellation*: "Interpellation occurs at the very moment one enters into a rhetorical situation, that is, as soon as an individual recognizes and acknowledges being addressed. An interpellated subject participates in the discourse that addresses him."[6] The key word in this definition is "participation," especially in light of analyzing a political movement.

Participation supplies democracy: the very institution under which campaigning, political movements, and mobilization takes place. Interpellation is the first necessary step in conjoining the *rhetor* (the producer of rhetoric and the creator of rhetorical situations)—in this case, the presidential candidate—and the audience. The rhetor must elicit the audience's participation before persuading them to act. In the Obama campaign, the chant "Yes We Can" calls upon the audience to become a "we," to enter into the rhetorical situation, and to recognize its own personal involvement in the unified community Obama's campaign creates. Obama proposed a presidential term that would not ride solely upon his singular leadership. Instead, he proposed a future characterized by the collective role of all Americans.

CONSTITUTIVE RHETORIC AND KENNETH BURKE

What is constitutive rhetoric, and who is Kenneth Burke? Burke was a prolific writer, a well-respected philosopher, and a pivotal figurehead within the rhetorical community. His works continue to challenge and instigate new perspectives on discourse, such that literary critics, when speaking of Burke, suggest:

> Years of study and contemplation of the general idea of effectiveness in language have equipped him to deal competently with the subject of rhetoric from its beginning as a specialized discipline to the present time. To his thorough knowledge of classical tradition he has added rich insights gained from serious study of anthropology, sociology, history, psychology, philosophy, and the whole body of human letters.[7]

Burke's principle works include *Permanence and Change, A Grammar of Motives, A Rhetoric of Motives,* and *Language as Symbolic Action.* He crossed over into other academic fields of study, and yet found fluid parallels to synthesize these fields together. Burke molded much of the scholarly discourse surrounding identity and notion of forming a constituted identity through rhetoric.

BURKE'S CONCEPTS OF DIVISION AND IDENTIFICATION

In any rhetorical situation, it is important to note the presence of *division* and *identification.* These two terms may not seem to oppose each other when viewed through their standard definitions, but the rhetor sees division (most simply) as the "places" where the audience is divided from him or herself. In other words, a rhetor does not enter instantly into communion or unity with his or her audience. The division between the audience and rhetor must be utilized as an opportunity for the rhetor to draw parallels and become one in perspective and potential with the audience. A rhetorical situation is "made up of persons, events, objects, and relations which . . . have the power to constrain decision and action needed to modify the exigency."[8] These conditions may limit or increase the candidate's ability to persuade, depending on how he or she chooses to utilize them.

Burke's *Rhetoric of Motives* establishes the concepts of division and identification as the goal and medium through which persuasion is enacted. When speaking of division and identification, Burke argues that

> the theologian's concerns with Eden and the 'fall' come close to the heart of the rhetorical problem. For behind the theology, there is the perception of generic divisiveness which, being common to all men, is a universal fact about them, prior to any divisiveness caused by social classes. Here is the basis of rhetoric. Out of this emerge the motives for linguistic persuasion.[9]

In other words, Burke contends that division is a natural state that calls for unity as its counterpart. Burke extends this line of argument on division and identification by stating, "Surely here is the point [the co-existence of unity and plurality] at which rhetoric merges into dialectic, and dialectic merges into the very nature of things. Just as we put things together and take things apart, so there are words that put things together and words that take things apart."[10]

Therefore, it may be argued that diversity, contention, and appeals from the American public for change in the 2008 presidential election were in fact the origins from which identification and unification—the "we"—developed. The first person pronoun, "we," is a primary example of a word that puts together that which was apart. In this word, a community, as well as dialectic, is formed.

Division and Identification in the 2008 Election

Political campaigns offer the opportunity to view the dynamic relationship between candidates, voters, and current political issues. In the *Grammar of Motives*, Burke titles these Agents, Audience, and Scene.[11] Let us identify the components of the rhetorical situation for the 2008 presidential campaign to better understand the discourse that occurred between the Agent (Barack Obama) and Audience (the "we").

CNN.com's "Election Center 2008" polls recognized that year's major campaign issues as concerns about the following: Iran, Iraq, and Afghanistan; health care; homeland security; abortion; energy; and, most significantly, the economy.[12] These contentious issues have provided grounds for some of the most significantly divisive and long-standing debates of this century. These debates instigated (and continue to instigate) quarrels antithetical to cohesive agreement. They also proved to be the most important and tenuous elements comprising the presidential candidates' political platforms from that election.

The 2008 campaign was also significantly characterized as the epilogue to the unpopular narrative defining President Bush's last days in office. Many perceived Obama's 2008 campaign as a direct reaction and response to the previous presidential administration. Bush's low approval ratings, political unrest tied to tensions surrounding the wars in Iraq and Afghanistan, and a declining economy had most candidates prefacing their political platforms as distinctly different, or even diametrically opposed to, the policies of the former administration. In effect, candidates hoped to set a uniquely different Scene as the perspective for their potential presidential role.

In addition to the significance, diversity, and contentious quality of the issues concerning the presidential candidates were the candidates themselves. The 2008 campaign introduced a diversity that the American campaign primaries had never witnessed before. The most serious contenders in the primaries included a woman, a man of African American descent, and a Mormon candidate. "Change had come to America," ("President-Elect") Obama voiced in his "President-Elect Victory Speech," but it had materialized even earlier than that moment. The diversity of the candidates reflected a growing diversity in America's demographic makeup and a shifting collective identity.

The "we" substantiating Obama's supporters also represented a significantly diverse body: "Senator Obama had to contend for the working class Democrats who were strongly supportive of Clinton while still securing educated liberals."[13] Obama's "message was designed to resonate with, first, a fractured Democratic electorate, and later the diversity of the general public."[14]

At the same time, younger voters added to the shifting demographic of the campaign audience, and technology was the principal source attracting the new voter base. Obama's campaign team tapped into this powerful congregation of supporters by using social media resources (most significantly, Facebook) to spur concentrated political movements on college campuses around the nation. The result of this younger, mobilized audience was a serious response from candidates to address appeals for change and transformation on Capitol Hill. It was declining attitudes toward the past administration; shifting views on race, gender, and power; the use of technologies in political campaigning; and a growing diversification of the American public supplying the conditions that created an exigent opportunity for Obama's campaign rhetoric and the slogan, "Yes We Can."

In the particular case of Obama's campaign slogan, he invites his audience and those previously divided from him to unify together into identification with him. In this "we," individuals from varied religious, social, and political backgrounds were brought into a common situation, now communicating through a unified dialectic. Out of the divided variety of voices involved in the debates came a call for a dialectic, or what Rafferty and Kephart define as polyphony, "the bringing together of many voices to perform one message," embodied in the words "Yes We Can."[15] Obama identifies this division as an exigency of the presidential campaign, and saturated his campaign with the repetition and consistency of a rhetoric that constituted a collective identity for his constituents.

After "call[ing the interpellated audience] into being," Obama needed to create their collective identity.[16] Obama sought to first and foremost represent the underrepresented, the lower and middle classes. He asserted that for too long, rich bureaucrats and politicians had directed American policy: For too long, opportunity was only ensured "for those with the most money and influence."[17] This rhetoric acts as a response to the demography of his constituency who, as mentioned earlier, were mainly composed of a younger age group and a more diverse ethnic base than his opponent, John McCain, sought to attract. In his Democratic Convention Speech, Obama asserted that during his presidency, the strength of the nation would not be measured by "the number of billionaires we have or the profits of the Fortune 500, but by whether someone with a good idea can take a risk and start a new business."[18] Obama speaks repeatedly about the American promise; this is simply another way to describe the American Dream. Because the American Dream is for the rich and for the poor, the young and the old, the struggling and the flourishing, all desire the fulfillment of its promise. Obama asks, "What is that American promise? It's a promise that says each of us has the freedom to make of our own lives what we will."[19] This brilliant appeal to constitutive rhetoric provides a foundation for the collective identity on an ideology devoid of specification. The promise offers more upward mobility for those from lower socio-economic backgrounds, but the chance for opportunity and success is non-exclusive. This principle represents the principle Obama chose to highlight as the connective "substance" joining himself to his constituency within identification.

STEPS TOWARD CONSTITUTING THE COLLECTIVE IDENTITY

To obtain the American promise, Obama most prominently emphasized the values of "hard work and sacrifice," "mutual responsibility" (DCS), "democracy, liberty, opportunity and unyielding hope," (AS) and "unity" (DCS and AS). These values constitute the American collective identity, the first step identified by Charland.[20] Hard work and sacrifice are the working tools pushing towards change. Mutual responsibility protects the less fortunate from neglect and monopoly by bureaucracy and political heads. Democracy is the forum in which the voices of change are heard. Liberty, opportunity, and unyielding hope are the vehicles in which the American people can most easily pursue the promise of the American Dream. Finally, above all else, unity is instrumental in any act of change. Power in numbers and the mobilization of the masses are the most effectual means of transformation. These values construct the identity of the "we" in Obama's campaign.

The second step in creating identification is to construct the audience as a subject in history. In one of the most poignant moments of his "Presidential Acceptance Speech," Obama described Ann Nixon Cooper, a 106 year-old woman, who lived to see some of the most formative moments in American history. After each point in history, he called on the audience to affirm the creed, "Yes we can." Obama declared, "When there was despair in the dust bowl and depression across the land, she saw a nation conquer fear itself with a New Deal, new jobs, a new sense of common purpose. Yes we can."[21] He went on to describe her birth in close relation to women's suffrage, the bombing of Pearl Harbor, World War II, the civil rights movement, and a man on the moon—each time following the event with a call to the audience to proclaim: "Yes we can." Not only are these moments of the speech a strong appeal to *pathos* (emotion), but they also construct the audience as a subject in history. Each moment experienced by Cooper was a moment re-experienced by the audience when they joined with Obama in repeating the creed. They were then collectively bound by a common past, formative in the construction of their constituted nature.

Obama's narrative depicted a woman who experienced America's triumph and progress in the midst of adversity. Ann Nixon Cooper viewed over one hundred years' worth of America's story. Obama called the audience to view their lives as small narratives within a larger story of the American promise. Most probably, their own narratives include adversity and triumph, success and failure, but most of all, change. This ideological narrative of progress and hope constituted the audience into a collective identity pushing towards change.

Finally, and most importantly, Charland argues that in a political election, constitutive rhetoric demands that subjects act in accordance with their identity.[22] Obama's own life story was the most persuasive tool he could use to inspire action in his audience. He was a product of the very promise of the American Dream he proposed. At the Democratic Convention, Obama narrated the story of his upbringing. He was raised from meager means by a single mother who relied on food stamps and worked the night shift to raise her children. Obama took advantage of student loans and scholarships to fund his schooling at Columbia University and Harvard Law School. His story is one of determination, ingenuity, and a hope for something better.

The Embrace of Obama's Identity as a Group Identity

Obama is also biracial, being both African American and Caucasian, and a product of a multi-cultural upbringing, being raised in Indonesia and in Hawaii. He represents the cultural plurality of America and the endless possibilities that await those with enough ingenuity and determination. Obama's story represents what Burke calls an "'ultimate' identification" that prevails over "divisive individual or class interests and concerns," and "transcends the limitations of the individual body and will."[23] Obama's story conjoins him with the audience through recognition of the social, racial, and economic boundaries he overcame to pursue the most worthy cause: change. If he could do it, so could they; Obama encourages this very act in his slogan "Yes We Can." The audience becomes the American Nation, pursuing the promise destined for them and written into their own national constitutions. For the audience to act in accordance with their constituted identity, they needed to vote for the very change with which they identified: they needed to vote for Barack Obama:

> On November 4th, Obama heard the news of his triumph and announced to America that:
>
>> This is our time, to put our people back to work and open doors of opportunity for our kids; . . . to reclaim the American dream and reaffirm that fundamental truth, that, out of many, we are one. . . . And where we are met with cynicism and doubts and those who tell us that we can't, we will respond with that timeless creed that sums up the spirit of a people: Yes, we can.[24]

Change had come to America because of the inspired communion Obama achieved. He stood as a president elect who was part of the collective people. Obama encourages the collective body by saying that his term would also be theirs; as he said, it "is our time." "Out of [the] many," Obama was able to create "one."[25]

Post-Election: Triumph and the Fall

Following Obama's election, posters publicizing his election were printed and distributed to the general public. Posters pronouncing "Yes We Did" were seen at universities, on main streets, condensed into bumper stickers, and in many other public meeting areas. Rhetorical response to the phrase and constitutive identity of Obama's campaign was extraordinary. The public continued to reconstitute itself as a unified body even after the campaign was over.

Not so long after the election, on the other side of the triumphant story of the election, came what seemed to be a political backlash from those who did not see themselves incorporated within the "we." Bookstore shelves housed literature with titles including: *The Case Against Barack Obama: The Unlikely Rise and Unexamined Agenda of the Media's Favorite Candidate* (David Freddoso), *Obama, the Man Behind the Mask* (Andy Martin), and *Conservative Victory: Defeating Obama's Radical Agenda* (Sean Hannity).[26] *The Daily Beast*, the online home of *Newsweek*, published an article on the "46 books demonizing the president" two years into Obama's presidency.[27] This resulting anti-Obama movement could be evidence that Obama's campaign and call for a certain unified body was actually very polarizing for some. A large contingent seemed to have grown from the desire to decidedly divide themselves from the "we."

One year after Obama was inaugurated into office, he delivered his first State of Union address. In this address, Obama was heard calling his audience back to the same message of unity he had pronounced in campaign speeches. He addressed the American public by prefacing the beginning lines of his speech with appeals to unity, identification, and the first person pronoun, "we." He announced:

> When the market crashed on Black Tuesday, and civil rights marchers were beaten on Bloody Sunday, the future was anything but certain. These were the times that tested the courage of our convictions, and the strength of our union. And despite all our divisions and disagreements, our hesitations and our fears, America prevailed because we chose to move forward as one nation, as one people.[28]

Again, Obama places the current rhetorical situation in the context of a broader narrative of American history. Black Tuesday became identified with the current recession, while tensions surrounding the civil rights movement and the nomination of America's first black president narrated a cyclical story of adversity in the midst of racial hostility and the unity required to overcome it. As Obama identifies in his speech, it was the efforts of one united collective that "prevailed" in this narrative—a fitting inference to the unity that must re-occur to triumph in the current writing of this nation's story.

Notably, the President's voice shows obvious frustration as he petitions Congress to diminish their strong penchant for division and partisanship.

Obama claims this division as antithetical to progress and change for the country. The unity, identification, and change he had pressed with so much dedication during his campaign seemed to have vanished just as he began his first term in office. As a result, he appeals to Congress, reprimanding them on behalf of the "we" that had once supported him:

> They're tired of the partisanship and the shouting and the pettiness. They know we can't afford it. Not now. . . . So we face big and difficult challenges. And what the American people hope—what they deserve—is for all of us, Democrats and Republicans, to work through our differences; to overcome the numbing weight of our politics. For while the people who sent us here have different backgrounds, different stories, different beliefs, the anxieties they face are the same.[29]

Unification did not last as a constant, as Obama proceeded to enact the change while in office that he proposed during the campaign. This unity is the principle he had so clearly identified as crucial to the enactment of change, and he identifies division within the House and the Senate as the leading obstruction to any path toward significant change. Obama recognizes the existence of segregation, and proposes congregation as its recourse. The "we" that had supported Obama during the campaign was not the only community involved in legislation on Capitol Hill.

If, as Burke argues, there is a "generic divisiveness which, being common to all men, is a universal fact about them," then Obama's call to unity and a constituted collective identity is a message that, although powerful, is finite in influence. Partisanship entrenched itself as one of the most significant issues Obama has faced during his presidency.[30] During a press conference in July, 2011, Obama was pressed on the topic of the national budget and recommendations that the National Commission for Fiscal Responsibility had made at the start of the recession: "[the Bowles-Simpson recommendations were] originally bipartisan legislation that some of the Republican supporters decided to vote against when I said I supported it—that seems to be a pattern that I'm still puzzled by."[31] The antithetical actions referred to here reflect the division Obama has battled repeatedly throughout his administration. With every proposed bill, address to Congress, and press briefing, Obama attempts to reify and evolve the message of his campaign against fraught tensions between liberals and conservatives, staunch bipartisanship, and a skeptical public bruised and wearied by a fragile economy.

Conclusion

In a political campaign, candidates do not step instantaneously into identification with voters; "A is not identical with his colleague, B."; it is only when "insofar as their interests are joined, A is identified with B. Or he may identify himself with B even when their interests are not joined, if he assumes that they are, or is persuaded to believe so."[32] This last line of reasoning is the basis of rhetoric and the foundation of Obama's campaign success. Obama provided not only the medium for identification in his campaign; he demanded it with the campaign's very first word. The nation's desire for change and a chance at the American Dream offered Obama an opportunity to create a narrative of his own story, one conjoined with the stories of many of America's people. He spoke to them out of his adversity and his diversity, two characteristics that strongly resounded with the American public. He made change seem possible for young and old, rich and poor, black, white, Latino, and Asian. Americans were confident of their representation in the White House, because Obama represented the very identity they also subscribed to, and a president who valued hard work, sacrifice, mutual responsibility, democracy, opportunity, and unyielding hope. They knew that their histories were intertwined because of the culminating narrative to create the story of the American people. Finally, they were ready to act upon the change they supported and lead the American identity into a new chapter of construction.

As history moves into the past, it will be most interesting to examine how Obama's rhetoric has evolved or re-positioned since 2008. Upcoming elections provide new rhetorical situations, characterized by change Agents and Audiences. While division continues to plague Capitol Hill, Obama will need to persist in the message of unification and identification. Obama has proven himself to be a most capable orator and rhetor, and, as Burke contends, out of this context of division and contention can in fact emerge the most exigent rhetorical situation providing the substance necessary for "linguistic persuasion."[33]

Notes

1. Obama announcement speech. http://www.washingtonpost.com/wp-dyn/content/article/2007/02/10/AR2007021000879.html, February 10, 2007; "Following is the text of Republican presidential candidate U.S. Senator John McCain's announcement speech." 4president.org. McCain 2000. Web. 19 Jan. 2010.

2. Peter du Preez. *The Politics of Identity: Ideology and the Human Image.* Oxford: Blackwell, 1980. Print, 3.

3. Erichsen, Gerald. "Does 'Sí, se puede' mean 'Yes, we can'?" About.com: Spanish Language. New York Times Company, 11 Apr. 2006. Web. 26 Jan. 2010.

4. "Political Music Video Inspired by Democratic Presidential Candidate Barack Obama Speech Wins Emmy Award." Marketwire.com. Marketwire, Incorporated. 16 Jun. 2008. Web. 30 Sep. 2010; "John Legend, will.i.am 'Yes We Can' Performance at the Democratic Convention (VIDEO)." HuffingtonPost.com. HuffingtonPost.com, Inc, 28 Sept. 2008. Web. 26 Jan. 2010.

5. "Barack Obama Democratic Convention Speech" *huffingtonpost.com,* 28 Aug. 2008. *The Huffington Post.* Web. 1 Apr. 2009.

6. "Constitutive Rhetoric: The Case of the Peuple Québécois." *Quarterly Journal of Speech* 73. 2 (May 1987): 138. Print.

7. Marie Hochmuth. "Kenneth Burke and the 'New Rhetoric.'" *Quarterly Journal of Speech, 38.* (1952), 144.

8. Lloyd F. Bitzer. "The Rhetorical Situation." University of Wisconsin, Madison. Nov. 1966. Lecture, 8.

9. Kenneth Burke. *A Rhetoric of Motives.* Berkeley: University of California Press, 1969. Print, 146.

10. Kenneth Burke. "The Rhetorical Situation." *Communication: Ethical and Moral Issues.* Ed. Lee Thayer. New York: Gordan and Breach Science Publishers, 1973, 265.

11. Kenneth Burke. *A Grammar of Motives.* Berkeley: University of California P, 1966. Print.

12. "Campaign Issues." CNNPolitics.com. Cable News Network, LLLP., n.d. Web. 01 Oct. 2010.

13. Kephart III, John M. and Steven F. Rafferty. "'Yes We Can': Rhizomic Rhetorical Agency in Hyper-Modern Campaign Ecologies." *Argumentation and Advocacy* 46 (Summer 2009): Print, 9.

14. Ibid.

15. Ibid.

16. Maurice Charland. "Constitutive Rhetoric: The Case of the Peuple Québécois." *Quarterly Journal of Speech* 73. 2 (May 1987): Print, 134.

17. Barack Obama. 2008 Democratic Convention Speech. http://www.nytimes.com/2008/08/28/us/politics/28text-obama.html?pagewanted=all&_r=0, August 28, 2008. Web.

18. Ibid.

19. Ibid.

20. "Constitutive Rhetoric".

21. "Text of president-elect Barack Obama's acceptance speech." Chron.com, 5 Nov. 2008. Associated Press. Web. 2 Apr. 2009.

22. "Constitutive Rhetoric".

23. Qtd. in Charland, 139.

24. Burke, Kenneth. *A Grammar of Motives.* Berkeley: University of California P, 1966. Print.

25. "Text of president-elect Barack Obama's acceptance speech."

26. Ibid.

27. "State of the Union Address." AmericanRhetoric.com. *American Rhetoric,* 27 Jan. 2010. Web. 01 Oct. 2010.

28. John Avlon. "The Obama Haters Book Club." Thedailybeast.com, 26 Oct. 2010. The Newsweek/Daily Beast Company. Web. 6 March 2012; David Freddoso. *The Case Against Barack Obama: The Unlikely Rise and Unexamined Agenda of the Media's Favorite Candidate.* Washington D.C.: Regnery Publishing, Inc., 2008. Print; Sean Hannity. *Conservative Victory: Defeating Obama's Radical Agenda.* New York: Harper Collins Publishers, 2010. Print; Andy Martin. *Obama, the Man Behind the Mask.* Forest Hills: Orange State Press, 2008. Print.

29. "State of the Union Address."

30. *A Rhetoric of Motives.* Berkeley: University of California Press, 1969. Print, 146.

31. "Transcript of Obama's News Conference." WallStreetJournal.com, 15 Jul. 2011. Dow Jones and Company, Inc. Web. 18 Jul. 2011.

32. *A Rhetoric of Motives,* 20.

33. The Rhetorical Situation." *Communication: Ethical and Moral Issues.* Ed. Lee Thayer. New York: Gordan and Breach Science Publishers, 1973. 263–275. Print.

3 Appointments and Disappointments: A Rhetorical Analysis of the Relationship Between President Obama, Catholics, and Their Church

John Jasso and Anthony Wachs

On May 17, 2009, President Barack Obama delivered a commencement speech at the University of Notre Dame. The speech was surrounded by controversy months before it was delivered. Many Catholics were upset with Notre Dame's administration for allowing an "ardently pro-choice" public figure the honor of speaking at the ceremony. Making matters worse in the eyes of many Catholics was the fact that the University was to award Obama an honorary doctorate in law. Obama addressed the controversy, and abortion's central role within it, by calling all sides of the debate to move past ideology and to work from the common ground of abortion reduction to promote an attitude of civility within the nation.[1] As such, President Obama rhetorically positioned himself within a long-standing discourse between Catholics over the issue of abortion. Indeed, this discourse had been coming to a head within the previous election cycles, leading up to Obama's ascension to the presidency.

During the 2008 election, the United States Conference of Catholic Bishops (USCCB) attempted to guide the formation of Catholics as citizens by issuing a document titled, "Forming Consciences for Faithful Citizenship." The document holds that Catholics can vote for a pro-choice candidate with the caveat that the vote not be specifically cast *because* the candidate is pro-choice.[2] As such, then-candidate Obama began a dialogue with the Catholic populous centered upon a fiscal policy to reduce abortions. While disagreement continued within the Church concerning the appropriateness of this stance, Obama extended an invitation for political action to mainstream Catholics that largely fell in line with their own ideologies.

Having won the Catholic vote, President Obama thus entered into a complex relationship with Catholics and their Church that was in need of constant management.[3] One avenue through which this dialogue has been managed is the numerous appointments of Catholic officials. Many of these appointments have a rhetorical dimension in-and-of-themselves, and have often been understood as a form of symbolic communication between the President and Catholic America. The appointments have been heralded as progress by some Catholics and as disappointments by others. Through an analysis of these appointments and the rhetoric surrounding them, this essay explores the effect this symbolic process has had in understanding what it means to be a Catholic politician, citizen, and member in good standing of the Catholic Church. Given President Obama's rhetorical posturing around the issue of abortion in his campaign, reiterated in the Notre Dame speech, appointments in positions dealing with abortion and health services are especially important in managing his relationship with Catholic citizens. For example, nominations to the Supreme Court or the Secretary of Health and Human Services are scrutinized by many Catholics. The significance of these appointments exponentially increases given that a number of Obama's relevant nominees are themselves Catholic.

This essay presupposes that appointments to political positions by the President of the United States often have a rhetorical dimension. The rhetorical aspect of appointments can be studied through analyzing the meaning of the political position for key constituencies. The politics of the nominee speaks to the relationship between the president and a given constituency. As such, a message is contained within the nominee, and the president is able to engage rhetorically with a specific group through such nominations. In this essay, facts surrounding key appointments are analyzed through the perspective of several different orientations. Depending upon one's position within the Church, various Catholics have interpreted the facts through different lenses. This essay presents these facts, and considers the multiple interpretations of the messages sent by the president.

STAGE SETTING

In many ways, the rhetorical stage was set for Obama to form a relationship with the Catholic Church long before the 2008 election cycle. Indeed, we see the beginnings of his strategy in the Catholic voter education con-troversies surrounding the 2004 election. In 2003, prior to the election cycle, the USCCB issued an official guide for Catholic voters—"Faithful Citizenship: A Catholic Call to Political Responsibility"—listing over fif-ty issues that Catholic voters should consider when going to the polls. The "Voter's Guide for Serious Catholics," issued by Carl Keating's conservative Catholic Answers, identifies five "non-negotiable" issues among those fifty on which Catholic voters could not, in good faith, oscillate their opinions: "abortion, euthanasia, fetal stem-cell research, human cloning, and homo-sexual 'marriage.'"[4] The guide is offset by the progressive Catholic Voting Project, founded by Chris Korzen. The group offered a guide of its own in the form of an online quiz. The quiz goes beyond the five non-negotiables, and includes a number of social justice issues important to Catholics men-tioned in "Faithful Citizenship," including minimum wage and tax cuts. Keating saw the Project as a direct response from the left to the voting guide's success. The problem for Keating is not that such issues of social justice are unimportant, but rather that "one is left with the impression that such things as the minimum wage are morally on the same level as abortion and that im-migration regulations are as important as euthanasia."[5]

This back and forth continued through the 2006 midterm elections, when the USCCB asked parishes not to hand out voting guides unapproved by the Church. Since their distribution was mainly online, Korzen and his associates, under the new moniker "Catholics United," interpreted this de-cision as a blow against Catholic Answers, who attempted "to undermine the Bishops' 2003 Faithful Citizenship voting guide—which lists more than fifty issues relevant to Catholic voters, and characterizes Catholic citizen-ship as a call to promote 'the common good.'"[6] The USCCB clarified its position, complicating the discussion, by publishing "Forming Consciences for Faithful Citizenship" in November of 2007. This document offers state-ments that fit neither the conservative nor the progressive interpretation of abortion. In effect, abortion was to be a heavily weighted issue according to the USCCB, although one that was possibly "negotiable" in the face of "other morally grave reasons." In short, according to the USCCB, Keating's "five non-negotiables" are too rigid, and Korzen's simplistic moral math is too bal-anced in its weighting.[7]

As a result, we see the evolution of key issues facing the Obama campaign and the subsequent administration in managing its relationship with the Catholic Church and its members throughout the United States. Thus, social justice issues like health care reform and the minimum wage are reframed by groups like Catholics United and Catholics in Alliance for the Common Good.[8] No longer were Catholics placed on equal footing with abortion, but became an integral part of the "abortion reduction" strategy in a manner that directly links them with mitigating the moral evil of abortion. In this way, the new progressive approach asks Catholic voters to weigh "tired" abortion criminalization rhetoric with innovative, results-oriented policies aimed at actually reducing the number of abortions.[9]

Although Catholics United and Catholics in Alliance set the stage, it was a different set of voices singing a very similar tune that garner the national spotlight and the attention of the Catholic community at large. When respected Catholic legal scholars such as Notre Dame's M. Cathleen Kaveny, and former Duquesne Law School Dean and Steubenville Trustee, Nicholas Cafardi, came out in support of Obama as not only a viable, but the preferred, Catholic choice, this discourse became a national concern. However, no endorsement was more surprising, and perhaps more powerful, than that of the conservative Reaganite Douglas Kmiec, who had just previously worked for the Mitt Romney campaign. In an article in *Slate*, Kmiec argues that "beyond abortion," Obama is the natural candidate to receive the Catholic vote.[10] In March of 2008, Kmiec formally endorsed Barack Obama's nomination for the presidency via *Slate*'s legal blog, "Convictions."[11] By October, Cafardi, Kaveny, and Kmiec presented Obama as the candidate who would most promote a culture of life.[12]

Eventually, the pro-choice candidate of the Democratic Party seemed to come out the victor in the rhetorical battle between progressive and conservative Catholics, as Obama garnered a majority of the Catholic vote and was elected to the office of President of the United States of America. However, in so doing, he makes a number of promises to the Catholic electorate concerning abortion reduction. More importantly, by paying direct attention to their concerns, Obama establishes an open dialogue with the Catholic Church he promised to carry into his presidency.

As the President-elect, however, conservatives and officials within the Church remained wary. When the Obama transition team met with Catholic leaders to address furthering their relationship after the inauguration, it was quickly pointed out by outlets like the conservative Catholic News Agency (CNA) that those invited to the meeting were all lay Catholics who hold memberships in progressive organizations that supported the Obama campaign.[13] Absent was any representative from the USCCB. Accordingly, the Bishop of Madison, Robert Morlino, notes: "Recognizing the stark contrast between the positions on abortion of the President-elect and the teachings of the Catholic Church, it would be a mistake for the President-elect's transition team to pretend that this meeting satisfied his promise of dialoguing with the Catholic community."[14] Here an official of the Church expressed discontent with the Obama administration's dialogue with Catholics, arguing that the administration merely spoke with one segment of the Catholic population, ignoring the segment that officially speaks on behalf of the Church in America.

At this point, Obama's appointments were already being read as the reality behind Obama's rhetorical posturing. As conservative Catholic lay leader Brian Burch noted regarding Obama's Cabinet, "the new Administration is composed of leading abortion advocates who are preparing to overturn a large number of existing pro-life laws, while providing hundreds of millions of new taxpayer dollars for abortion."[15] His outlook for the ability of progressive Catholic groups to provide adequate oversight is, in a word, "doubtful."

APPOINTMENTS

Secretary of Health and Human Services I—Tom Daschle

The first Catholic nomination important to understand President Obama's rhetorical management of the Catholic electorate is that of former senator of South Dakota, Tom Daschle, to the position of Secretary of Health and Human Services. He was nominated on December 11, 2008.[16] In his announcement of Daschle, President-elect Obama framed the need for health care reform in terms of social justice that matches the rhetorical strategy that worked so well among Catholic voters during the election. In listing Daschle's many qualifications—health care expert, gifted manager, Congressional leader—Obama characterized Daschle as a compromiser who is able to heal divisions rather than cause them: "He knows how to reach across the aisle and bridge partisan divides. And he has the trust of folks from every angle of this issue: doctors, nurses and patients; unions and businesses; hospitals and advocacy groups—all of whom will have a seat at the table as we craft our plan."[17] According to Obama, the current system of health care places a great economic burden on individuals and families, and reform is needed to alleviate the burden on those families. To accomplish reform, the Secretary of Health and Human Services needed to be someone the people could trust. Along these lines, Obama stated that Daschle was one of America's foremost experts on healthcare, and that he knew "how to reach across the aisle and bridge partisan divides and he has the trust of folks from every angle of this issue."[18] Moreover, Daschle would be appointed as Director of the White House Office of Health Reform. As such, he would both craft and implement the necessary reforms to health care policy.

What Obama had to be aware of was that Daschle, a Catholic, was already a divisive figure among members of the Church, given his views on issues that directly affected the office to which he would be appointed. While Daschle was Senator of South Dakota and Senate Minority Leader, Bishop Robert J. Carlson of the Diocese of Sioux Falls, wrote him a letter "directing him to remove from his congressional biography and campaign documents all references to his standing as a member of the Catholic Church."[19] On account of his public persona, Daschle had developed a unique relationship between the Catholic Church and its members. Bottum states that, "Daschle's consistent political opposition to Catholic teachings on moral issues—abortion, in particular—has made him such a problem for ordinary churchgoers that the Church must deny him the use of the word 'Catholic'"[20] Essentially, Daschle was told not to publicly call himself Catholic because his support of pro-choice legislation is contrary to Church teachings, and because his self-identification as a Catholic leaves the impression that one could remain in good standing as a Catholic while also rejecting the moral teachings of the Church. As the Secretary of Health and Human Services and the Director of the White House Office on Health Reform, Daschle would have had an important, executive role concerning abortion and medical research with stem cells.[21] A dissenting Catholic was nominated for a position in which his dissent is made all the more obvious. Consequently, this early nomination is of particular importance, since Obama must have known how the message of this particular appointment would be read by the Church and its members.

The position itself is described as important because its holder would be in charge of "implementing one of Obama's top campaign promises to overhaul the health system in a country where 45 million people have no health insurance."[22] The job was also seen as especially difficult to accomplish on account of the economic situation at the time.[23] However, CNA looked beyond the position and straight to the nominee, noting immediately that Daschle is known for his "anti-life initiatives," and that he was asked to stop calling himself Catholic by then Bishop Carlson.[24] The initial response by CNA consisted of an analysis of how Daschle's stance on abortion had changed over the years. They note that he shifted his position from having the nuns that educated him write a letter in 1978, confirming that he would always fight against abortion, to writing fundraising letters for NARAL in 2002. The article ends by summarizing several of his positions that conflict with Church teachings:

> Before he failed to be re-elected to the Senate in 2004, Tom Daschle had a 50% NARAL rating. His mixed rating is the result of voting for a ban on partial-birth abortions and a vote for penalties for those who harm fetuses while committing a violent crime. On the other hand, Daschle voted to

allow human cloning, expand research on human embryos
and against banning privately funded abortions on U.S.
military installations.[25]

The article provides no real commentary for or against Daschle, but represents a desire to frame Daschle's nomination around his positions concerning abortion and other issues pertinent to the Catholic Church. CNA never
states that the nomination is problematic, but leaves this as an enthymematic
conclusion for readers.

Other Catholic groups and individuals responded in various ways to the
nomination. In particular, the Catholic Health Association (CHA) issued
a statement welcoming the choice (CNA, Catholic Health).[26] Sister Carol
Keehan, President and CEO of CHA, said that the organization was pleased,
and that the nomination shows that the President-elect understands the need
for overhauls to healthcare.[27] In the same article, CNA juxtaposes the CHA's
response with the response of pro-life groups that are not exclusively Catholic. These groups are quoted as describing the nomination as a "disaster appointment" and a "deep disappointment."[28] This article shows once again the
CNA's framing of the appointment around issues of life.

Eventually, on February 3, 2009, Daschle withdrew his nomination for
Secretary of Health and Human Services because of tax problems. Catholics
in Alliance for the Common Good responded by posting an article from *The
Economist* explaining why the withdrawal is a "pity."[29] Its coverage of Daschle's nomination is centered on his qualifications for the position.[30] He is
described by this group as the perfect person for the job because of his past
experience in Congress and because of the political knowledge and connections that come from such experience. Thus, we can begin to see how Catholics responded to Obama's important nominations. Those who worked from
the Church's teachings on social justice responded favorably to the Daschle
nomination. They tended to focus upon his qualifications to accomplish the
task of reforming the health care system, and do not mention his stance on
life issues. Conservative outlets reported on the acceptance of the nomination by Catholics who were experts in related fields, but also brought to the
fore the fact that Daschle did not follow official Church teachings in regards
to issues of life.

Secretary of Health and Human Services II: Kathleen Sebelius

On March 2, 2009, the White House officially announced that then Governor
of Kansas, Kathleen Sebelius, was nominated as Secretary of Health and
Human Services, the position that Daschle failed to fill. As with Daschle,
Obama spoke of the bipartisan nature of the duty that Sebelius would take

on, and of her ability to accomplish such work, noting her experience as "time and again, on energy and education, jobs and health care, she's bridged the partisan divide and worked with a Republican legislature to get things done for the people of Kansas."[31] What he did not mention was that some of her most public clashes with the Republican legislature came not only on health care, but on abortion policy, specifically, vetoing pro-life legislation in 2003, 2005, 2006, and 2008 (Novak).[32] Curiously, he does not mention common ground or shared values in this speech; rather, he took a more pragmatic stance, characterizing Sebelius as one of the "exceptional individuals who stand on the side of the American people, who push politics aside in favor of proven science, who eschew stale ideology for sound ideas and a focus on what works."[33] For Catholic leaders in Kansas, the stale ideology that Sebelius eschewed was, quite simply, the Church's stance on abortion.

Similar to the reception of Daschle, two Catholic camps emerged in response to the Sebelius nomination. This time there was more of a response by lay-Catholics and Church officials. To begin with, the Archbishop of Kansas City, Joseph F. Naumann, had already told Sebelius that she could no longer present herself for Holy Communion within the diocese. The Archbishop argued that Sebelius's example was harmful to other Catholics:

> Writing in the Archdiocesan paper, The Leaven, the archbishop also pointed out that Governor Sebelius' support for abortion leads others to question the "moral gravity" of abortion. The governor's continued reception of Holy Communion, coupled with her support for legalized abortion, convey the erroneous message that, "You can be a good Catholic and support legalized abortion," he wrote.[34]

Appointing Sebelius to such a position only highlighted the controversy and scandal. Michael Gerson, op-ed columnist for the *Washington Post*, called the nomination a humiliation:

> It is probably not a coincidence that Obama has chosen a Roman Catholic—Kansas Gov. Kathleen Sebelius—to implement many of these policies as secretary of the Department of Health and Human Services. Obama has every right to a pro-choice Cabinet. But this appointment seems designed to provide religious cover. It also smacks of religious humiliation—like asking a rabbi to serve the pork roast or an atheist to bless the meal.[35]

Consequently, many highlight the fact that the nominations of Sebelius, as well as Catholic nominees similar to her, created a degree of ambiguity regarding the relationship between Catholic doctrine, the hierarchy, and the individual consciences of Catholic citizens. It seems as if dissident Catholics are held up publicly as exemplar Catholics precisely because of their dissent.

CNA's article on Sebelius centers on her views on abortion and her relationship to her local bishop. Worth noting is that the archbishop gave a nod to Sebelius fulfilling the Church's social teachings through her work on health care, but that he was saddened by the positions she had taken in opposition to the Church.[36] Archbishop Raymond Burke, "head of the Roman Catholic Church's highest office overseeing Church law," commented that because Sebelius is Catholic, the nomination served as the "greatest embarrassment because she has publicly and repeatedly betrayed her Catholic faith."[37] Especially important here is that the Archbishop was embarrassed that this specific Catholic filled the position, not that Obama chose a pro-abortion nominee. That Obama's nominee would be pro-abortion was expected, but that it would be a Catholic not in communion with the Church is viewed by some as scandalous. Catholic League president Bill Donohue expressed the same sentiment. He stated that "Catholics do not expect that abortion-rights presidents will go out of their way to choose pro-life Catholics to be in their administration. But they also don't expect them to go out of their way to offend them. Obama has done just that."[38] Thus, like Daschle, this appointment was viewed by Burke, Donohue, and the like as controversial, and more importantly, as deliberate because the appointee was a well-known Catholic who publicly held beliefs contrary to Church teachings and would, in turn, perform an executive role in which those very teachings would be aggressively challenged.

Other Catholics responded favorably to Sebelius's nomination. In fact, twenty-six prominent Catholic leaders, scholars, and theologians signed a statement in support of Sebelius's nomination.[39] They argued that she had two qualities that helped to qualify her for the position, but, unlike Daschle, the qualities did not concern political knowledge and networking connections to aid in instituting health care reform. Rather, they cited her hard work at improving the social environment from immigration to health care, and more importantly, they defended Sebelius for "significantly reducing the abortion rate in Kansas."[40] These more progressive Catholics had begun to respond to the comments of conservative Catholics and the Church hierarchy. This opposition to more conservative elements in the Church was made even more apparent in the statement's rejection of "the tactics of those who would use Gov. Sebelius' faith to attack her. As Catholics, we find such partisan use of our religion regrettable and divisive."[41] The statement was prepared by Catholics United[42], the organization that also started Catholics for Kathleen Sebelius. Once again, we see a greater divide being established between some progressive Catholics and the hierarchy of the Church.

Ambassador to the Holy See

Although not a cabinet appointment, the discussion of the Obama administration's appointment to the post of Ambassador to the Holy See is important in understanding the overall symbolic maneuvering that took place between the administration and the Catholic Church. However, the discourse is also relatively difficult to analyze because most of the so-called "nominees" were merely informal suggestions that the two governments discussed back and forth through unofficial channels. Perhaps what is most ironic is that these least public discussions are also recognized among observers as the most symbolic.

As early as November 23, 2008, progressive Catholics, such as Michael Sean Winters of *America Magazine*, discussed Douglas Kmiec as a good choice for the ambassadorship to the Vatican.[43] As early as November 25, 2008, the CNA made it clear that, in the words of one unnamed Vatican official, Kmeic's appointment "will never happen."[44] The initial reason appears to be quite political, as the Vatican official commented that Catholics inside the Vatican, like Cardinal James Francis Stafford or Archbishop Raymond Burke, "look at Kmiec as a 'traitor' and 'their opinion will certainly count heavily'."[45] More importantly, according to the source, the Vatican did not want to risk straining relationships with important U.S. Catholic organizations, such as the Knights of Columbus and the American branch of the Knights of the Holy Sepulcher, who voiced their disappointment with Kmiec's role in the election.[46] However, in January of 2009, it was made clear that the Vatican would not officially veto any nominee for the ambassadorship, as "Rejecting an ambassador for those kinds of political motives [supporting a given candidate] is not in the tradition of Vatican diplomacy and would, in fact, be very dangerous."[47] The anonymous Vatican source asserted that the main issue is neither religious nor political at its core, but rather deals with Kmiec's relationship with the community he would serve: "There are many other candidates, Catholic or not, that would not spark the kind of antagonism and division that Professor Kmiec has sparked, as he himself has recently admitted" (CNA, Kmiec Considers).[48] At this stage, the argument against Kmiec was one of symbolic significance—given a selection of equally qualified candidates for the ambassadorship, don't choose the one that would be seen as explicitly divisive by the nation with which you are trying to establish diplomatic relations.

By April, observers exchanged allegations. The Vatican was accused of being too demanding on the one hand, and the White House was charged with being deliberately insulting on the other. According to CNA, the Vatican countered the claim of being overly demanding by referencing the "simple standard" by which it had always judged the qualifications of ambassadorial candidates: "the person should not be in opposition to fundamental teachings of the Church that belong to our common shared humanity. He or she may not believe in Catholic dogma if he or she is not a Catholic, but we could not accept someone who is in favor of abortion, or (human) cloning or same-sex unions equated to marriage," noting the ease with which progressive governments such as Spain, Cuba, and the United States under the Clinton administration had understood and complied with these criteria.[49] As such, although denying that Kmiec's name ever appeared on the list of possible appointees, the final rejection of his possible nomination is framed in light of his "disappointing position on embryonic stem cell research" (CNA, Obama Candidates). Thus, the reasoning against Kmiec had moved from one of political consideration, to one of relational incompatibility, to one of failing a simple standard set for all diplomats to the Vatican.

Three other candidates were rejected in the informal back and forth for similar reasons, although it is not clear exactly who they were. When asked whether Caroline Kennedy, a prominent, pro-choice Catholic and speculated nominee, was on the list, the simple response was "no comment," with the addendum that "obviously she would not fit the profile."[50] However, days later, on April 15, 2009, the Vatican dismissed new reports that they had vetoed Kennedy's nomination, stating simply that they had never received a nomination to veto.[51] Some news reports characterize these unofficial problems as a symbolic struggle between the Obama administration and the Church,[52] while conservative Catholic leaders characterize the attempted nomination of Catholics in such discord with basic Church doctrine as "inappropriate" at best, and at worst, as "a calculated insult to the Holy See."[53]

Calculated or not, the Obama administration settled on an official nominee for the office who passed the "simple standard" in Professor Miguel Diaz of St. John's University, on May 27, 2009. The nomination garnered comparatively little condemnation from conservative Catholics. CNA simply noted that he is a "liberation theologian" in their press release (carrying its own stigma as a heretical theological position), and otherwise did not question his appropriateness as a nominee.[54] However, CNA did offer an interesting rhetorical read of the appointment, characterizing it as "the first return that Catholics who have unconditionally supported Obama's policies and appointments have received for their investment in the ticket," noting Diaz was listed as a member of pro-Obama Catholics in Alliance for the Common

Good—an association he attempted to downplay as "a response to an invitation to become a theological advisor."[55] CNA further noted that:

> Miguel Diaz served in 2008 on the Obama campaign's Catholic advisory board. Also in 2008, he donated $1,000 to the Obama Victory Fund. Although he claims to be a "defender of life in all of it stages," Diaz was among 26 Catholic leaders and scholars who signed a statement supporting the nomination of staunch pro-abortion Catholic Kathleen Sebelius as Health and Human Services Secretary.[56]

The charge then seemed to be of standard political cronyism mixed with an indirect questioning of his pro-life *bona fides*. In many ways, he was a less public version of Kmiec, who had the benefit of never having been a conservative stalwart, meaning he was a Catholic Obama supporter who did not ruffle conservative feathers. One might point out the dislike of his policy positions or sophisms in his support of certain dissident Catholics, but he could himself be labeled neither a religious dissident nor a political traitor.

The main question, from a rhetorical perspective, is: With such a well-qualified, pro-life Catholic candidate already on the Obama administration's radar who had yet to raise the ire of conservative Catholics, why wait so long to appoint him? Why float a number of names that would so obviously cause discord with the country with whom he is trying to establish diplomatic relations? The natural inclination might be to assume that Obama had indeed been dealing in some sort of symbolic maneuvering with his earlier picks. It might also be that Obama was just beginning to realize the ways the administration and the Church could find common ground. This is the read that the more progressive *National Catholic Reporter* offers. They saw the appointment of a pro-life ambassador as Obama successfully passing his second major Catholic test.[57] NCR is quick to bring up the two worries mentioned by CNA. The first is that it is political pay-back for a staunch Obama supporter and member of the Catholic Alliance. The second is that Diaz is a "liberation theologian." The charge of cronyism is left unaddressed, but NCR pointed out the inaccuracies in labeling Diaz as a liberation theologian just because he is sympathetic to such theories. Overall, NCR emphasized the Vatican's pleasure with the choice, noting that he has no official track record of challenging U.S. Bishops on doctrinal issues. Noting his Hispanic background, NCR characterized Diaz as a smart choice who can speak to issues of immigration, Cuba, reconciling relations between North and South America, and the changing demographics of the Church in America; issues on which the Holy See would be interested in obtaining U.S. cooperation and vice versa. As we will see, the lengthy saga of appointing a Vatican ambassador might have culminated in a possible template of appointments on which both the Church and the Obama administration could agree.

Supreme Court Justice and Surgeon General

Finally, let us consider the Catholic nominations for Supreme Court Justice and Surgeon General, first together, and then in turn. The reason for this is that relatively little controversy surrounded their nominations, despite following similar patterns. This may be because, by May of his first year of office, Obama seemed to have cracked the Catholic code; at least according to Deal Hudson, President Bush's Catholic Outreach Director:

> If you take some of their Catholic nominations, they seem to have a common thread. Sonia Sotomayor and/or surgeon general nominee Regina Benjamin—they are presented as Catholics, but the part of their story that the White House highlights is something that is compelling from another direction . . . by having stories ready that they know will appeal to Catholics and blunt criticism from the pro-life side.[58]

Indeed, President Obama highlighted the childhood and young adult struggles of each as minority women, and the life experiences these struggles would bring to their positions. He highlighted the fact that, after her father's death, Sotomayor's mother worked tirelessly for her children's well-being: "Sonia's mom bought the only set of encyclopedias in the neighborhood, sent her children to a Catholic school called Cardinal Spellman, out of the belief that with a good education here in America all things are possible."[59] He highlighted the fact that Benjamin rebuilt a clinic for the poor three times after various disasters knocked it down.[60] Hudson failed to mention that neither of these nominees were ever subjects of controversy the way that Daschle, Sebelius, or Kmiec had been. Sotomayor and Benjamin did not have a public record of dissent from Church teachings. A brief examination of each nominee shows that Obama adopted a new pattern of communicating with Catholics via appointments, a pattern perhaps acquired by his Vatican trials. There was a common ground to be reached between Catholics and the Obama administration, and it is miles away from the issue of abortion.

On May 26, 2009, President Obama made one of his most significant and long-lasting appointments when he nominated Sonia Sotomayor for a position on the Supreme Court. Sotomayor was received in a fairly positive, universal manner by her fellow Catholics. Even Bill Donohue responded favorably to her nomination. He stated that he would "quietly root" for Sotomayor because she is not "brandishing" her faith.[61] Additionally, he notes that the qualifications for a Catholic judge are different than the qualifications that make for a good Catholic legislator. CNA, once again, gave no direct commentary on the appointment. However, it did run articles about Sotomayor receiving positive reviews from pro-abortion groups, such as NARAL, but that other abortion advocates were leery about the nomination.[62] Eventually, Sotomayor was appointed to the Supreme Court. Some pro-lifers protested, but the majority of Catholic commentators left this appointment alone.

On July 13, 2009, Regina Benjamin was nominated to Surgeon General, the nation's "chief health educator." Benjamin presents a unique case for this study because of the praise that she has received. In 2006, Benjamin was awarded the Pro Ecclessia et Pontifice medal by Pope Benedict XVI himself.[63] CNA noted that, at that point, her position on abortion was in line with the Church's teachings as far as one could tell, but that "it would be 'difficult' to adhere to Catholic moral teaching in a position with the Obama Administration."[64] Thus, her views on life issues were called into question, though they were relatively unknown. In the same article, CNA quoted Sr. Keehan of CHA, stating that her position on abortion should not matter because she is not in a "'specialty that would do abortion,' and that her work to provide health care to the poor and elderly demonstrates her 'tremendous attention to the issue of life.'" She also defended Benjamin by saying that a Catholic does not receive the Pro Ecclessia medal for being a "token Catholic"[65] CNA ends its coverage by noting that, "In December 2008 a coalition of several dozen pro-abortion groups released a strategy document titled 'Advancing Reproductive Rights and Health in a New Administration' calling on Obama to improve access to 'abortion care.' The document named the surgeon general's office as a 'position of interest'."[66] Thus, CNA concludes the article by, again, framing its coverage around the issue of abortion.

Conclusion: Rhetorical Readings of the Appointments

It has been asserted that President Obama viewed the relationship between his administration and the Church as one that required a good deal of symbolic management. While much of this management has taken the form of speeches, press releases, and policy statements that require consideration in order to fully grasp the complexity of Obama's relationship with the Church, the realm of appointments provides a rhetorical microcosm that allows us to more clearly view the relevant, interacting forces. The analysis of Obama's various Catholic appointments provide the elements for a compelling narrative that tells the story of a developing relationship between the President, Catholic voters, and official voices of the Catholic Church. However, the elements are such that they offer themselves up to a multitude of interpretations, depending on one's point of view.

As we have documented, nominations made after May of 2009 were much less controversial among the lay Catholic faithful and the Church hierarchy. Of the various reads that one might give concerning this change of tact, four seem most prominent. The most positive of these reads is offered by Kelley, Korzen, and other Catholic voices who supported Obama even before the election. They maintained from the outset that each and every appointment, whether Catholics in good standing or not, is consonant with the larger Catholic concern for abortion reduction through increased social justice. For some commentators, like Donohue, there is no doubt that earlier appointments sent a clear message to conservative forces within the Church, while presenting a pretense of cooperation, to Catholic voters, most of who were not fooled. As such, the shift in strategy signaled a practical realization on Obama's part of what the Catholic polity was willing to put up with. A much more cynical read is given by some conservative observers who, like Kelley and Korzen, see no real change in the narrative and claim that Obama had just better learned how to smokescreen the problematic aspects of his Catholic appointees.[67] By far, the most nefarious read permeates the conservative Catholic blogosphere, as they characterize Obama's appointments as continual attempts to redefine Catholicism for Americans by presenting dissident views, whether they be about abortion, stem cell research, gay marriage, or liberation theology, as legitimate Catholic views worthy of emulation.

These interpretations are by no means exhaustive. For instance, by simply looking at the timeline of events, we could interpret the narrative as one in which the President had to adjust to a learning curve whereby he himself was educated on what it means to be Catholic, and that his genuine desire for interfaith dialogue and cooperation caused him to re-examine the nature of his appointees. Conversely, we could note that his later appointees were indeed different in their adherence to Catholic doctrine, not as a product of discovery, but rather out of a shrewd political calculation that allowed him to "come to a realization" of what genuine dialogue means only after his most important policy posts were already filled by dissident Catholic voices. Given the elements themselves, we can endorse none of the reads offered above since the key to their legitimacy resides within the unknowable motives of the President Obama. However, further insight can be gleamed by reviewing the controversy surrounding the final rule, issued by the Department of Health and Human Services, mandating the coverage of contraceptive services for women in the final year of the President's first term. While the rhetoric surrounding the HHS mandate is worthy of its own analysis, a digest of the controversy provides a fitting conclusion to the current study.

Throughout the rest of President Obama's first term, his administration and Catholic groups continually dialogued concerning his aim to reform health care in the United States. In general, groups ranging from the Conference of Bishops to the Catholic Health Association were supportive of the administration's efforts to create a more socially just system of health care. However, with the passing of the Affordable Care Act in 2010, the USCCB and CHA split their endorsement of the administration's efforts, with Sr. Keehan and CHA being a major supporter of the bill, and the Bishops voicing concern that it would lead to a rise in access to abortion and the deterioration of conscience protections.[68] On January 20, 2012, the Bishops and other Catholic skeptics were apparently proved correct when Secretary Sebelius delivered a surprising blow to the Catholic community, announcing that contraception, sterilization, and potentially abortion-causing drugs would be mandatorily covered by all employers, except for narrowly defined religious institutions.[69] The announcement was met with immediate public backlash from Catholics across the political spectrum, and many of Obama's previous supporters publically interpreted it as a personal affront to the Catholic community issued from the President himself. In an open letter, Douglas Kmiec asked the President why he would "put the cold calculus of politics above faith and freedom," and noted that this move is not the move of the man and friend he supported (Catholic Online).[70] Sr. Keehan professed on behalf of the CHA that the "impact of being told we do not fit the new definition of a religious employer and therefore cannot operate our ministries following our consciences has jolted us" (Something).[71]

Less than a month later, in response to a great deal of public criticism, the Obama administration promised a compromise to the mandate that required insurance companies to pay for these drugs and procedures, rather than nonprofit religious employers directly. The promise of such a compromise satisfied many Catholic allies of Obama, garnering public statements of support from the likes of Cafardi, Kmiec, Keehan, and Notre Dame President, Fr. John Jenkins (Catholic World News; Ford; Keehan, Catholic).[72] Even the Bishops were momentarily inclined to call the compromise "a first step in the right direction," before concluding that no such compromise was possible.[73] Indeed, the Bishops launched a vigorous campaign against the mandate, and by the early summer months, even Notre Dame and CHA voiced their opposition to the promised compromise due to lingering concerns (Jenkins, Message; Keehan, Stanek, and Swedish).[74] As the presidential election approached, the rhetorical force of the Bishops' campaign faded, and its substance devolved into partisan cries about the "War on Religion!" and the "War on Women!"

By September of 2012, Kmiec was able to frame the HHS mandate as a tactless mishandling due to bad advice: "Yes, he could have handled the HHS contraceptive issue in a more accommodating and sensitive way to the formal teaching of my church, and he was again given some very poor advice on the scope of religious exemption that should have been provided an institution like his honorary alma mater, Notre Dame."[75] To the casual observer, it would seem this argument is just like Kmiec and others claimed; i.e., a rhetorical and political misstep. However, such a defense, while plausible, only gives credence to the readings of Obama's early symbolic interactions with the Church and its members as shrewd and calculating rather than sympathetic and sincere. On the sincere reading, as we have pointed out, Obama's policies would have always been in concert with the true spirit of the Church, or else he would have learned in the first year of his administration where the common ground between his administration and the Church lies. The HHS mandate was far from such common ground. Moreover, when we account for who the advisors were and what the advice was, sincerity is a tougher pill to swallow. The list of Catholic organizations and individuals that offered advice on the proposed final rule during the commenting period between August and September of 2011 consisted, in part, of: CHA, Notre Dame, and an "ad hoc" group of Catholic academics and public figures (including Cafardi and many others who supported Obama and defended his appointments). These letters employed the same rhetoric of conscience, dialogue, and service to the common good they had used while supporting the President, and often reminded the administration of its own rhetorical posturing.[76] Indeed, even top Catholic officials, such as Vice President Joe Biden, Defense Secretary Leon Panetta, and then White House Chief of Staff Bill Daley, advised against the mandate.[77] In the end, it seems as if Secretary Sebelius was the lone Catholic advisor pushing for the mandate. As such, the "bad advice" to which Kmiec had dismissively referenced was exactly what skeptical readers of the earlier symbolic interactions had worried about—Obama had held up a dissident Catholic as an exemplar and then used her "exemplary" advice to justify his interactions with the Church. This is either a rookie mistake or a failed gamble by an otherwise shrewd gambler. Our analysis indicates that by 2012, Obama should be well beyond such rookie mistakes.

However, as the election drew nearer, the mandate issue was drowned out for many Catholic voters by the more immediate, but less substantive, contrast between Joe Biden and Paul Ryan. Past sparring over policies and appointments were replaced with verbal sparring between "social justice" and "moral doctrine." When the dust of the election settled, President Obama had won 50% of the Catholic vote, whereas Romney garnered 48% (Pew Forum).[78] The Obama administration lost 4% of the Catholic electorate to the Republicans from 2008. Certainly there were a number of factors that played into the decrease in votes, but the feelings of distrust that were seeded during the early cabinet appointments, and exposed during the ongoing mandate dialogue between Obama and Catholics, had to have played a part. As of the writing of this coda, President Obama has nominated John Kerry to the position of Secretary of State—a nomination much more in the mold of Daschle and Sebelius than of the Benjamin and Sotomayer—and the HHS mandate has taken effect without any further details on the promised compromise. Ultimately, the dialogue between Catholics and President Obama will continue throughout his second term, and will likely continue to play on the rifts outlined in this article. While many conservative Catholics will interpret his forthcoming interactions with skepticism, the Bishops enduring concern for the poor, for immigrants, for the unborn, and for all God's children will ensure that there is rhetorical room at the table for both political parties. Both parties, however, would wisely take note of how the Catholic Church in America understands itself.

NOTES

1. Obama, Barak. "Obama Notre Dame Speech: Full Text, Video." *Huffingtonpost.com*. 17 Aug.
2009. Web. 20 April 2010. http://www.huffingtonpost.com/2009/05/17/obama-notre—dame-speech-f_n_204387.html

2. Forming Consciences for Faithful Citizenship: A Call to Political Responsibility." *Faithful Citizenship*. 2007. Web. 1 Apr. 2010. http://www.usccb.org/faithfulcitizenship/FCStatement.pdf, 11.

3. According to the Pew Research Center, President Obama garnered 54% of the Catholic vote, while candidate McCain was only able to gain 45% The Pew Forum on Religion & Public Life. "How the Faithful Voted: 2012 Preliminary Analysis." *Pewforum.org*. 7 Nov. 2012. Web. 15 Dec. 2012. http://www.pewforum.org/Politics-and-Elections/How-the-Faithful-Voted-2012-Preliminary-Exit-Poll-Analysis.aspx

4. "Faithful Citizenship: A Catholic Call to Political Responsibility." *Faithful Citizenship*. 2003. Web. 1 Apr. 2010. http://www.usccb.org/faithfulcitizenship/faithfulcitizenship03.pdf, 6-8.

5. Keating, Karl. "Karl Keating's E-Letter." *Catholic Answers*. 14 Sept. 2004. Web. 10 Apr. 2010. < http://www.catholic.com/newsletters/kke_040914.asp>

6. "Catholic Bishops Put Kibosh on Partisan Voting Guides." *Catholics—united.org*. 3 Nov. 2006. Web. 12 Apr. 2010. http://www.catholicsunited.org/?q=node/39

7. Ibid., 11.

8. Alliance for the Common Good was founded in 2005 by Alexia Kelley, the former religious outreach director for the 2004 Kerry campaign.

9. It is worth noting that "abortion reduction" did not become a prevalent concept within either Catholics United or Catholics in Alliance until after the US-CCB's 2007 document.

10. Douglas W. Kmiec. "Reaganites for Obama? Sorry, McCain. Barack Obama is a Natural for the Catholic Vote." *Slate*. 13 Feb. 2008. Web. 9 Apr. 2010. <http://www.slate.com/id/2184378>

11. Kmiec. "Endorsing Obama." *Convictions. Slate*. 23 March 2008. Web. 8 Apr. 2010. http://www.slate.com/blogs/blogs/convictions/archive/2008/03/23/endorsing-obama.aspx

12. Newsweek. "A Catholic Brief for Obama: Why the Faithful can in Good Conscience Back the Democrat." *Newsweek.com*. 17 Oct. 2008. Web 8 Apr. 2010. http://www.newsweek.com/2008/10/16/a-catholic-brief-for-obama.html

13. "Social Justice Groups Meet with Obama Team, Catholic Bishops Express Doubt." *Catholicnewsagency.com*. 18 Dec. 2008. Web. 8 Apr. 2010. http://www.catholicnewsagency.com/news/social_justice_groups_meet_with_obama_team_catholic_bishops_express_doubt/

14. Ibid.

15. Ibid.

16. Though he was officially nominated on this date, the discussion surrounding the Daschle nomination began on November 19, 2008, when it was first unofficially leaked that he would be nominated.

17. "Remarks of President-Elect Barack Obama as Prepared for Delivery Thursday, December 11, 2008 Chicago, Illinois." *Change.gov*. Web. 13 Apr. 2010. <http://change.gov/newsroom/entry/president_elect_obama_nominates_senator_daschle_as_secretary_of_hhs/>

18. Ibid.

19. Bottum, J. "Tom Daschle's Duty to be Morally Coherent." *Weeklystandard.com*.17 April 2003. Web. 16 Apr. 2010. http://www.weeklystandard.com/Content/Public/Articles/000/000/002/559jrrei.asp

20. Ibid.

21. Catholic News Agency. "Catholic Health Association Welcomes Daschle Appointment Called Disastrous' by Pro-lifers.'" *Catholicnewsagency.com*. 17 Dec. 2008. Web. 2 Apr. 2010. http://www.catholicnewsagency.com/news/catholic_health_association_welcomes_daschle_appointment_called_disastrous_by_pro-lifers/

22. AFP. "Obama Picks Former Senate Leader Daschle to Lead Healthcare Reform." 19 Nov. 2008. Web. 17 Apr. 2010. http://www.google.com/hostednews/afp/article/ALeqM5iRH14RvRDzSBH3NvOVm0WnvXg0A

23. Cooper, Heline, and Peter Baker. "Daschle to Be Nominee for Health Post in Obama Cabinet." *Nytimes.com*. 19 Nov. 2008. Web. 15 Apr. 2010. http://www.nytimes.com/2008/11/20/us/politics/20transition.html

24. "Obama Picks Abortion Supporter Daschle to Head HHS." *Catholicnewsagency.com.* 19 Nov. 2008. Web. 17 Apr. 2010. http://www.catholicnewsagency.com/news/obama_picks_abortion_supporter_daschle_to_head_hhs/

25. Ibid.

26. "Catholic Health Association Welcomes Daschle"

27. Keehan, Sr. Carol, DC, Robert V. Stanek, and Joseph R. Swedish. Letter to Marilyn Tavenner 15 June 2012. *Modernhealthcare.com.* 15 June 2012. Web. 20 Dec. 2012. http://www.modernhealthcare.com/assets/pdf/CH80052615.PDF

28. "Catholic Health Association Welcomes Daschle"

29. Catholics in Alliance for the Common Good. "Stealth Care." *Catholicsinalliance.org.* 11 Feb. 2009. Web. 12 May 2010. http://www.catholicsinalliance.org/node/20514

30. This article was housed on Catholics in Alliance for the Common Good's website. The webpage no longer exists.

31. "President Barack Obama Delivers Remarks with Secretary of Health and Human Services Nominee Governor Kathleen Sebelius." galegroup.com. 2 Mar. 2009. Web. 10 Apr. 2010. http://go.galegroup.com/ps/i.do

32. Robert D. Novak. "A Pro-Choicer's Dream Veep." Washington Post,. May 28, 2008. Web. http://www.washingtonpost.com/wp-dyn/content/article/2008/05/25/ AR2008052502275.html

33. "President Barack Obama Delivers Remarks with Secretary of Health"

34. "Pro-abortion 'Rights' Catholic Governor Possible Pick for HHS Secretary." *Catholicnewsagency.* 10 Feb. 2009. Web. 16 Apr. 2010. http://www.catholicnewsagency.com/news/proabortion_rights_catholic_governor_possible_pick_for_hhs_secretary/>

35. Gerson, Michael. "Sebelius's 'Choice:' Obama's Messenger for Moral Incoherence." *Washingtonpost.com.* 11 March 2009. Web. 12 Apr. 2010. <http://www.washingtonpost.com/wp-dyn/content/article/2009/03/10/AR2009031002838.html>

36. Shelly, Barb. "Why Sebelius's Archbishop is Unhappy." *Kansascitystar.com.* 5 March 2009.Web. 14 Apr. 2010. <http://voices.kansascity.com/node/3927>

37. Catholics in the Public Sphere. "Archbishop Raymond L. Burke: Sebelius' Appointment'Greatest Disappointment Because she has Publicly and Repeatedly Betrayed her Catholic Faith." thepublicsquare.blogspot.com. 14 March 2009. Web. 12 Apr. 2010. < http://thepublicsquare.blogspot.com/2009/03/archbishop-raymond-1 -burke-sebelius.html>

38. Catholic League. "Obama Chooses Pro-Abortion Zealot for HHS." CatholicLeague.org. 2 March 2009. Web. 13 Apr. 2010. < http://www.catholicleague.org/release.php?id=1564>

39. Fox, Thomas. "26 Prominent Catholics Back Sebelius Pick." *Ncronline.org.* 1 March 2009. Web. 17 Apr. 2010. http://ncronline.org/news/politics/26-prominent-catholics-back-sebelius-pick

40. Ibid.

41. Ibid.

42. Ibid.

43. Winters, Michael Sean. "Kmiec for Vatican Ambassador." *In All Things.* *America.* 23 Nov.2008. Web. 25 Apr. 2010. <http://www.americamagazine.org/blog/entry.cfm?blog_id=2&id=CBCE4400–1321-AEAA-D38BB214E0D504BA>

44. Why Kmiec Will Not Become the New Vatican Ambassador." *Catholicnewsagency.com.* 25 Nov. 2008. Web. 27 July 2010 <http://www.catholicnewsagency.com/news/why_kmiec_will_not_become_the_new_vatican_ambassador/>

45. Ibid.

46. Ibid.

47. "Kmiec Considers Himself a Candidate for Vatican Ambassadorship." *Catholicnewsagency.com.* 26 Jan. 2009. Web. 28 Apr. 2010. <http://www.catholicnewsagency.com/news/kmiec_considers_himself_a_candidate_for_vatican_ambassadorship/>

48. Ibid.

49. Obama's Candidates for Vatican Ambassador Failing 'Simple Standard.'" *Catholicnewsagency.com.* 9 Apr. 2009. Web. 2 Apr. 2010. http://www.catholicnewsagency.com/news/obamas_candidates_for_vatican_ambassador_failing_simple_standard/

50. Ibid.

51. Vatican Spokesman Denies 'Veto' of Caroline Kennedy." *Catholicnewsagency.com.* 15 April 2009. Web. 28 Apr. 2010. <http://www.catholicnewsagency.com/news/vatican_spokesman_denies_veto_of_caroline_kennedy/>

52. McGreal, Chris. "Vatican Vetoes Barack Obama's Nominees for US Ambassador." *Guardian.co.uk.* 14 April 2009. Web. 29 Apr. 2010. <http://www.guardian.co.uk/world/2009/apr/14/vatican-vetoes-obama-nominees-abortion>

53. Steven Ertelt. "Caroline Kennedy Reportedly Rejected as Potential Vatican Ambassador Over Abortion." *Lifenews.com.* 13 Apr. 2009. Web. 2 Apr. 2010. <http://www.lifenews.com/2009/04/13/int-1157/>

54. Obama Picks Cuban Liberation Theologian as U.S. Ambassador to the Holy See." *Catholicnsewsagency.com.* 28 May 2009. Web. 28 Apr. 2010. <http://www.catholicnewsagency.com/news/obama_picks_cuban_liberation_theologian_as_u.s._ambassador_to_the_holy_see/>

55. Ibid.

56. Ibid.

57. Allen, John L., Jr. "With Diaz Nomination, Obama Passes Major Catholic Test." *Ncronline.org.* 28 May 2009. Web. 29 Apr. 2010. http://ncronline.org/blogs/all-things-catholic/diaz-nomination-obama-passes-major-catholic-test. The first test was the success, in NCR's view, of Obama's speech at Notre Dame.

58. Gilgoff, Dan. "Bush's Catholic Outreach Director Assesses Obama's Catholic Outreach." *US News.* 23 July 2009. Web. 13 Apr. 2010. http://www.usnews.com/news/blogs/god-and-country/2009/07/23/bushs-catholic-outreach-director-assesses-obamas-catholic-outreach

59. President Barack Obama Delivers Remarks Regarding the Nomination of Judge Sonia Sotomayor to the Supreme Court."*galegroup.com.* 26 May 2009. Web. 20 Sep. 2011. < http://go.galegroup.com/ps/i.do?&id=GALE%7CA200593047&v=2.1&u=upitt_ main& it=r&p=ITOF&sw=w>

60. "President Barack Obama Delivers Remarks on His Nominee for Surgeon General." *galegroup.com.* 13 July 2009. Web. 21 Sep. 2011. < http://go.galegroup.com/ps/i.do?&id =GALE%7CA203502841&v=2.1&u=upi tt_main&it=r&p=ITOF&sw=w>

61. Waldman, Steve. "Bill Donohue: Will Likely 'Quietly Root for' Sotomayor (!)." *Beliefnet.net.* 28 May 2009. Web. 30 Apr. 2010. <http://blog.beliefnet.com/stevenwaldman/2009/05/bill.html>

62. Pro-Abortion Groups Praise Nomination of Sotomayor to Supreme Court." *Catholicnewsagency.com.* 29 May 2009. Web. 18 Apr. 2010. http://www.catholicnewsagency.com/news/proabortion_groups_praise_nomination_of_sotomayor_to_supreme_court/; "Sotomayor Receives NARAL Endorsement." *Catholicnewsagency.com.* 22 June 2009. Web. 1 Apr. 2010. <http://www.catholicnewsagency.com/news/sotomayor_receives_naral_endorsement/>

63. "Obama Nominates Rural Catholic Doctor as Surgeon General." *Catholicnewsagency.com.* 13 July 2009. Web. 17 Apr. 2010. <http://www.catholicnewsagency.com/news/obama_nominates_rural_catholic_doctor_as_surgeon_general/>

64. Ibid.

65. Keehan, Sr. Carol, DC. "Catholic Health Association is Very Pleased with Today's White House Resolution that Protects Religious Liberty and Conscience Rights." *Chausa.org.* 10 Feb. 2012. Web. 20 Dec. 2012. <http://www.chausa.org/Pages/Newsroom/Releases/2012/ Catholic_Health_Association_is_Very_Pleased_with_Todays_White_House_Resolution_that_Protects_Religious_Liberty_and_Conscience_Rights/>

66. "Obama Nominates Rural Catholic Doctor"

67. See, for instance, the comments of Deal Hudson as reported by CNA ('Smart' Obama).

68. Gilbert, Kathleen. "USCCB President: CHA's Keehan is 'to Blame' for ObamaCare Passage."*LifeSiteNews.com.* 17 June 2010. Web. 20 Dec. 2012. < http://www.lifesitenews.com/ news/archive/ldn/2010/jun/10061705>

69. Even the list of grievances has been the subject of rhetorical interpretation, since the Church defines an abortion as any destruction of a fertilized egg, while the Obama administration relegates usage of the term to the period after the egg is implanted in the uterus.

70. Doug Kmiec Writes President Obama: 'Friendship Will Not Permit Me to Disregard Duty to Faith and Country' http://www.catholic.org/national/national_story.php?id=44667

71. "Something has to be Fixed." *Chausa.org.* 15 Feb. 2012. Web. 20 Dec. 2012. <http://www.chausa.org/Something_has_to_be_fixed.aspx>

72. This support ranged from outright endorsement to cautious optimism.

73. Cooper, Heline, and Laurie Goodstein. "Rule Shift on Birth Control is Concession to Obama Allies." *Nytimes.com.* 10 Feb. 2012. Web. 20 Dec. 2012. http://www.nytimes.com/ 2012/02/11/health/policy/obama-to-offer-accommodation-on-birth-control-rule-officials-say.html?pagewanted=all&_r=3&

74. Jenkins, Fr. John, C.S.C. "A Message from Father Jenkins on the HHS Lawsuit." *President.nd.edu.* 21 May 2012. Web. 20 Dec. 2012. http://president.

nd.edu/ communications/a-message-from-father-jenkins-on-the-hhs-lawsuit/; Keehan, Sr. Carol, DC, Robert V. Stanek, and Joseph R. Swedish. Letter to Marilyn Tavenner 15 June 2012. *Modernhealthcare.com.* 15 June 2012. Web. 20 Dec. 2012. http://www.modernhealthcare.com/assets/pdf/CH80052615.PDF

75. Avlon, John. "Many 2008 Conservative Obama Backers, or ObamaCons, Will Stay True." *Thedailybeast.com.* 4 Sep. 2012. Web. 20 Dec. 2012. http://www. thedailybeast.com/ articles/2012/09/04/many-2008-conservative-obama-backers-or-obamacons-will-stay-true.html

76. Letter to Kathleen Sebelius 28 Sep. 2011. *President.nd.edu.* 28 Sep. 2011. Web. 20 Dec. 2012. http://president.nd.edu/assets/50056/comments_from_rev_john_i_jenkins_notre_ dame_3_.pdf; "Catholic Health Association Response to Women's Preventive Services Regulations."*Chausa.org.* 2 Aug. 2011. Web. 20 Dec. 2012. http://www.chausa.org/Pages/ Newsroom/Releases/2011/ CHA_Response_to_Women__39;s_Preventive_Services_Regulation; "Prominent RCs Write to Sebelius on Conscience Protections." *Ncronline.org.* 26 Aug. 2011. Web. 20 Dec. 2012. http://ncronline.org/blogs/distinctly-catholic/prominent-rcs-write-sebelius-conscience-protections

77. Lopez, Kathryn Jean. "Panetta, Biden, Daley vs. Cecile Richards." *National review.com.* 9 Feb. 2012. Web. 20 Dec. 2012. < http://www.nationalreview. com/corner/290689/panetta-biden-daley-vs-cecile-richards-kathryn-jean-lopez#>

78. The Pew Forum on Religion & Public Life. "How the Faithful Voted: 2012 Preliminary Analysis." *Pewforum.org.* 7 Nov. 2012. Web. 15 Dec. 2012. <http:// www.pewforum.org/Politics-and-Elections/How-the-Faithful-Voted-2012-Preliminary-Exit-Poll-Analysis.aspx>

WORKS CITED

AFP. "Obama Picks Former Senate Leader Daschle to Lead Healthcare Reform." 19 Nov. 2008. Web. 17 Apr. 2010.

Allen, John L., Jr. "With Diaz Nomination, Obama Passes Major Catholic Test." *Ncronline.org.* 28 May 2009. Web. 29 Apr. 2010.

Avlon, John. "Many 2008 Conservative Obama Backers, or ObamaCons, Will Stay True." *Thedailybeast.com.* 4 Sep. 2012. Web. 20 Dec. 2012.

Bottum, J. "Tom Daschle's Duty to be Morally Coherent." *Weeklystandard.com.*17 April 2003. Web. 16 Apr. 2010.

Catholic Answers Action. "Voter's Guide for Serious Catholics." *Caaction.com.* 2006. Web. 18 Apr. 2010.

Catholics in Alliance for the Common Good. "Stealth Care." *Catholicsinalliance. org.* 11 Feb. 2009. Web. 12 May 2010.

Catholics in the Public Sphere. "Archbishop Raymond L. Burke: Sebelius' Appointment 'Greatest Disappointment Because she has Publicly and Repeatedly Betrayed her Catholic Faith." thepublicsquare.blogspot.com. 14 March 2009. Web. 12 Apr. 2010.

Catholic League. "Obama Chooses Pro-Abortion Zealot for HHS." CatholicLeague.org. 2 March 2009. Web. 13 Apr. 2010.

Catholic News Agency. "Catholic Health Association Welcomes Daschle Appointment Called 'Disastrous' by Pro-lifers.'" *Catholicnewsagency.com.* 17 Dec. 2008. Web. 2 Apr. 2010.

—. "Colorado's Politicians React to Denver Archbishop's Strong Words." *Catholicnewsagency.com.* 19 April 2004. Web. 16 Apr. 2010.

—. "Kmiec Considers Himself a Candidate for Vatican Ambassadorship." *Catholicnewsagency.com.* 26 Jan. 2009. Web. 28 Apr. 2010.

—. Obama's Candidates for Vatican Ambassador Failing 'Simple Standard.'" *Catholicnewsagency.com.* 9 Apr. 2009. Web. 2 Apr. 2010.

—. "Obama Nominates Rural Catholic Doctor as Surgeon General." *Catholicnewsagency.com.* 13 July 2009. Web. 17 Apr. 2010.

—. "Obama Picks Abortion Supporter Daschle to Head HHS." *Catholicnsewsagency.com.* 19 Nov. 2008. Web. 17 Apr. 2010.

—. "Obama Picks Cuban Liberation Theologian as U.S. Ambassador to the Holy See." *Catholicnsewsagency.com.* 28 May 2009. Web. 28 Apr. 2010.

—. "Pro-Abortion Groups Praise Nomination of Sotomayor to Supreme Court." *Catholicnewsagency.com.* 29 May 2009. Web. 18 Apr. 2010.

—. "Pro-abortion 'Rights' Catholic Governor Possible Pick for HHS Secretary." *Catholicnewsagency.* 10 Feb. 2009. Web. 16 Apr. 2010.

—. "'Smart' Obama Outreach to Catholics Seeks to Offset Abortion Concerns, Commentator Says." *Catholicnewsagency.com.* 24 July 2009. Web. 12 Apr. 2010.

—. "Social Justice Groups Meet with Obama Team, Catholic Bishops Express Doubt." *Catholicnewsagency.com.* 18 Dec. 2008. Web. 8 Apr. 2010.

—. "Sotomayor Receives NARAL Endorsement." *Catholicnewsagency.com.* 22 June 2009. Web. 1 Apr. 2010.

—. "Vatican Spokesman Denies 'Veto' of Caroline Kennedy." *Catholicnewsagency.com.* 15 April 2009. Web. 28 Apr. 2010.

—. "Why Kmiec Will Not Become the New Vatican Ambassador." *Catholicnewsagency.com.* 25 Nov. 2008. Web. 27 July 2010.

—. "Catholic Bishops Put Kibosh on Partisan Voting Guides." *Catholics—united.org.* 3 Nov. 2006. Web. 12 Apr. 2010.

—. "'Catholics United' Welcomes Church Reproach of Controversial Voting Guides." *Catholics-united.org.* 6 Nov. 2006. Web. 10 Apr. . 2010.

Catholic World News. "Notre Dame, Jesuit Colleges Welcome HHS mandate 'Compromise.'" *CatholicCulture.org.* 15 Feb. 2012. Web. 20 Dec. 2012.

Chaput, Archbishop Charles. "Little Murders." *Public Discourse: Ethics, Law, and the Common Good. Thepublicdiscourse.com.* 18 Oct. 2008. Web. 14 Apr. 2010.

Cooper, Heline, and Peter Baker. "Daschle to Be Nominee for Health Post in Obama Cabinet." *NYTimes.com.* 19 Nov. 2008. Web. 15 Apr. 2010.

Cooper, Heline, and Laurie Goodstein. "Rule Shift on Birth Control is Concession to Obama Allies." *Nytimes.com.* 10 Feb. 2012. Web. 20 Dec. 2012.

Ertelt, Steven. "Caroline Kennedy Reportedly Rejected as Potential Vatican Ambassador Over Abortion." *Lifenews.com.* 13 Apr. 2009. Web. 2 Apr. 2010.

Ford, Kristin. "Prominent National Faith Leaders Celebrate White House's Common-Ground Solution on Contraception Coverage." *Faithinpubliclife.org.* 10 Feb. 2012. Web. 20 Dec. 2012.

Fox, Thomas. "26 Prominent Catholics Back Sebelius Pick." *Ncronline.org.* 1 March 2009. Web. 17 Apr. 2010.

Fournier, Deacon Keith A. "Doug Kmiec Writes President Obama: 'Friendship Will Not Permit Me to Disregard Duty to Faith or Country.'" *Catholic.org.* 7 Feb. 2012. Web. 20 Dec. 2012.

Gerson, Michael. "Sebelius's 'Choice:' Obama's Messenger for Moral Incoherence." *Washingtonpost.com.* 11 March 2009. Web. 12 Apr. 2010.

Gilbert, Kathleen. "USCCB President: CHA's Keehan is 'to Blame' for ObamaCare Passage." *LifeSiteNews.com.* 17 June 2010. Web. 20 Dec. 2012.

Gilgoff, Dan. "Bush's Catholic Outreach Director Assesses Obama's Catholic Outreach." US News. 23 July 2009. Web. 13 Apr. 2010.

Jenkins, Fr. John, C.S.C. "A Message from Father Jenkins on the HHS Lawsuit." *President.nd.edu.* 21 May 2012. Web. 20 Dec. 2012.

—. Letter to Kathleen Sebelius 28 Sep. 2011. *President.nd.edu.* 28 Sep. 2011. Web. 20 Dec. 2012.

Keating, Karl. "Karl Keating's E-Letter." *Catholic Answers.* 14 Sept. 2004. Web. 10 Apr. 2010.

Keehan, Sr. Carol, DC. "Catholic Health Association is Very Pleased with Today's White House Resolution that Protects Religious Liberty and Conscience Rights." *Chausa.org.* 10 Feb. 2012. Web. 20 Dec. 2012.

—. "Catholic Health Association Response to Women's Preventive Services Regulations." *Chausa.org.* 2 Aug. 2011. Web. 20 Dec. 2012.

—."Something has to be Fixed." *Chausa.org.* 15 Feb. 2012. Web. 20 Dec. 2012.

Keehan, Sr. Carol, DC, Robert V. Stanek, and Joseph R. Swedish. Letter to Marilyn Tavenner 15 June 2012. *Modernhealthcare.com.* 15 June 2012. Web. 20 Dec. 2012.

Kmiec, Douglas W. "Endorsing Obama." *Convictions. Slate.* 23 March 2008. Web. 8 Apr. 2010.

—. "Reaganites for Obama? Sorry, McCain. Barack Obama is a Natural for the Catholic Vote." *Slate.* 13 Feb. 2008. Web. 9 Apr. 2010.

Lopez, Kathryn Jean. "Panetta, Biden, Daley vs. Cecile Richards." *National review. com.* 9 Feb. 2012. Web. 20 Dec. 2012.

McGreal, Chris. "Vatican Vetoes Barack Obama's Nominees for US Ambassador." *Guardian.co.uk.* 14 April 2009. Web. 29 Apr. 2010.

Newsweek. "A Catholic Brief for Obama: Why the Faithful can in Good Conscience Back the Democrat." *Newsweek.com.* 17 Oct. 2008. Web 8 Apr. 2010.

Novak, Robert D. "A Pro-Choicer's Dream Veep." Washington Post,. May 28, 2008. Web.

Obama, Barak. "Obama Notre Dame Speech: Full Text, Video." *Huffingtonpost. com.* 17 Aug. 2009. Web. 20 April 2010.

—."President Barack Obama Delivers Remarks Regarding the Nomination of Judge

Sonia Sotomayor to the Supreme Court." *galegroup.com.* 26 May 2009. Web. 20 Sep. 2011.

—. "President Barack Obama Delivers Remarks on His Nominee for Surgeon General." *galegroup.com.* 13 July 2009. Web. 21 Sep. 2011.

—. "President Barack Obama Delivers Remarks With Secretary of Health and Human Services Nominee Governor Kathleen Sebelius." galegroup.com. 2 Mar. 2009. Web. 10 Apr. 2010.

—. "Remarks of President-Elect Barack Obama as Prepared for Delivery Thursday, December 11, 2008 Chicago, Illinois." *Change.gov.* Web. 13 Apr. 2010.

Office of the Press Secretary. "President Obama Will Nominate Governor Kathleen Sebelius Secretary of HHS, Announces Release of $155 Million of ARRA Funds for Health Clinics Across America." *whitehouse.gov.* 2 March 2009. Web. 14 Apr. 2010.

Pew Forum on Religion & Public Life. "How the Faithful Voted: 2012 Preliminary Analysis." *Pewforum.org.* 7 Nov. 2012. Web. 15 Dec. 2012.

Peters, Thomas. "Breaking: Obama Picks Tom Daschle for HHS Secretary." *Americanpapist.blogspot.com.* 19 Nov. 2008. Web. 15 Apr. 2010.

Shelly, Barb. "Why Sebelius's Archbishop is Unhappy." *Kansascitystar.com.* 5 March 2009. Web. 14 Apr. 2010.

USCCB. "Faithful Citizenship: A Catholic Call to Political Responsibility." *Faithful Citizenship.* 2003. Web. 1 Apr. 2010.

—. "Forming Consciences for Faithful Citizenship: A Call to Political Responsibility." *Faithful Citizenship.* 2007. Web. 1 Apr. 2010.

Waldman, Steve. "Bill Donohue: Will Likely 'Quietly Root for' Sotomayor (!)." *Beliefnet.net.* 28 May 2009. Web. 30 Apr. 2010.

Winters, Michael Sean. "Kmiec for Vatican Ambassador." *In All Things. America.* 23 Nov. 2008. Web. 25 Apr. 2010.

—. "Prominent RCs Write to Sebelius on Conscience Protections." *Ncronline.org.* 26 Aug. 2011. Web. 20 Dec. 2012.

4 Barack Obama, Islam, and the Discourses of American Racial Belonging

Steven Salaita

The 2008 American presidential election brought into lucid focus long-standing discourses of racial belonging in the United States. I argue in this chapter that the discourses underlying the 2008 election were not novel or new-fangled, but those discourses invigorated dormant or tacit narratives of American nationhood. These narratives of nationhood are replete with nostalgia and the implicit belief that a true American is somebody who is white and Christian. This problem isn't new. Numerous scholars have analyzed it—Valerie Babb, for instance, in *Whiteness Visible*, and, more recently, Joel Olson in *The Abolition of White Democracy*.[1] The conflation of whiteness with American normativity is an age-old story that has inspired a luminous tradition of scholarship. It would be useful at this point to focus on how this conflation became a central component of an American presidential election. It would be foolish to argue that valuations of whiteness have been marginal to American electoral politics. In fact, the white majoritarian fear of various minorities, African Americans particularly, has long been a crucial feature of presidential campaign strategies. Even Bill Clinton, often lauded for his honorary blackness, expertly parlayed white fears and their dislike of blacks into electoral success. In this essay, I highlight the uses of racial innuendo in the media inventions of Obama, paying special attention to the introduction of Islamophobia into the process.

The uses of racialist innuendos in American elections aren't new, but rarely have they been so explicit in recent American history. In many ways, tropes of white belonging and minority foreignness were the central component of the 2008 election, especially when it became clear in the late summer of 2008 that Obama would win. There is a causal relationship between the strength of Obama's poll numbers and the level of vitriol directed against him. Of special interest is the role of Islamophobic discourses in the idea of American belonging. Islamophobia was its own rhetorical monster during the election, but it intersected in notable ways with extant ideologies of foreign encroachment on a pristine, Pax Americana. Because of its connotative and political problems, I use "Islamophobia" here, in a basic form, to describe a dislike of Muslims (and those seen to be Muslim) based on their innate fealty to an imagined set of ingrained commitments and characteristics (e.g., jihad, sharia law, the destruction/conversion of Christians, tribalism, and so forth).

Let's look at some of the ways that Islamophobia is exhibited; it is possible even to say that it was performed, for its exhibition, in many cases, follows ideas scripted onto American racial history. First, during the election, there was a pervasive conflation of disparate vocabularies underlying the election, as is generally the case when racism flares up: Obama is secretly an Arab; Obama is secretly a Muslim; Obama is secretly a foreigner. For instance, Michael Goldfarb of *The Weekly Standard* expresses anxiety about both Obama's religion and his linguistic acumen: "With even the White House now smearing Obama as a Muslim, one wonders if the president hasn't been concealing some greater fluency with the language of the Koran."[2] A study conducted by Mahzarin Banaji and Thierry Devos finds that volunteers "were quicker to associate former British Prime Minister Tony Blair with being American than Obama."[3] The main reason for this ambiguity, according to Banaji and Devos, is because Blair is white. Throughout the election season and into the present, the descriptors "Arab," "Muslim," and "foreigner" have been used interchangeably, sometimes as a deliberate strategy and other times out of old-fashioned ignorance.

Moreover, the accusations Obama faced give us a clear sense of how racist ideas can be articulated in an ever-shifting marketplace of public opinion. In today's United States, the risk associated with Islamophobia is minimal; in some cases, articulating Islamophobia can actually be helpful. Glenn Beck has seen his popularity increase since his days at CNN, when he warned that if "Muslims and Arabs don't act now by step[ping] to the plate to condemn terrorism, they will be looking through a razor wire fence at the West."[4] The ever-influential Rush Limbaugh explained in 2007 that Muslims "can't turn their back or face Mecca when they use the bathroom. What do they do on an airplane? Go to the cockpit and say, 'I got some box cutters, and if you don't turn this airplane 45 degrees for the next two minutes I'm going to hijack you?'"[5] This reality clarifies some of the Muslim-bashing directed against Obama that I will examine momentarily. At this point, I suggest that the expression of a particular form of racism in the United States doesn't necessarily denote a specific or isolated prejudice, but the type of prejudice that acceptably can be expressed.

Finally, it is important that we not view Obama merely as a victim of these racialist discourses. Although he was often their target, he is also one of their instigators. Obama didn't actively instigate Islamophobia, but he reinforced it by not condemning it and through his modes of response—something I discuss momentarily. First, let's explore the discourses of American racial belonging.

If one looks closely at the evolution of the racist and Islamophobic narratives during the election, it is clear that there is a causal relation between Obama's poll numbers and the intensity of the attacks directed against him. The attacks, then, are rooted in the material considerations of the American electoral structure, highlighting some of the inherent problems within the American electoral structure itself. It is a structure arising from a capitalistic economy, and as such, it emphasizes the commerce of electability and the business of governance, rather than the sincere representation of citizen-subjects in the body politic. The American democratic structure is only democratic insofar as (most) people have a right to vote for a pre-packaged candidate; it is not a democracy in the sense of shared power or genuinely representative politics. These shortcomings of the American system underline the usefulness of the racist and Islamophobic discourses that emerged *en masse* in 2008.

The idea that Obama is an Arab reflects a majoritarian identification with whiteness. The incorrect and contradictory deployment of this identification highlights the desire of the imperiled white majority to retain the special status that has attended whiteness since America's inception. "Arab," then, doesn't necessarily describe Arabs. It can describe anybody who exists outside the boundaries of proper American-ness, as the election made clear. Such outsiders include Muslims, Africans, African-Americans, South Asians, and even socialists, who were somehow outfitted with atavistic characteristics as if they constitute a racial group themselves. Former Republican congressman Tom Tancredo, for example, proclaims Obama "a committed socialist ideologue," a choice of language that intimates an atavistic devotion to harmful ideology.[6] Connections with racial politics are evident in the conflation of socialism with ontology, a practice that usually involves racial valuation. As Sherene Razack explains, after 9/11, "We can see how race thinking (the clash of modern and pre-modern civilization) is annexed to a political project (control of oil, capitalist accumulation, power) and erupts into a full-blown racism when united with ideas about universal values, individualism, and the market."[7]

Take the infamous John McCain town hall meeting—another capitalist appropriation of something originally democratic—in which a supposedly wayward attendee charged Obama with the crime of being Arab. McCain's troublesome response, that Obama is not an Arab but a good family man, drew lots of attention and some outrage, but most responses missed the point. Here is the exchange:

> Audience Member: I got to ask you a question. I can't trust Obama. I have read about him. He's not, he's um, he's an Arab.
>
> McCain: No ma'am, no ma'am. He's a decent family man, a citizen that I just happen to have disagreements with on fundamental issues and that's what this campaign is all about. He's not, thank you.

McCain's response drew some boos and some heckles from the audience. It is certainly true, as most point out, that McCain's juxtaposition of the Arab against the good family man (whatever that is) was a deeply racist formulation, but it seemed that no one noticed that McCain also called Obama a "citizen," which presents another notable binary.

The idea that an Arab is dialogically opposed to a normative American, the "citizen," is actually more prevalent, and more perilous, than the idea that an Arab is incapable of being a good family man. It is in the prejudicial notions of citizenship, defined here as national belonging, that the racialized criteria for American normativity are given their moral and discursive power. In order for the individual to qualify as a citizen, McCain implies, he or she must contravene the physical and cultural qualities of the Arab. This Arab, I point out, is an invention of the very same discourse by which it is buttressed—a result of the fact that, as Razack explains, "Whites remain individuals while Arabs and Muslims are understood only as a group with the group characteristic of violence."[8]

Of comparable peril is the majority response to the notorious exchange. Most folks rushed to condemn the woman for intolerantly proclaiming that Obama is an Arab, or they complained that Republicans were creating an atmosphere of intolerance. These are all worthy laments, but they omit any acknowledgement of the most conspicuous victims of the exchange: Arabs and Muslims. By constantly defending Obama against the false charges of his shady Arab and Muslim origin, his open-minded defenders ensured that the categories of Arab and Muslim remain consigned to an inflexible alterity.

Obama's campaign handlers, and Obama himself, share the guilt in this problem. They were presented with countless opportunities to note that being Arab or Muslim is not an inherently negative attribute. Instead, they indignantly proclaimed that Obama is most certainly not of such mysterious background. The discourse was unchallenged during the election, and Obama only offered explicit support to Arabs and Muslims after the election.[9] This inaction can be taken as a strategy: By disavowing Obama's connection to Arab and Muslim alterity, his campaign, like McCain's, sought to benefit from the discourses of American racial belonging that pervaded election conversations. In fact, it was important that Obama was able to benefit from a phenomenon that could have harmed his campaign. If one looks at the anxieties generated by his alleged sinister origin, it becomes clear that Islamophobia acted as the acceptable cover for the more un-politically correct phenomenon of anti-black racism. This isn't to say that the Islamophobia and xenophobia directed against Obama were insincere. They were very real, and it is very important that we confront them. From an intellectual standpoint, however, the dialectic between the more deeply-inscribed issue of anti-black racism and the more new-fangled Islamophobia presents us with numerous socio-cultural developments that are of interest.

When faced with accusations that Obama is an Arab or Muslim, his advisors denied those accusations and then appropriated them tacitly into their own candidate's public identity. Obama's vehement denial that he is Arab or Muslim didn't merely represent an unwillingness to stand up for an embattled minority community; it actually further ostracized that minority community by enabling Obama to position his blackness as adequately normative vis-à-vis the immutable foreignness of Arabs and Islam. This strategy hasn't worked completely, however. Suspicions of Obama's foreignness, both figurative and physical, remain a crucial part of American political discourse. If we go back to McCain's assertion that Obama is a citizen, as opposed to an "Arab," we see that the invention of the normative citizen in the present United States underlies the frequent demands that Obama produce his birth certificate.

The idea of citizenship in the United States is invested with racialized valuations, as is, in some cases, its legal practices. This problem is one that spans the American political spectrum from liberal to conservative. As I have already argued, the main target of these tendentious notions of national belonging, Obama, contributed tangibly to the problem. The interaction of black and Muslim bodies that ensued arose from a fantasy of a perpetual white Americana—in other words, from the timeless idea that a stable national identity can survive the encroachment of racialized objects. If Obama was best challenged through explicit and implicit charges that he is either a foreign interloper or inadequately American, then Obama's best defense was to point to even more foreign objects to presuppose his own belonging. In this way, the liberal discourses of tolerance reified the exclusionary discourses of American racial belonging.

Post-election phenomena are equally instructive. Immediately after Obama's victory was confirmed, grandiose fantasies of a post-racial United States emerged. The mythologized versions of Islam reinforced during the 2008 election became subsumed to the new ideology of an unprecedented colorblindness. Amid the 2008 election, Jim Hoaglund of the *Washignton Post* opined,

> Barack Obama has succeeded brilliantly in casting his candidacy—indeed, his whole life—as post-racial. Even before the votes have been cast, he has written a glorious coda for the civil rights struggle that provided this nation with many of the finest, and also most horrible, moments of its past 150 years. If the results confirm that race was not a decisive factor in the balloting, generations of campaigners for racial justice and equality will have seen their work vindicated.[10]

Nearly a year later, in the *Los Angeles Times*, Jim Rutten figuratively traipsed across the Atlantic to express a comparable sentiment:

> Obama remains a powerful voice of hope and change for many Europeans, not only because of his eloquence and his reassertion of America's role as a leader of international diplomacy, but also because he physically embodies change as progress. In this country [Norway], most people have taken their cue from a president determined to govern as chief executive of a post-racial society.[11]

This sort of sentiment predominated in the immediate aftermath of Obama's victory. Many discerning commentators and scholars have deconstructed the mythology of a post-racial America, and so I will not concentrate on its general problems. Instead, I would like to comment on the relationship of this mythology with the preponderance of Islamophobia unleashed during the election.

The idea of post-racialism in the United States excludes Arabs and Islam. Obama can thus benefit from the idea and from the modes of racism directed at Arabs and Muslims. The normative national identity Obama's camp attempted so vigorously to enter into relies on a collective retreat from the dark and un-modern spaces inhabited by Muslims, regardless of their actual geographical location. The Arab and Muslim, then, cannot achieve American normativity, for American normativity is immediately negated by the presence of the Arab and Muslim. As Ali Behdad points out, "Often treated as an exception to the prevailing myth of immigrant America, nativism is almost never acknowledged as a driving force behind much of the nation's immigration policy, one that continues to define citizenship and national identity in exclusionary terms and in a normalizing fashion."[12] To be sure, there are complexities and variations in the post-election conceptions of American national identity, but on the whole, it remains a racialized phenomenon, one in which the splendors of modernity derive meaning from a distinctly white and Christian taproot. Even the new multicultural modern in the United States is inclusive of people of color only when they, too. accept the limitations of an American normativity that can accommodate diversity, but cannot accommodate racial provocation. The Arab and Muslim are innately provocative.

This ontological provocation highlights matters of belonging and symbolic citizenship. From a legal standpoint, many Muslims are American, having been born in the United States. Many Muslim immigrants are in possession of a United States passport, an item that ideally would be the only criterion by which one is judged "American." National identity is only partly informed by formal citizenship, however. In the United States today, as throughout its history, citizenship is invested with crucial symbolic features. Most of the symbolic features of proper American-ness involve race or religion (wherein, say, Jews or African Americans aren't seen to be fully American ideologically or, in some cases, legally). Another, often related, feature is political belief: Dissent from what politicians and corporate media deem the national interest isn't traditionally a welcome feature of true American-ness (i.e., the normative American). In turn, the politically mainstream white Christian is the truest American of all.

Current conceptions of the normative American can best be detected in the recent imbroglio over the "ground-zero mosque," a histrionic misnomer popularized by right-wing media. The proposed Muslim community center two blocks from the northeastern tip of ground zero, actually called Cordoba House, has created a national frenzy that compels us to reassess the symbolic qualities of citizenship in the United States. By expressing such loud opposition to the community center, a significant portion of Americans has again reinforced a limited definition of American-ness. In this case, it is one that excludes Muslims from the full rights of citizenship. The debate over the community center in the United States is framed by troublesome assumptions and implications. Most commentators focus on moral questions about the purported insensitivity of constructing a mosque so close to the site of one of America's deepest tragedies. Because Muslims perpetrated 9/11, the reasoning goes, their association with ground zero is absolute and irreparable.

Otherwise, the conversation revolves around a rights-based discourse. Supporters of the Cordoba House invoke constitutional rights as a reason the community center ought to exist.

It would be useful to look beyond these morals- and rights-based discourses, and instead examine the issue from the perspective of belonging and citizenship. If the proposed Cordoba House is simply a matter of constitutional rights, then its inability to function (whether legally or by popular decree) merely formalizes the reality that Muslims have constricted access to the rights of American citizenship. If the rights of the Cordoba House planners are upheld, but those planners are impelled by widespread outrage to abandon the project, then Muslims are delimited in their moral and ontological rights. These matters come down to the fact that most Americans (as polling suggests) are unwilling to perceive Muslims as normatively American. The categories "American" and "Muslim" in the popular imagination are mutually exclusive. Normal privileges of citizenship for Muslim Americans, then, can be circumscribed without abandoning the ideals of democratic belonging. For this reason, a cross can be mounted above the Oklahoma City memorial without controversy, even though the bombing of the Alfred Murrah Federal Building was an act of terrorism carried out by Christians. Unlike Christians, the embodiment of a Messianic America, Muslims can be readily associated with the behavior of extremists, while Christians are freed from the burden of their own fanatical ideologues.

Even the sporadic defense of Muslim Americans does little to clarify their restricted access to the ideals of citizenship. Trying to allay his readers' fear of Muslims, Nicholas Kristof of the *New York Times* writes, "My hunch is that the violence in the Islamic world has less to do with the Koran or Islam than with culture, youth bulges in the population, and the marginalization of women. In Pakistan, I know a young woman whose brothers want to kill her for honor—but her family is Christian, not Muslim."[13] Kristof enters into dangerous territory here by indicating that the very *culture* of the East is indelibly different than that of his idealized America. (Kristof is also tendentious: Many women in the United States are murdered by angry husbands or male family members who happen to be Christian, without even mentioning culture or religion.)

In Kristof's formulation, Muslims can be defended on legal and ideological grounds, but nevertheless remain outside the boundaries of normative American-ness. This is made clear when he invokes the seemingly requisite specter of Osama bin Laden: "Osama abhors the vision of interfaith harmony that the proposed Islamic center represents."[14] For Kristof, Cordoba House is emblematic of the proverbial "good Muslim"—the pro-American, moderate, assimilated, ecumenical fantasy of xenophobic reactionaries—and he does little to foster the acceptability of Islam itself. Too frequently ignored or over-looked in the great ground zero mosque debate is the attribution of irrational violence to Islam, as it effectively subdues acknowledgment of the profound violence perpetrated by the American state (including military intervention, police brutality, labor exploitation, torture, and legislative racism). The debate is fundamentally incomplete: It begins with the assumption that all Muslims are subsumed in a religious violence that is somehow non-existent in Christian modernity. Muslim Americans are thus endowed a historical burden that no community could ever possibly overcome.

As to the question of whether a Muslim can ever truly be American, the answer at present is no. The current perceptions of the normative American do not provide space in the national community to Muslims who do not dis-avow the forms of Islam invented by patriotic interrogators. For the Muslim to truly become American, it is not the Muslim who must change, but the restrictive and racialized ideals of the American national identity. Religion is an important factor in this racialized American identity: One of the primary arguments in opposition to the Cordoba House either proclaims or intimates that white Christianity is the primary basis on which American normativity should be judged. In this schema, even secular logic is inherently religious. The logic is also specious. If America, in essence if not in law, is in fact a Christian nation, then no crosses should be allowed in Panama, Iraq, Palestine, Nicaragua, the Philippines, Grenada, Lebanon, Haiti, Hawaii, Puerto Rico, East Timor, Somalia, Afghanistan, Mexico, and Japan. In these places, American violence caused extraordinary destruction, and in that destruction, all Christians are implicated. Indeed, given the countless atrocities committed directly against Indigenous peoples in the name of Christianity in the so-called New World, it is certainly insensitive to build churches anywhere in the United States.

In the meantime, the logic that would lead to the banishment of churches in the United States proceeds unmolested when it is aimed at Islam, and questions about Obama's real religion and his secret place of birth continue steadily. There is even a group, informally known as "the birthers," that devotes time to proving that Obama isn't a true American. In the birther lexicon this means that he is foreign born. Even though most of those who impugn Obama's nebulous origin appear to be extreme or ultra-conservative, it is important to remember that on this particular issue, they are more vocal than they are extreme. That is to say, they crudely articulate a sentiment that is widespread in the United States, one that attaches a proper American identity to racialized values and phenotypes. Most liberals despise the birthers, but they don't really do much to get at the structures of the problem birthers so exuberantly represent. In fact, most liberal commentators are eminently complicit in the problem, because, in their zeal to prove that Obama is just as American as the next person, they ensure that the next person remains a metaphorical certainty, a synecdoche of a receding white majority desperate to retain ownership of the America they worked so hard to invent.

NOTES

1. Valerie Babb, *Whiteness Visible* (New York: New York Univ. Press, 1998); Joel Olson, *The Abolition of White Democracy* (Minneapolis: Univ. of Minnesota Press, 2004).

2. Michael Goldfarb, "Does Obama Speak Arabic?" *The Weekly Standard*, June 3, 2009.

3. Shankar Vedantam, "Does Your Subconscious Think Obama is Foreign?" *Washington Post*, October 13, 2008.

4. Beck cited in Robert Dietz, "Beck again warned that if Muslims don't "act now" by "step[ping] to the plate" to condemn terrorism, they "will be looking through a razor wire fence at the West." Media Matters for America, September 7, 2006. http://mediamatters.org/mmtv/200609070002.

5. Limbaugh cited in Adam Serwer, "Limbaugh: Would Muslims threaten hijacking if airplane toilet was not properly aligned with Mecca? Media Matters for America, January 31, 2007. http://mediamatters.org/mmtv/200701310012.

6. Brian Montopoli, "Tom Tancredo Laments Obama's 'Socialist Government,'" *CBS News*, http://www.cbsnews.com/8301–503544_162–6178114–503544.html.

7. Sherene Razack, *Casting Out: The Eviction of Muslims from Western Law and Politics* (Toronto: Univ. of Toronto Press, 2008), 9.

8. Ibid., 33.

9. It was actually a Republican Colin Powell who spoke up on behalf of Muslims during the election, telling Tom Brokaw of *Meet the Press*, "Well, he's not a Muslim. He's a Christian. He's always been a Christian. But the right answer is, Well, what if he is? Is there something wrong with being a Muslim in America? Is there something wrong with some seven year old Muslim-American kid believing that he could be president?" See Kaitlin's "What's Wrong with Being a Muslim in America," October 27, 2008. http://insideislam.wisc.edu/2008/10/whats-wrong-with-being-muslim-in-america/

10. Jim Hoaglund, "The Post-Racial Election," *Washington Post*, November 2, 2008.

11. Jim Rutten, "Prized for His Noble Words," *Los Angeles Times*, October 10, 2009.

12. Ali Behdad, *A Forgetful Nation* (Durham: Duke Univ. Press, 2005), 10.

13. Nicholas Kristof, "Taking Bin Laden's Side," *New York Times*, August 21, 2010.

14. Ibid.

5 THE NEW CULTURAL POLITICS OF OBAMA: RACE, POLITICS AND UNITY IN OBAMA'S "A MORE PERFECT UNION"

Erec Smith

After the reverend Jeremiah Wright implored church goers to replace "God Bless America," with "God Damn American," and after blaming the 9/11 attacks on the American government in no uncertain terms[1] many spelled the beginning of the end for erstwhile candidate Barack Obama's campaign for presidency. However, it is quite accurate to say that Jeremiah Wright's words provided the perfect *kairos* (i.e., the appropriate window of opportunity) for a necessary move in Obama's run for the presidency. The issue of race had been a large elephant in America's room for quite some time, and it is not a stretch to say that many wanted to know who Obama was as an African American male running for president in a country infamous for its oppressive and draconian treatment of African Americans. Not only did Barack Obama take the Wright opportunity to broach the issue of race, but he also used it to define himself as a candidate, make strong connections to the American people, and present himself as a model citizen and ideal president.

Ultimately, Obama's response to Wright can be interpreted as an especially strong push (if only rhetorically) toward a transcendence of race and a "neutrality of culpability" (the erasure of a victim/oppressor mentality) in North American society. However, it can also be seen as a call toward a more unitary and participatory democracy in which realistic dialogue between parties with long-standing but, perhaps, illusory conflicts of interest can take place. In fact, Obama needed to establish the former before he could accomplish the latter. He needed to show, in a sense, that disparate factions—Blacks and Whites, in this case—were situated on a relatively equal moral playing field, one hidden by a conscious or subconscious adherence to arbitrary notions of difference by both "oppressor" and "oppressed."

What cannot be forgotten is that Obama only could have pulled this off after the Wright incident, as it produced the *kairotic* moment of truth for such a call to occur. Those critics who see "A More Perfect Union" as a ploy to distract voters from the fact that Jeremiah Wright was, indeed, Obama's pastor for several years assume that Obama always held the perfect opportunity to effectively refute the sentiments expressed by Wright. Even if Obama's ethos is a fiction, one cannot rightly determine this from the timing of his refutation of Wright; the Wright incident presented an opportunity for what David Eisenhower calls a "teaching moment"[2] in American race relations, a moment not possible on such a grand scale prior to Wright's vitriol. The coincidence of Obama's self-construction as a "post-racial" icon with Wright's anti-White and anti-American diatribe provided the best opportunity to effectively address race relations since the movement for civil rights. What looked like passive acceptance of hate speech by Obama can also be construed as a patient—even if subconsciously so—biding of time for a more favorable and efficient opportunity.

Thus, my goal for this essay is to show how presidential candidate Obama used the Jeremiah Wright incident for purposes beyond damage control. "A More Perfect Union" is an "all-purpose" speech that allowed Obama to buttress his candidacy by presenting himself as a model American; alleviating racial anxieties around his campaign by creating a "neutrality of culpability" between Blacks and Whites; and constructing a call towards a more participatory democracy by showing, upon acknowledging a neutrality of culpability, American race relations can be significantly assuaged by the citizens themselves. Thus, he effectively addresses those who doubted his ethos as an American, those who may have feared the motives of a Black male President, and those who sought a push toward progressive, citizen-based politics—all in about forty minutes.

Before getting into "A More Perfect Union," Obama's oratorical response to the Jeremiah Wright fallout, I would like to set up the cultural context with Cornel West's 1993 essay, "The New Cultural Politics of Difference." West defines what he considers a new racial situation in America and the challenges any leader for equality will face; He does this in a way that is almost prophetic in its relevance to the middle months of the 2008 presidential campaign. The prophecy is in his description of what he calls a "new cultural politics of difference":

> Distinctive features of the new cultural politics of differ-
> ence are to trash the monolithic and homogenous in the
> name of diversity, multiplicity, and heterogeneity; to reject
> the abstract, general, and universal in light of the concrete,
> specific, and particular; and to historicize, contextualize,
> and pluralize by highlighting the contingent, provisional,
> variable, tentative, shifting, and changing. . . . To put it
> bluntly, the new cultural politics of difference consists of
> creative responses to the precise circumstances of our pres-
> ent moment—especially those of marginalized First World
> agents who shun degraded self-representations, articulating
> instead their sense of the flow of history in light of the con-
> temporary terrors, anxieties, and fears of highly commer-
> cialized North Atlantic capitalist cultures.[3]

So, in a society that is more culturally and racially eclectic, there are more
ways of responding to the apparently monolithic projections of a historically oppressive institution. For West, it was becoming harder to pigeonhole
people into distinct categories, and this difficulty was being effectively—
and affectively—used by those very people. Obama fits into this situation
nicely: a son of a Midwestern mother and African immigrant who excelled
in the ivory tower of the Ivy League as well as the neighborhoods of Chicago.
Obama embodies eclecticism. However, this is not where West's definition of
the new cultural politics of difference ceases to be relevant. West continues:

> The new cultural politics of difference is neither simply op-
> positional in contesting the mainstream (or male-stream)
> for inclusion nor transgressive in the avant-gardist sense of
> shocking conventional bourgeois audiences. Rather, it is
> distinct articulations of talented (and usually privileged)
> contributors to culture who wish to align themselves with
> demoralized, demobilized, depoliticized, and disorganized
> people in order to empower and enable social action and, if
> possible, to enlist collective insurgency for the expansion of
> freedom, democracy and individuality.[4]

Obama is, indeed, a "talented contributor to culture." However, Obama's
situation is distinct because he is both inside and outside of the people West
identifies as demoralized, depoliticized, etc. That is, the talented contributor
is the face of the traditionally downtrodden. This may seem like a benefit,
but only after Obama articulately defines *himself* as such. Jeremiah Wright
provided the stage for just that.

"A More Perfect Union"

As a response to Jeremiah Wright's comments, Obama gave a speech titled "A More Perfect Union." In this speech, Obama consistently used the concept of Definition as a topic of invention and an appeal to tradition as his major rhetorical move.[5] Definition, to Aristotle, is an excellent way to draw syllogistic and logical conclusions about a topic.[6] To Obama, that topic is himself.

It is important to remember that Obama begins this speech by pointing out the hypocrisy of the Declaration of Independence and its American Creed: "that all men are created equal, that they are endowed by their Creator with certain unalienable Rights, that among these are Life, Liberty and the pursuit of Happiness."[7] This is hypocritical because, as Obama states, the Declaration "was stained by this nation's original sin of slavery."[8] It is fitting that he then goes into his driving topic of invention, Definition; it is the original hypocrisy of the American Creed that gives his self-definition its power.

After pointing out the inherent contradiction in the Declaration's opening lines, Obama goes on to define what it truly is to be an American, based on the Declaration's implied expectations of citizenship and deliberative democracy. He states:

> This was one of the tasks we set forth at the beginning of this campaign—to continue the long march of those who came before us, a march for a more just, more equal, more free, more caring and more prosperous America. I chose to run for the presidency at this moment in history because I believe deeply that we cannot solve the challenges of our time unless we solve them together—unless we perfect our union by understanding that we may have different stories, but we hold common hopes; that we may not look the same and we may not have come from the same place, but we all want to move in the same direction—towards a better future for our children and our grandchildren.[9]

The theme of unity, to Obama, reflects those strong supporters of the American Creed, who, regardless of difference, are all striving for equality, life, liberty, and the pursuit of happiness. It was from this definition of a Declaration of Independence-based America that Obama moved into a *self*-definition as a well-educated son of a Kenyan man and white woman from Kansas, a man married to a Black woman "who carries within her the blood of slaves and slaveowners," and a man with close relatives "of every race and every hue, scattered across three continents."[10] Obama punctuates his self-definition by recognizing, appropriate to the occasion, that subject and context are, indeed, consubstantial; that is, they coexist interdependently. He states, "I will never forget that in no other country on Earth is my story even possible."[11]

It would seem that the erstwhile Democratic candidate Barack Obama is a living personification of the American melting pot that so many have passed off as myth. However, it is his next statement that wraps up his definition, and sets us up for the remainder of his speech: "It's a story that hasn't made me the most conventional candidate. But it is a story that has seared into my genetic makeup the idea that this nation is more than the sum of its parts—that out of many, we are truly one."[12] By using Definition as his preferred topic of invention—a tactic in which he systematically sets up a topic (Obama, himself) via a definitive syllogism—Obama tries to make it clear that he embodies not only the diversity of a new cultural politics of difference, but also the unity that is this ideology's sought-after result. Obama *is* the answer. Now that he *is* America, he can justify his actions *as* American.

Despite his artful construction of character, conservative critics felt they saw past this justification, calling it a decoy to distract the American people from Obama's apparent tolerance, if not support, of Wright's hate. Charles Krauthammer referred to the speech as a "shameful, brilliantly executed, 5,000-word intellectual fraud" when suggesting that Obama's contextualization of the incident is an exercise in deception.[13] David Barnett refers to the speech as "an unbecoming slipperiness."[14] In an article in *The Weekly Standard*, he writes:

> What the analysts who are gushing over Obama's sentiments regarding race relations are missing is not only did Obama fail to accomplish the mission he needed to, he didn't even really try. He made no attempt to explain his relationship with Wright and why he hung around a man who habitually offered such hateful rhetoric. Obama instead offered a non-sequitur on race relations.[15]

Charles Wehner questions Obama's cognitive ability, shunning the candidate's speech while inquiring into the depths of Obama's relationship to Wright and the level of concurrence Obama may have had with Wright's sentiments. Wehner attempts to provide his own answers:

> The answers, as best we can tell at this stage, is that Obama heard some very harsh things said from the pulpit of Trinity United Church of Christ; that Obama heard them said a long time ago and probably repeatedly; and that he did little or nothing about it. This from a man who tells us at

almost every stop along the campaign trail that he has the "judgment to lead."[16]

These pundits ignore both the concept of *kairos* and the exposition of a leveled moral playing field that distributes culpability as well as innocence. What's more, much of this criticism is just incorrect. Obama does explain his apparent nonchalance amidst Wright's dithyrambs, and does so quite explicitly.

First, let's look at his rhetoric when dealing with the Jeremiah Wright case. Obama tends to perform, on at least three occasions in the talk, a kind of *Ad hominem Tu Quoque*.[17] This rhetorical construction says, "Hey, you do it, so it's okay that I did it," and is usually considered a logical fallacy. However, after Obama defines himself as the personification of America, such a statement becomes less fallacious and more an extension of an already established syllogism: "If I represent America, and you are Americans, than what I do is probably what all of you do." He admits that he heard Wright say some questionable and objectionable things during sermons. Did he clearly hear them? "Absolutely," he says, "just as I'm sure many of you have heard remarks from your pastors, priests, or rabbis with which you strongly disagreed."[18] He later expresses his inability to fully disown Jeremiah Wright as the same feeling he has about his own white grandmother, who has said racial slurs in his midst on more than one occasion. He explains, "These people are a part of me. And they are a part of America, this country that I love."[19] Finally, he utilizes this strategy when talking about how the deep-seated, underlying anger that can be found in some Black communities is also present in some white communities. He states,

> They've worked hard all their lives, many times only to see their jobs shipped overseas or their pension dumped after a lifetime of labor. They are anxious about their futures, and feel their dreams slipping away; in an era of stagnant wages and global competition, opportunity comes to be seen as a zero sum game, in which your dreams come at my expense. So when they are told to bus their children to a school across town; when they hear that an African American is getting an advantage in landing a good job or a spot in a good college because of an injustice that they themselves never committed; when they're told that their fears about crime in urban neighborhoods are somehow prejudiced, resentment builds over time.[20]

As mentioned earlier, the fallacious potential of the *ad hominem tu quoque* tactic is assuaged—if not outright eradicated—by the context set up to construct Obama as the embodiment of America. In fact, all such statements take place in the midst of Obama's challenge/plea with Americans to embrace unity and diversity instead of separation. In fact, this is the salient part of his presentation; his critique of Wright begins with a critique of divisiveness "at a time when we need unity" to deal with issues that apparently transcend race: "two wars, a terrorist threat, a falling economy, a chronic health care crisis and potentially devastating climate change."[21] Wright is therefore wrong because he focuses on division when America—and real Americans—wants and needs unity and a level playing field, one where genuine dialogue is able to alleviate racial tension.[22] Again, Obama—the product of a diverse group of united people and of an America that is a space for unity and diversity—has the ethos to say these things.

The themes of unity and diversity move throughout Obama's critique of Wright, Obama's construction of himself, and, as we soon see, culminates in calling Americans toward a more unified and deliberative citizenry. In fact, according to Obama, Wright's biggest mistake is his tendency to thwart this theme.[23] Obama echoes this sentiment when critiquing Wright, stating that (a) the man is a great leader trying to do his best in a society where he doesn't feel comfortable; but that (b) he has chosen a method that is counterproductive. He says that the combination of these two things often produces a frustration that often "finds voice in the church on Sunday morning, in the pulpit and in the pews"; that is, in a place often designated as a space to alleviate the pains of American racism. Obama admits that such a vitriolic alleviation isn't always productive, but that it must be acknowledged, for "the anger is real; it is powerful; and to simply wish it away, to condemn it without understanding its roots, only serves to widen the chasm of misunderstanding that exists between the races."[24] To Obama, Wright's anger is understandable, but his tactics are antithetical to effective collaboration among apparently disparate factions, an obstacle blocking efforts at unification.

Obama and anyone wanting unity and diversity would prefer a person who acts as what West calls "a critical organic catalyst"; West describes such a person as one "who stays attuned to the best of what the mainstream has to offer—its paradigms, viewpoints, and methods—yet maintains a grounding in affirming and enabling subcultures of criticism."[25] Does this not sound like the self Obama has constructed in his "A More Perfect Union" speech? Does he not seem to embody this? In fact, Obama concludes his speech in this vein, claiming that he, as a critical organic catalyst will start the conversation and challenge race once and for all. Regarding the racial divide that has been an inherent part of America, and had brought about his speech in the first place, Obama holds no delusions "that we can get beyond our racial divisions in a single election cycle, or with a single candidacy."[26] However, he does express his erstwhile trademark hope for future success in this area: "But I have asserted a firm conviction—a conviction rooted in my faith in God and my faith in the American people—that working together we can move beyond some of our old racial wounds, and that in fact we have no choice if we are to continue on the path of a more perfect union."[27]

Obama utilized a *potentially* devastating event about an *actually* disquieting subject in a way that strengthened his image as the embodiment of unity and diversity, constructs his character into one with the ethos to carry out a successful campaign, and presents himself as the very symbol of the American Creed. (Note his rhetoric of solidarity and cohesion as well as his faith in American citizenry. I address this later.) In order to work together and attempt to move beyond "some of our old racial wounds," we must look closer at what Obama's speech declared and invoked.

A Neutrality of Culpability?

Obama's ability to construct himself *as* America helped to get him elected, and continued to be the implied platform that justified his first two years in office.[28] However, "A More Perfect Union" and its controversial impetus say much more about the direction of race relations in America. I believe we must focus on this speech's potential effects on current definitions of terms like "race," "victim," "oppressor," and "identity." By doing so, we can glean the explicit and implicit power behind Obama's speech: the major push toward an alleviation of racial tension in America. I also see Obama's speech as a call for a more deliberative democracy characterized by authentic public dialogue on race issues. The *kairos* presented by the Jeremiah Wright incident, and the resulting speech given by Obama, did more than just give the future President an opportunity to solidify an all-American ethos and address race once and for all. "A More Perfect Union" is also one of the strongest rhetorical influences toward a "cure" for race and racism in post-Civil Rights America.

A dependence on race as a lens through which we see the world, embodied in Paul Gilroy's term, *raciology*, is alive and well in America, but Obama's speech did a very good job of pointing out the reasons why it is still alive. Raciology, a term Gilroy defines as "the lore that brings the virtual realities of 'race' to dismal and destructive life,"[29] is perpetuated by those traditionally victimized and by those who hold the role of "oppressor." Obama seeks to acknowledge and transcend both camps in his speech, thus bringing on the idea—if not the reality—of deliberations toward a post-racial America.

Gilroy's initial reason for the need to transcend race based on the fundamental sameness of all people is systemic in "A More Perfect Union." Gilroy
writes,

> These groups [oppressor and oppressed] will need to be per-
> suaded very carefully that there is something worthwhile
> to be gained from a deliberate renunciation of "race" as the
> basis for belonging to one another and acting in concert.
> They will have to be reassured that the dramatic gestures
> involved in turning against racial observance can be accom-
> plished without violating the precious forms of solidarity
> and community that have been created by their protract-
> ed subordination along racial lines. The idea that action
> against racial hierarchies can proceed more effectively when
> it has been purged of any lingering respect for the idea of
> "race" is one of the most persuasive cards in this political
> and ethical suit.[30]

Gilroy's point that the "crisis of raciology" is the discomfort felt by oppres-
sors (i.e., those who use race to maintain power) and the oppressed (i.e., those
who have appropriated racial distinction to construct positive identities and
racial pride) is the problem that Obama attempts to transcend. The problem
must be transcended if American citizens will have effective dialogue. The
passage above is echoed in Obama's speech:

> I chose to run for presidency at this moment in history be-
> cause I believe deeply that we cannot solve the challenges of
> our time unless we solve them together—unless we perfect
> our union by understanding that we may have different sto-
> ries, but we hold common hopes; that we may not look the
> same and we may not have come from the same place, but
> we all want to move in the same direction—towards a bet-
> ter future for our children and our grandchildren.[31]

What's more, the perceived benefits of raciology, felt by both the oppressor
and the oppressed, are also addressed when Obama defines Reverend Wright
as a man fighting for power and racial pride in ways that are divisive and
ultimately bad for democracy: "That anger is not always productive; indeed,
all too often it distracts attention from solving real problems; it keeps us
from squarely facing our own complicity in our condition, and prevents the
African-American community from forging the alliances it needs to bring
about real change."[32]

The crisis of raciology is fully acknowledged by Obama, but as he forges his identity as primarily American and incidentally African-American, he acknowledges that race is still an issue. Regarding the anger that drives Wright and many other African-Americans, Obama states, "But the anger is real; it is powerful; and to simply wish it away, to condemn it without understanding its roots, only serves to widen the chasm of misunderstanding that exists between the races."[33] What we can strongly infer from "A More Perfect Union" is a plan for the crisis of raciology that can be understood as a need to acknowledge our collective complicity in it. This must necessarily be prefaced by a neutrality of culpability.

This neutrality of culpability has always been a presence in want of an eloquent and timely justification. Obama's "More Perfect Union" may have been a manifestation of this, with its connections to the concept of "post-race." As a professor of rhetoric and composition and a former diversity officer, I have much to say about the presence and nature of diversity initiatives on college and university campuses. I have been pulled by a campus' desire for unity in diversity, and pushed by the same campus' resistance to being "forced" to open its collective mind. I have seen the oppressor become the oppressed, and vice versa. I have seen diversity activities backfire, making dominant and subordinate people more solidified in these roles.

Throughout all of this, I've noticed that many who attempt to promote diversity seem to focus on the effects instead of the causes, the symptoms instead of the disease. (This trend is clearly reflected in the fact that on most campuses, the diversity officer is a glorified ombudsperson only called upon when something racist occurs, and not to celebrate or promote diversity.) A first step in the right direction is to revise the term "post-racial" for a more accurate view of society. "Post-racial" is not to say that racism does not exist. It is to say that it indeed does exist, but the perpetrators are not members of a homogenous, easily identified cohort. In a post-racial America, there is a "neutrality of culpability" that pits us all as identity-creating beings dealing with the seemingly involuntary drive to *essentialize*. Again, this is not to say that Obama skirted the too real existence of racial discrimination. Of course, the monolithic issues of institutional and environmental racism should not be ignored, but approached differently—by deducing general modes of identity and meaning-creation toward more specific moments of xenophobia.

A neutrality of culpability suggests that the key to diversity studies and to an alleviation of racial tension may be inherent in an exploration of subject positions—its construction, maintenance, and benefits. I believe too many of us focus so much on the trees that we do not see the forest. That is, if we focus too heavily on particular races or sexualities—or race and sexuality, specifically—we may miss the larger issues that induce racial separation and discrimination in the first place: the individual's role in the creation of identity. Again, too many diversity initiatives focus on the symptoms and not the sickness.[34]

The desire to focus on the sickness has already been articulated by *the* projected harbinger of a post-racial America: Barack Obama. However, I think that Obama's description of contemporary America strongly implies a definition of the term *post-racial* that echoes a neutrality of culpability. Remember, Obama describes himself as an example of diversity personified, and praises America for being the sole place where such a person could exist. By setting up his comparison of White and Black racial issues, he also promotes the idea of a neutrality of culpability:

> As imperfect as [Wright] may be, he has been like family to me. He strengthened my faith, officiated my wedding, and baptized my children. . . . I can no more disown him than I can disown the Black community. I can no more disown him than I can my white grandmother—a woman who helped raise me, a woman who sacrificed again and again for me, a woman who loves me as much as she loves anything in this world, but a woman who once confessed her fear of Black men who passed by her on the street, and who on more than one occasion has uttered racial or ethnic stereotypes that made me cringe.[35]

Many voices have said that Obama's rhetoric on race relations was political and not actual. Besides those exhibiting what Gilroy calls "new hatreds," caused not by the concerted maintenance of racial distinctions but by the inability to maintain those distinctions,[36] liberals who consider themselves supporters of Obama also take issue. The Jewish writer Adam Mansbach, in an essay titled "The Audacity of Post-Racism," complains, "I watched the speech in my living room, on a laptop computer with tiny speakers, and I was with Obama until he let white people off the hook."[37]. These sentiments may come from people who identify themselves with a group typically labeled "victims" by themselves and by others. Perhaps, to a large extent, they *are* victims; they may have been treated unfairly due to arbitrary features of their bodies, races, or cultures. However, I would like to invite those people to recognize the potential benefits of rhetorically constructing themselves as a victimized subject or in a victimized group. I also invite them to recognize how others may possibly see them as members of groups categorized not as subordinates, but as dominants. This is not to say that discrimination is okay or erased, but such recognition may present a different perspective that may create different results—results that might quicken our pace on a road to Obama's, and the Declaration's—more perfect union. Based on "A More Perfect Union," perhaps where "racial" America saw racial difference as a cause for the construction of identity, "post-racial" America may see the construction of identity as the cause of racial difference. The prefix "post" may merely denote a switch in cause and effect.

This is well illustrated by Diane Goodman in her book, *Promoting Diversity and Social Justice*. Goodman lists several types of oppression (sexism, racism, heterosexism, etc.), their corresponding dominant groups (males, whites, heterosexuals, etc.) and subordinate groups (females, people of color, homosexuals, etc.). She does this to show how one person can embody both a dominant and a subordinate membership, but, for one reason or another, tends to embrace just one. She writes that she may inhabit the subordinate groups of "Jew" and "woman," but she also enjoys the privileges of being "White, heterosexual, able-bodied, middle-class, and in my middle-adult years," and explains that our choices about which labels we embrace and relinquish may tell us something about our senses of self and the world.[38] Goodman is careful not to dismiss people's reasons for embracing one group identity over the other, but she does point out the idea that some members of dominant groups double as subordinate group members, and vice versa. The purpose: to expose the arbitrary nature of group position in a way that does not alienate people but brings them together in their human tendency to categorize for the sake of security and—voluntarily or involuntarily—power.

The point is that we are all, to a large degree, constructions and abstractions. This realization lends some insight into how we see others who we've constructed as different from our constructed selves. This is not to say that racism does not exist and does not affect our lives, but a neutrality of culpability may alleviate "diversity fatigue" among traditionally oppressive and oppressed groups and re-construct diversity studies in the future. Racial injustice does exist and does have a detrimental potential that should be guarded against, but if we understand race as a symptom of illusive demarcations of judger/judged—thus acknowledging each other as both judger *and* judged—we can more easily embrace the commonalities we already have.

I am confident in saying that if people really want to improve diversity and diversity relations, they will broach the subject by exploring the social construction of subject/group position; if taken to its nascent state, such an exploration may conclude with the idea that we are not as guilty or innocent as history or the media may make us out to be. Generally, people may see that social construction is part individual will, part societal influence, and part circumstance. (In the specific situation of "A More Perfect Union," this translates into autonomy, society, and the Jeremiah Wright situation.) Obama seems to understand this, and he presents this understanding as a necessary first step toward a unification based on common humanity and, at its narrowest, a common membership in a diverse society. He says that one of Wright's most common mistakes was his attempt to help people under the assumption that society cannot change—a notion antithetical to Obama's statements of change and hope that were ubiquitous throughout his presidential campaign. Obama acknowledges Wright's "profound mistake," and continues: "But what we know—what we have seen—is that America can change. That is the true genius of this nation. What we have already achieved gives us hope—the audacity to hope—for what we can and must achieve tomorrow."[39]

Obama's "A More Perfect Union" is historic for many reasons: a prominent and probable future U.S. president gives the first honest speech on race relations by a person of such stature; a man that would most likely be the first African-American President addresses his country on its most controversial characteristic; and a man that most ideally embodies the concept of "melting pot" delivers a speech to remind us of how badly we've maintained such an ideal. These would be understandable, if not obvious, lessons learned. However, I invite you to take other things away from the speech: first, an exploration of how we define ourselves as Americans, and second, an idea of the roles we play in interpersonal and intergroup race relations. If we can explore how Obama constructs himself and his position as a citizen of the United States of America, we can also get a better idea of how we construct ourselves as such. Any kind of civil deliberation, any kind of honest dialogue about American race relations, must start there.

CITIZENS TOWARD A MORE PERFECT UNION

This brings me to my conclusion regarding the efficacy of this speech as a call for citizen participation. Many regard "A More Perfect Union" as a groundbreaking speech, but most only see it as such from a rhetorical standpoint; Obama doesn't make good on any promises (at best), or uses this speech to placate and sedate the American public (at worst). Obama's speech may be accused of exemplifying what Herbert Marcuse called "repressive desublimation": the acceptance or gratification of countercultural values just enough to assuage the champions of that value while still maintaining power.[40] "A More Perfect Union," as a direct address of America's problem with race, provided starving progressive and anti-racist masses a crumb that, compared to nothing, was substantial enough to create an air of satisfaction and accomplishment. Basically, some level of acceptance of a value and of a principle creates satisfaction, but only "satisfaction in a way which generates submission and weakens the rationality of protest"[41] Obama himself was seen

as an agent of repressive desublimation, even before his speech on race. Paul
Street, in *Barack Obama and the Future of American Politics*, writes:

> [Obama's] outwardly revolutionary image and "change"
> persona promised to divert, capture, and safely control cur-
> rent and coming popular rebellions; to stealthily prick and
> smoothly drain the alternating boils of mass disgust and
> mass elation (at the impending passing of the Bush regime);
> and to simultaneously surf, de-fang, and "manage" the citi-
> zenry's hopes for radical structural change—perhaps even
> revolution.[42]

"A More Perfect Union" could be construed as a tactic to silence activists who
would rock the boat in the name of racial equality and justice, to "de-fang"
the frustrated masses. What's more, support of this speech by Whites may
also denote repressive desublimation; strong acceptance of the speech as brilliant, honest, and respectable could be given in lieu of real activity toward the
promotion of racial harmony.

However, if all this does amount to repressive desublimation—either
purposeful or inadvertent—can we really blame Obama? Throughout his
speech, he challenges American citizens to think differently, empathetically,
and actively about race. The speech is more a call for what Benjamin Barber
calls "Strong Democracy": a mode of participatory politics in which dialogue
among citizens "transforms conflict" and "turns dissensus into an occasion
for mutualism and private interest into an epistemological tool of public
thinking."[43] It is much less a promise that he, Barack Obama, would finally
fix the problem of race in America. The fact that most of his administration
has not focused on race relations is not neglect on his part, but on the citizenry of the United States. Obama's charge to the American public is clear:

> I would not be running for President if I didn't believe with
> all my heart that this is what the vast majority of Americans
> want for this country. This union may never be perfect, but
> generation after generation has shown that it can always be
> perfected. And today, whenever I find myself feeling doubt-
> ful or cynical about this possibility, what gives me the most
> hope is the next generation—the young people whose atti-
> tudes and beliefs and openness to change have already made
> history in this election.[44]

A bit later, as Obama wraps up an anecdote of solidarity and interdependence
between a young, White activist and an older, Black activist. Obama says,
"By itself, that single moment of recognition between that young white girl

and that old black man is not enough. It is not enough to give health care to the sick, or jobs to the jobless, or education to our children."[45] When Obama does use the subjective singular, he does so to express his relationship to the subjective plural; the former is the effect to the latter's inspirational presence. Throughout this entire speech, Obama expresses the need for a movement driven by citizens through conciliatory and cohesive language.

Barber's "Strong Democracy" seems to be the necessary attitude and course of action. Barber writes that such a democracy "is defined by politics in the participatory mode: literally, it is self-government by citizens rather than representative government in the name of citizens. Active citizens govern themselves directly here, not necessarily at every level and in every instance, but frequently enough and in particular when basic policies are being decided and when significant power is being deployed."[46] Regarding race, once a neutrality of culpability is accepted, or at least considered as a pragmatic principle, citizens can more easily begin to dialogue as citizens. In fact, Obama is only a let-down in the realm of race politics if citizens see politics as representative, as something others do for them. According to Barber, however: "Strong democracy is the politics of amateurs, where every man is compelled to encounter every other man without the intermediary of expertise.[47]

The speech was interpreted by many as the birth of a new figure of social justice, a new embodiment of Martin Luther King, Jr.[48] The ethos created by Obama throughout this speech—that of a charming African American of mixed ethnicity and wide-spread compassion—drove people to assume that Obama would carry the torch of racial justice on his own. However, the speech was not that at all. In addition to explaining his connection to what seemed to be hate speech from Wright, this is a speech that both explains the racial condition in America, and invokes the American citizenry to stand together to do something about it.

Robert C. Rowland and John M. Jones come to a similar conclusion when analyzing the American Dream as myth narrative used by Obama for ideological purposes. The American Dream is an ideology that is "a narrative embodiment of classical liberalism" which presents unity and liberation as "the responsibility of the entire community."[49] Rowland and Jones hear Obama say that the failure to achieve the American Dream is a reflection of a failure to work together,[50] and hear him define this dream as a narrative driven not by an iconic individual (even if he does stand as a symbol of America), but by ordinary people. They write that "the heroes of the American Dream are both ordinary people and the personification of something larger. It is the very fact that they are ordinary that makes their actions so extraordinary. In the progressive vision of the American Dream, it is not the larger-than-life hero who achieves the "more perfect union" but the ordinary citizen."⁵¹ The American Dream, as a narrative of powerful individuality, will never create the ideal democracy of equity and liberation. Only the collaboration of the people, the "ordinary" citizens, can make that happen.

Most agree that "A More Perfect Union" was successful in defining Obama as an ideal presidential candidate addressing the current state of race relations. Those who would call it a failure are often those who, in hindsight, see a failure on the part of the Obama administration to make good on an imagined promise within this speech. Obama does not claim to be some kind of race savior; he merely sets the stage for American citizens—Black and White—to be a collective savior through dialogue and understanding. "A More Perfect Union" is not the beginning of a movement, but a call for a movement to begin.

The Jeremiah Wright incident presented a *kairotic* moment, both dynamic and fecund, for erstwhile candidate Obama. In one historic moment, he addresses a controversial affiliation with Wright, addresses the lingering and haunting issue of race in America, creates an air of neutral culpability, and expresses a belief that American citizens have what it takes to work together toward the eradication of racism. As we all know, this speech succeeded in helping Obama win the presidency; he did, indeed, solidify an ethos worthy of the office. The efficacy of the rest of the speech, however, still remains to be seen.

Notes

1. Brian Ross and Rehab El-Buri, "Obama's Pastor: God Damn America, U.S. to Blame for 9/11," *ABC News.* March 13, 2009, http://abcnews.go.com/Blotter/DemocraticDebate/story?id=4443788&page=1#.UcDq_nliBKY

2. Albert R. Hunt, "Obama Provides Eisenhower a Teaching Moment," *Bloomberg News*, March 23, 2008, http://www.bloomberg.com/apps/news?pid=newsarchive&sid=aVwYL7ci__aM.

3. Cornell West, "A New Cultural Politics of Difference," *Beyond a Dream Deferred*: Multicultural *Education and the Politics of Excellence*, Ed. Becky W. Thompson and Sangeeta ., MN: University of Minnesota Press, 1993), 18-19.

4. Ibid., 19

5. In rhetoric, *Invention* is one of the canons of rhetoric (along with Arrangement, Style, Memory, and Delivery) that concerns a speaker's or writer's mode of thought when conveying an idea. The commonplace modes of thought are called *Topics* and include Definition, Relationship, Comparison, and Testimony.

6. Aristotle, *On Rhetoric: A Theory of Civic Discourse*, Trans. George A. Kennedy (New York: Oxford University Press, 1991), 195.

7. "The Declaration of Independence," *The Charters of Freedom*, http://www.archives.gov/exhibits/charters/declaration_transcript.html.

8. Barack Obama, "A More Perfect Union," *Presidential Rhetoric*, March 18, 2008, http://www.presidentialrhetoric.com/campaign2008/obama/03.18.08.html.

9. Ibid.

10. Ibid.

11. Ibid.

12. Ibid.

13. Charles Krauthammer, "The 'Race' Speech Revisited," *The Washington Post*, May 2, 2008, http://articles.washingtonpost.com/2008-05-02/opinions/36798301_1_race-speech-reverend-wright-barack-obama.

14. Dean Barnett, "Obama the Ditherer," *The Weekly Standard*, March 19, 2008. http://www.weeklystandard.com/weblogs/TWSFP/2008/06/obama_the_ditherer.asp

15. Ibid.

16. Peter Wehner,. "The Wright Stand," *The National Review Online*, March 20, 2008, http://www.nationalreview.com/node/223973.

17. This kind of fallacy is deemed specifically psychological by W. Ward Fearnside and William B. Holther in *Fallacy: The Counterfeit Argument,*(Englewood Cliffs, NJ: Spectrum Books, 1959). Its purpose is not necessarily to damn one's interlocutor, but to point out the inconsistencies between the interlocutor's ethos and his or her claim. Damning Obama for associating with someone as misguided as Jeremiah right may seem hypocritical, since so many of Obama's critiques are doing or have done the same.

18. Obama, "A More Perfect Union."

19. Ibid.

20. Ibid.

21. Ibid.

22. See Cornel West, "A New Cultural Politics of Difference," *Beyond a Dream Deferred:* Multicultural *Education and the Politics of Excellence*, Ed. Becky W. Thompson and Sangeeta (Minneapolis, MN: University of Minnesota Press, 1993), 35-36. West says that the most difficult challenge for leaders of color is trying to acquire and maintain "the self-confidence, discipline, and perseverance necessary for success without an undue reliance on the mainstream for approval and acceptance." It seems that Wright is stuck in this situation and, out of the three options West says leaders of color typically choose (a preoccupation with the mainstream, a talented tenth conception, and a "Go-It-Alone" methodology), Wright chooses the "Go-It-Alone" option. This option shuns the other two, but, obviously, isn't perfect. West writes that the Go-It-Alone option "is healthy in that it reflects the presence of independent, critical, and skeptical sensibilities toward perceived constraints on one's creativity. Yet it is, in the end, difficult if not impossible to sustain if one is to grow, develop, and mature intellectually, as some semblance of dialogue with a community is necessary for almost any creative practice."

23. See "A New Cultural Politics of Difference," *Beyond a Dream Deferred:* Multicultural *Education and the Politics of Excellence*, Ed. Becky W. Thompson and Sangeeta ., MN: University of Minnesota Press, 1993). The relevant passage reads:

As such, Reverend Wright's comments were not only wrong but divisive, divisive at a time when we need unity; racially charged at a time when we need to come together to solve a set of monumental problems—two wars, a terrorist threat, a falling economy, a chronic health care crisis, and potentially devastating climate change; problems that are neither Black or white or Latino or Asian, but rather problems that confront us all.

24. Obama, "A More Perfect Union."

25. West, "The New Cultural Politics of Difference," 36.

26. Obama, "A More Perfect Union."

27. Obama, "A More Perfect Union."

28. Obama's goal of unity in diversity is seen as a necessary first step toward tackling the list of "monumental problems" that America faces. An understandable conclusion to his speech's logic may be that we cannot agree on the solutions to these problems because we have yet to truly see ourselves as a unified society.

29. Paul Gilroy, *Between Camps: Nations, Cultures and The Allure of Race* (London: Routledge Press, 2004), 11.

30. Gilroy, *Between Camps*, 12-13.

31. Obama, "A More Perfect Union."

32. Ibid.

33. Ibid.

34. See Kwame Anthony Appiah, *The Ethics of Identity* (Princeton: Princeton University Press, 2005), 62-64. Appiah provides a fine example of approaching race through the phenomenon of identity construction is Kwame Anthony Appiah's *The Ethics of Identity*. In a chapter titled "The Demands of Identity," Appiah begins to address and defend "the not-uncontroversial assumption that differences of identity are, in various ways, prior to those of culture" (64). Appiah initially uses the example of the Robbers Cave experiment, in which two groups of White, Protestant, middle-class boys were placed on a Robbers Cave State Park campsite in close proximity—but separate—to each other. After each group had a few days to bond, it was told of the existence of the other group, and after challenging each other in competitive sports, "tempers flared and a violent enmity developed between the two groups, the Rattlers and the Eagles (as they came to dub themselves)" (62). Each group created identities for themselves and the others, and each group proudly wore the negative descriptions thrown at it by the other group as badges of pride (63).

35. Obama, "A More Perfect Union."

36 Paul Gilroy, *Against Race: Imagining Political Culture Beyond the Color Line* (Cambridge, MA: Harvard University Press, 2000), 105-106.

37. Adam Mansbach, "The Audacity of Post-Racism," *The Speech: Race and Barack Obama's "A More Perfect Union,"* Ed. Denean Sharpley-Whiting (New York: Bloomsbury Press, 2009), 69.

38. Diane Goodman, *Promoting Diversity and Social Justice* (Thousand Oaks, CA: Sage Publications, 2001), 8.

39. Obama, "A More Perfect Union."

40. Herbert Marcuse, *One-Dimensional Man* (Boston: Beacon Press, 1964), 75.

41. Ibid.

42. Paul Street, *Barack Obama and the Future of American Politics* (Boulder, CO: Paradigm Press, 2009), 174.

43. Benjamin Barber, *Strong Democracy: Participation for a New Age* (Berkeley: University of California Press, 2003), 151.

44. Obama, "A More Perfect Union."

45. Ibid.

46. Benjamin Barber, *Strong Democracy*, 151.

47. Ibid, 152.

48. Paul Street, *Barack Obama and the Future of American Politics,*185-186.

49. Robert C. Rowland and John M. Jones, "One Dream: Barack Obama, Race, and the American Dream," *Rhetoric and Public Affairs,* 14:1 (2011): 132.

50. Rowland and Jones, "One Dream," 134-135.

51. Ibid, 148.

6 Obama's West Point Address: The Symbolic Construction of Policy and Authority

Michael Kleine

On the day following Obama's address at West Point (delivered December 1, 2009), in which the president announced both an increase in troop deployments to Afghanistan and also a timetable for withdrawal, Dan Balz, a staff writer for the *Washington Post*, asserted that despite the President's assumption of "full ownership of the war in Afghanistan," and his argument that "The fastest way out of the conflict is a rapid and significant escalation of it," the immediate public reception of the speech was somewhat discouraging.[1] In fact, as Balz argues, Obama's policy claim advanced in the speech was met with "muted response from key Democratic congressional leaders," and "skepticism from Republicans" regarding Obama's timetable for troop withdrawal.[2] Balz writes that Obama gives his policy speech as "a clear acknowledgement of the fragile state of public opinion after eight years of conflict in Afghanistan." Although Balz commends Obama's efforts to assume responsibility for escalating the War in Afghanistan, and praises a speech that is "clearly argued," he notes that the "president's main audience was the American public, which has soured on the Afghanistan conflict and on Obama's handling of it in recent months."[3] In an effort to underscore how deeply divided the American public was before, and remained after, the West Point Address, Balz gestures to a recent poll conducted by the *Washington Post*/ABC News regarding the war in Afghanistan. The poll reported that only 52% of the "respondents said the war there was worth fighting, with Republicans agreeing by two to one,

Democrats disagreeing by more than two to one, and independents split down the middle."[4]

As a rhetorician interested in both the vagaries and successes of persuasion—as measured by persuasion's *effectiveness* at influencing, changing, or moving to action diverse audiences (including the persuaders themselves)—I was the most impressed with Balz's analysis of the audiences addressed and evoked by Obama's West Point address. As Balz notices, though the present and putative audience of West Point cadets seemed to be the target audience, Obama was most interested in communicating remotely with the military establishment as a whole, the legislative branch of our government, the American public (Balz sees this public as the most important audience), Afghani President Hamid Karzai, Pakistan, and NATO allies. With Balz, I believe that the West Point Address, beyond its articulation of policy, accomplishes a number of other rhetorical purposes. Certainly the address by itself cannot immediately and effectively accomplish Obama's persuasive agenda regarding policy, but perhaps its ultimate effectiveness must be evaluated in the fullness of time, must be followed by other acts of persuasion, and must be considered in light of the unfolding of future events the policy address might set in motion.

In this chapter, I analyze Obama's West Point Address using perspectives offered by classical Greek and Roman rhetoricians. I claim that despite the failure of the address to decisively unify and mobilize its diverse audiences, to achieve total persuasive "effectiveness," Obama manages to construct himself as a public orator and political leader who is decidedly of the lineage of the Greek sophists (Protagoras and Isocrates), the premier theorist of classical Greek rhetoric (Aristotle), and the brilliant Roman rhetorician and orator (Cicero). Furthermore, Obama succeeds in recuperating ancient strategies for oral persuasion in a "classical oration" that displays remarkable range and complexity, synthesizing, as it does, both Greek and Roman approaches to its construction and arrangement. Although Obama's West Point Address asserts a policy claim, it also employs rhetorics of fact and value, both of which help him enhance and contextualize his core policy argument. What is *effective*, then, about the West Point Address is that Obama can now better assume a presidential *ethos*, an authoritative posture that had been repeatedly called into question by his opponents. Whether he is right or wrong about the need for a troop surge in Afghanistan, he can, as his political future unfolds, at least posture more strongly (and symbolically) as the commander in chief and as the moral leader of the kind of republic invented and enacted by the best of the Greeks and the Romans. After his publically criticized silence about Afghanistan (albeit a studied silence), he had, at last, arose and spoke.

THE RHETORICAL SITUATION AND THE SOPHISTIC
CONSTRUCTION OF A POLICY CLAIM

Despite many Americans' association of "rhetoric," and especially "sophistic rhetoric," with language devoid of action or even of "Truth," I would like to clarify here the values and claims of two of the most important Greek sophists and rhetoricians: Protagoras and Isocrates. Although much of what we know of Protagoras (481–411 BCE) comes from Plato's critical dialogue that bears this sophist's name,[4] and although Isocrates (436–338 BCE) is not considered a sophist by all rhetoricians, we can read in Plato's dialog *Isocrates*[5] enough to form a kind of general idea of what I call "sophistic political rhetoric." I recommend that interested readers go to a secondary source that in my view, best recuperates, revalues, and reclaims the importance of sophistic rhetoric to the political progress of ancient Athens: *Rhetoric Reclaimed*, by Janet Atwill. Atwill points out that sophism, or that which associates linguistically with the word "wisdom," was developed and applied by teachers of rhetoric deeply concerned with the kind of policy-driven persuasion at the heart of Athenian democracy, and that waned as the Roman Republic gave way to empire.[6]

It is with the work of sophists like Protagoras and Isocrates, then, that I begin my analysis of Obama's West Point Address.[7] It is an address that has to do with policy and with a decidedly problematical and unknown future. Following a largely symbolic gesture toward his putative audience, the cadets at West Point, and a lengthy narration in which Obama tells the story of our involvement in Afghanistan, he succinctly makes his policy claim: "And as commander in chief, I have determined that it is in our vital national interest to send an additional 30,000 troops to Afghanistan. After 18 months, our troops will begin to come home. These are the resources that we need to seize the initiative, while building the Afghan capacity that can allow for a responsible transition of our forces out of Afghanistan." The claim itself is followed by personal reflection, a three-part explanation of the strategic course Obama wants us to follow, arguments, counter-arguments, and other elements that I discuss later.

From a sophistic point of view, Obama's claim is not a claim of Truth, but one that is forged from ongoing, deliberative political and public discourses concerning the reemergence of the Taliban in Afghanistan. Sophists reject truth's foundational basis, embracing the view that it is socially constructed. The question Obama asks and answers is, quite simply, "What should we do at this point in time?" Here I employ concepts key to ancient Athenian sophists to examine how, exactly, Obama's claim is constructed. The exact, exigent moment (*kairos*, or "knowing when" to speak) of the address must first be considered, along with the strategic and rhetorical expertise (*techne*, or "knowing how" to speak effectively). In terms of time and timing, despite the strong urging of his critics to address the Afghanistan issue, Obama had long remained silent until the public and political pressure to speak grew to a nearly clamorous pitch. Indeed, the nation seemed to be at a point of political impasse and rancor (an *aporia*) that constrained Obama at last to rise and speak in an effort to find a pathway forward (a *poros*) that would, if not perfectly forge an effective military policy in regard to Afghanistan, at least enable him to reassert his leadership in a decidedly fractured nation. Thus, we must look to Obama's claim not as a claim of truth, but as a political act aimed at indicating, to his multiple audiences, that he is fully cognizant of the competing policy impulses of both the United States and its allies. The claim, then, is one that is contingent and mediated, even problematic and compromised; it is also one that the president felt he needed to make to be perceived as a fair, decisive, and an effective commander in chief. Of course, critics from both the left and the right were not satisfied by the policy claim, but, were they to fully reflect on it, they would be forced to agree that their own positions had in some way been acknowledged and incorporated in Obama's remarks.

The rhetorical context and timing of the claim was inordinately complicated, but Obama's symbolic move to speak before an assembly of West Point cadets suggests the underlying issue and motive impelling his address. Increasingly, public perception of his presidency—both nationally and globally—had reached an untenable nadir. He seemed weak, incapable of acting and speaking strongly, perhaps even incompetent. To reestablish his presidential authority and his role as commander of our military (his *ethos*), he needed to speak forcefully in a place symbolic of our military preparation and also during a moment (and in a way) by delivering a number of potent statements to a number of audiences available to him—all thanks to television and the Internet. To the American left, he endeavored to say that this time, in contrast to our botched military policy regarding Iraq, he would provide a timetable and an exit strategy. To the American right, he endeavored to say that he, in contrast to strong liberal opponents of yet another troop surge, would act decisively to continue the war against global terrorism. To Hamad Karzai and his corrupt government, he endeavored to say that business as usual would no longer be possible, due to the impending withdrawal of American troops. To our NATO allies, he endeavored to say that our alliance with them needed to be honored, and that his proposed course of action is both rational and potentially effective. Finally, to the people of Pakistan, he endeavored to say that our troop surge in their country would in no way jeopardize the sovereignty of their nation, but instead would provide a firm basis for further cooperation between the United States and Pakistan. To restore his political and moral authority among multiple audiences on both global and national levels, he was driven to make a single policy claim before a single assemblage that was packed with a number of speech acts, each one decidedly political and, from Obama's point of view, situationally necessary.

In many ways, then, Obama's observance of *kairos* and his strategic, deliberative *techne* establish him as a kind of latter-day sophist, speaking not about what is true or obvious, but to set into motion a process that might lead our nation beyond a critical impasse and clearly establish the presidential authority of the speaker.

Invention and Arrangement of the Elements of the West Point Address

When I heard the televised Obama address at West Point, I first became aware of its classical orientation when I thought I heard the psychological progression of the six-part arrangement structure (some rhetoricians say seven-part) recommended by the greatest orator and rhetorical theorist of the Roman Republic: Cicero. Cicero (106–43 BCE), whose early work, *On Invention*, and more mature work, *On Oratory*,[8] dramatically influenced the shape of persuasive orations and written texts for many years, even into our twenty-first century. For classical rhetoricians, the construction of persuasive discourse involved a linear process consisting of five "canons": first, the persuasion was "invented"; next, it was "arranged"; then it was "styled"; because the focus was on oral persuasion mainly, it then needed to be "memorized"; finally, it was "delivered." Although the great Greek rhetorician, Aristotle (384 BCE-322 BCE), years before Cicero, had focused his attention on the canon of "invention" in perhaps the most important of ancient classical works concerning persuasion, his seminal *Rhetoric*,[9] it was Cicero who most fully explicated the canon of arrangement. In my view, Cicero's six-part structure, a "progression" really, is itself a *techne* that serves as the sort of dynamic strategy that would have been of great interest to the sophists, given its focus on a process approach to laying out persuasive discourse in relationship to the changing psychology of resistant audiences. I avoid Cicero's Latin names for the six parts, endeavoring instead to name those parts to emphasize their relationship to audience psychology. Following an explanation of each, I offer a brief explanation of how Obama displays rhetoric that is attentive to Cicero's approach to arrangement.

Part 1, or, the salutation and suggestion of an issue or problem or question of vital and timely interest to an immediate audience

In the case of writing and other technologies of delivery, though, remote and peripheral audiences may be of most importance to the persuader. The desired effect is that the audience assents to the salience of the problem and becomes interested enough to pay attention during the rest of the delivery.

Obama begins his address with a salutation directed at "the men and women of our armed services," and also his "fellow Americans."[10] Because he knows that his audience is already well aware of the problem, he does not belabor his introductory remarks, but instead clarifies that his address will focus on "the nature of our commitment there," "the scope of our interests," and especially, "the strategy that my Administration will pursue to bring this war to a successful conclusion."[11] In so speaking, he establishes the deliberative, policy-oriented purpose of the address. He concludes his rather short introduction with a move that is decidedly symbolic, gesturing at the physical location of the address (West Point), "where so many men and women have prepared to stand up for our security and to represent what is finest about our country."[12]

Part 2, or the presentation of background information or narration

This serves to fully inform the audience and, even more importantly, prepare them to receive the claim at the heart of the persuader's message. Here, the desired effect is that the audience might become better prepared to process the claim, and also more predisposed to at least consider it as viable.

Cicero named the second element of his recommended persuasive arrangement the *"narratio,"* and in so doing, intimated that this might be an appropriate slot not only for background information, but background information presented in the form of a story. Obama does indeed tell a story—a lengthy one—regarding the history of our involvement in Afghanistan following the events of 9/11. Ordinarily, the *narratio* is rather brief, but Obama's narration proceeds for well over a page of the printed version of his address. He begins his narration with this sentence: "To address these issues, it is important to recall why America and our allies were compelled to fight a war in Afghanistan in the first place."[13] He then proceeds to vilify Al Qaeda and the Taliban in Afghanistan who "harbored" them as "a group of extremists who have distorted and defiled Islam. He is careful, at the same time, to honor Islam as "one of the world's great religions."[14]

What is especially interesting about the narrative is the way it brackets our preemptive invasion of Iraq as a distraction from our original and, in his view, justifiable presence in Afghanistan. Thus, Obama's narrative indirectly critiques the decision of the Bush administration to veer from its primary mission, a costly interruption of the *real* war, the war in Afghanistan. He emphasizes that our misstep in Iraq for the following six years "drew the dominant share of our troops, our resources, our diplomacy, and our national attention," causing "significant rifts between America and much of the world."[15] Before continuing his lengthy narrative, Obama points out that "we are bringing the Iraq war to a responsible end" by emphasizing that all of our troops there will be gone before the dawn of 2012. Obama continues by asserting that the situation in Afghanistan "has deteriorated," that the Taliban has now "begun to take control over swaths of Afghanistan," and that the Taliban's re-emergence has spilled over into Pakistan in "increasingly brazen and devastating acts of terrorism against the Pakistani people." After acknowledging that Afghanistan has been, and is now, "hampered by corruption, the drug trade, an under-developed economy, and insufficient Security Forces," Obama relates the deteriorating situation in Afghanistan to insufficient troop numbers, comparing the 32,000 troops there to "162,000 in Iraq at the peak of the war."[16] The narrative moves toward closure as Obama reinforces his concern about the future of Pakistan, tells of modest successes despite our low troop level, and concludes with a gesture at military authority (Aristotle might view this gesture as "testimony" aimed at building a persuasive *ethos*): "Our new Commander in Afghanistan—General McChrystal—has reported that the security situation is more serious than he anticipated. In short: the status quo is not sustainable."[17]

Classical rhetoricians interested in the canon of arrangement might see Obama's extended narration as a violation of the usually short length of the *narratio*, and the resultant delay of his policy claim as vexing; however, new rhetoricians interested in narrative persuasion would most certainly regard Obama's lengthy story as a kind of preparatory argument, one justifying the policy claim Obama will articulate next. In terms of emphasis, then, Obama finds in narrative a powerful way to frame the story of Afghanistan in such a way that his various audiences might see his policy claim as both morally and pragmatically necessary.

Part 3, or the assertion of the claim and an indication of the forthcoming division of arguments that will be used to support the claim

After this assertion, audience resistance might well be at its greatest, but the persuader hopes that the audience might at least be reassured that the policy will be more fully outlined and articulated and, especially, that good reasons for accepting the claim will follow.

I have already discussed the policy claim itself, as it appears near the top of the third of six pages of a printed version of the address, but it is important to notice that, in addressing the cadets directly, Obama first defends the deliberative review time he took before speaking to them. He says, observing the *kairotic* aspects of the time delay that had been so strongly criticized by his political opponents, "There has been no delay or denial of resources necessary for the conduct of the war. Instead, the review has allowed me to ask the hard questions, and to explore all of the different options along with my national security team, our military and civilian leadership in Afghanistan, and with our key partners."[18] This assertion enables Obama to establish solidarity with his putative audience of cadets, for, as he explains, "I owe you a mission that is clearly defined, and worthy of your service."[19] In some ways, this preamble to the policy claim refutes the criticism that the extended review time is partly responsible for the deterioration in Afghanistan.

After articulating the claim, and before moving on to full explanation and conventional argumentation, it is telling that Obama engages in a personal digression, within which he twice repeats: "I do not make this decision lightly."[20] This reminds his audiences that he had himself opposed the war in Iraq, and that he believes personally in the "exercise of restraint in the use of military force."[21] Furthermore, the digression enables Obama to develop an emotional appeal having to do with his deep sympathy for those soldiers who had already sacrificed their lives, and with their families, to express his understanding of the war-weariness of the American public. Finally, the digression speaks to another audience, our international allies, urging them to join us in our escalation of troop activity in Afghanistan, claiming that "This burden is not ours alone to bear." Obama's powerful digression lends credence to the assertion of Richard Leo Enos, in his recent, brilliant book, *Roman Rhetoric: Revolution and the Greek Influence*,[22] that, in fact, Cicero observed not a six-part arrangement structure for effective persuasion, but a seven-part structure. For Cicero, this seventh part offers a space for a digression aimed at enhancing the moral authority (or *ethos*) of the persuader.

Part 4, or the provision of the details of the proposed policy and good reasons (or arguments) for acceptance of the claim

With this move, the persuader hopes that audience resistance will be, if not eliminated, at least largely diminished, and that both rationally and emotionally, the audience will be further moved to accept or to act upon the claim.

Nearly halfway through his West Point Address, Obama explains, with a three-part enumeration, the strategic objectives that accompany his policy claim. "First," he asserts, "we will pursue a military strategy that will break the Taliban's momentum and increase Afghanistan's capacity over the next 18 months." He continues: "Second, we will work with our partners, the UN, and the Afghan people, to pursue a more effective civilian strategy, so that the government can take advantage of improved security." He concludes, stating, "Third, we will act with the full recognition that our success in Afghanistan is inextricably linked to our partnership with Pakistan." Each of these objectives is followed by detailed explanation and, when necessary, argumentation. Clearly, the objectives, as they are articulated and argued, are aimed at multiple audiences, including not only the American public, but also our NATO allies and, most interesting to me, the government and people of Pakistan.

Following his announcement of the first objective, Obama mainly concerns himself with explaining *how* the objective will be accomplished. Following the second objective, he clarifies *what* the objective will entail, especially in terms of providing, instead of American domination of Afghanistan, a partnership with an elected government that seems to be increasingly at risk.

However, it is the argumentation following the third objective that appears to be most important to Obama, given his focus on fully addressing the systemic terrorist threat that involves not only Afghanistan, but also Pakistan. Too, Obama seems to be arguing before both Pakistanis and Americans. He begins his arguments for a more robust partnership with Pakistan with an analogy (one of the Aristotelian topics for invention) that endeavors to address *why* we need to focus on developing such a partnership: "We are in Afghanistan to prevent a cancer from once again spreading through that country. But this same cancer has also taken root in the border region of Pakistan. That is why we need a strategy that works on both sides of the border." Anticipating strong resistance from key Pakistani factions, and before developing a formal refutation, Obama says, "In the past, there have been those in Pakistan who have argued that the struggle against extremism is not their fight, and that Pakistan is better off doing little or seeking accommodation with those who use violence." In the refutation that follows, Obama argues that it is, in fact, in the interest of the people of Pakistan—and with those he calls the "innocents"—to join in our struggle against Al Qaeda and the Taliban: "But in recent years, as innocents have been killed from Karachi to Islamabad, it has become clear that it is the Pakistani people who are the most endangered by extremism." The appeal here is somewhat emotional, but through it, Obama is able to suggest to his Pakistani audience that we share a common enemy. Of course, he also speaks to the American people, who (he hopes) will see Islamic Pakistan not as an enemy, but as an important ally and as a potential partner. Obama concludes by focusing directly on his Pakistani audience, reminding them of the ongoing American support of Pakistan, both in terms of necessary resources and also shelter for Pakistanis displaced by terrorist activities. He expresses respect for the "great potential" of Pakistan that might be "unleashed" in the fullness of partnership and alliance.

The compression and rhetorical complexity of Obama's enumeration and explication of his objectives is remarkable. In this element of his address, he must speak to a variety of audiences and for a variety of purposes.

Part 5, or the development of a refutation (or counter-arguments)

This part addresses the remaining reservations of the audience. This may well be the most important element of the persuasion's progress, for here the persuader can show the audience direct attention to their needs, interests, beliefs, etc., and, if necessary, the persuader can qualify the initial claim so that it better accords with the changing psychology of the audience.

In the fashion of Cicero, Obama turns to a full-blown refutation of the counter-arguments that he anticipates. In relationship to the various audiences he addresses, this turn is extremely interesting. It is not only a turn from argument to counter-argument, but it is also a turn away from an international audience (particularly a Pakistani audience), and toward the American public and a political audience. In three short paragraphs of refutation (beginning near the bottom of page four of a printed version of the address), Obama makes three "sub-turns," if you will. His first turn is toward the American faction that likens Afghanistan to Vietnam, and insists that we must withdraw from Afghanistan completely. The second turn is toward the American faction that insists we remain in Afghanistan while retaining the current level of troops there. The third and final turn is toward the faction that insists on a troop surge, but resists the notion of a timetable for withdrawal.

In light of the first faction's potential resistance of his policy claim and clamor for complete withdrawal, he argues these points: Vietnam and Afghanistan are not comparable; we are not facing, as we did in Vietnam, "a broad-based popular insurgency"; in the case of the war in Afghanistan, our own homeland was first attacked by extremists enjoying sanctuary in Afghanistan; and failure to "abandon this area now—and to rely only on efforts against Al Qaeda from a distance—would significantly hamper our ability to keep the pressure on Al Qaeda, and create an unacceptable risk of additional attacks on our homeland and our allies." In light of the second faction's potential resistance and clamor that we maintain current troop levels, he argues pragmatically that a failure to increase troop levels permits "a slow deteriora-

tion of conditions there" that would "ultimately prove more costly and pro-
long our stay." In light of the third faction's potential resistance and clamor
that announcing a timetable for withdrawal jeopardizes our mission and our
troops, he argues that we cannot achieve an "open-ended escalation of our
war effort—one that would commit us to a nation building project of up to
a decade" because such a goal is "beyond what we can achieve at a reasonable
cost," and that Afghanis must become aware "that America has no interest in
fighting an endless war in Afghanistan."

From Aristotle on, rhetoricians have noticed that deliberative discourse—
the discourse of policy—draws its arguments from two warranting values,
the "good" and the "expedient." Clearly, Obama's refutation draws mainly
from the value of the expedient, or the pragmatic. As he makes his turns from
one national faction to another, we begin to understand even more clearly
his attachment to a pragmatic and sophistic rhetoric, where his policy claims
have less to do with what is true or obvious, and more to do with symbolic
mediation. Rhetorically, then, Obama's claim and refutation have much to
do with the dynamic and provisional assertion of a policy that might be, if
not acceptable to the entirety of an audience, at least attuned to the various
opinions, ideologies, and positions of that audience. Sensitive to the classical values of balance and moderation, Obama says, "I refuse to set goals that
go beyond our responsibility, our means, or our interests." In an extremely
interesting rhetorical move, he evokes the authority of a past, Republican
president, President Eisenhower, in a final assertion of the value of balance:
"I am mindful of the words of President Eisenhower, who—in discussing
our national security—said, 'Each proposal must be weighed in the light of a
broader consideration: the need to maintain balance in and among national
programs.'"

Aristotle, among others, notices the importance of employing the warranting value of "the good," but we must go to Obama's action-oriented closing to find such warranting and argumentation.

Part 6, or the articulation of an action-oriented closing

In an action-oriented closing, the persuader assumes that the audience has
been largely or partially persuaded, and that it awaits answers to remaining
questions: What should we do? What are the implications of fully accepting
the claim? How will a change in our psychological stance toward the claim
affect our lives and the future of our community?

Like his unusually long background section, or *narratio*, Obama's action-
oriented close to his West Point Address, or his *peroration*, exceeds the expected length for conclusions. In the Web version, his final remarks occupy

nearly two of the six printed pages. Perhaps the conclusion's length can be explained by its purpose: to remind Americans of the key values that must undergird all of its future actions both at home and abroad, of "the good" that was neglected during the Bush administration and that must now be reasserted. In the concluding section of this chapter, I discuss more fully the ceremonial significance (and style) of the conclusion. For now, I want to associate it with the kind of value-laden and nearly transcendent rhetoric with which Martin Luther King closes his moving and decidedly persuasive "Letter from Birmingham Jail."[23] King, like Obama, uses the Ciceronian approach to arrangement, though his refutation is much longer than Obama's and his final *peroration* is much shorter. Both conclusions, despite their difference in length, are noteworthy for their evocation of values that transcend immediate context and expediency; both exemplify a remarkable use of style to move their audiences toward a focus on moral transformation.

Obama begins his conclusion by lamenting the loss of the kind of "balance" that might "appreciate the connection between our national security and our economy." He identifies with his audience of ordinary Americans by saying, "In the wake of an economic crisis" (presumably exacerbated by our involvement in Iraq), "too many of our friends and neighbors are out of work and struggle to pay the bills, and too many Americans are worried about the future facing our children. Meanwhile, competition within the global economy has grown more fierce. So we simply cannot afford to ignore the prices of these wars." This turn toward the economy, and Obama's identification with working-class Americans, is clearly intended to enlarge his *ethos* in such a way that he appears not only to be a strong commander in chief, but also a president sensitive to the domestic needs of his public audience. From such a concerned and sympathetic position, he can use the topic of comparison to point out that, "All told, by the time I took office the cost of the wars in Iraq and Afghanistan approached a trillion dollars. Going forward, I am committed to addressing these costs openly and honestly. Our new approach in Afghanistan is likely to cost us roughly 30 billion dollars for the military this year, and I will work closely with Congress to address these costs as we work to bring down our deficit."

He then proceeds to make a number of value-laden assertions that might turn us away from the policies of the past—policies that were focused on military aggression and control of the globe—and instead move us toward policies that are both more balanced and more moral. For example:

- "We must rebuild our strength at home."
- "America will have to show our strength in the way that we end wars and prevent conflict."
- "We cannot count on military might alone."

- "We will have to take away the tools of mass destruction . . . to stop the spread of nuclear weapons . . . and to pursue the goal of a world without them."
- "We will have to use diplomacy."
- "We must draw on the strength of our values—for the challenges that we face may have changed, but the things that we believe in must not. That is why we promote our values by living them at home—which is why I have prohibited torture and will close the prison at Guantanamo Bay."

As the end of the address nears, Obama evokes Franklin Roosevelt as a great exemplar of leadership that focuses on the value of the unity of our nation. He observes that "Our security and leadership does not come solely from the strength of our arms. It derives from our people." Clearly, he turns away from his immediate audience of West Point cadets and speaks instead on behalf of the "workers," "the researchers," "the teachers," "the diplomats and Peace Corps volunteers," and includes "the men and women in uniform" as simply another part of the totality of Americans who comprise his larger public audience.

The freedom to disagree, the necessity of overcoming those forces that would cause us to be "split asunder by the same rancor and cynicism and partisanship that has in recent times poisoned our national discourse," the primacy of "common purpose"—these, Obama asserts, are the "values" that "are not simply words written into parchment," but instead, "are a creed that calls us together, and that has carried us through the darkest of storms as one nation, one people."

It is in his conclusion that Obama evinces the values underlying his policy claim. That claim, a mediated claim, is in the end justified by its balance and by its most important purpose: to respect the factions that constitute our nation by articulating a claim that, if not acceptable to all Americans, at least shows the President's driving desire to be seen as a unifier and to work toward not only national unity, but also international unity.

Obama's Unification of Aristotle's Three Types of Persuasion in the Discourse of Policy

As I move toward my own close here—if not an action-oriented close, at least one that considers the implications of my claim that Obama is a contemporary sophist and a brilliant classical rhetorician—I would like to consider the problem of classifying the West Point Address as solely deliberative and of working in strict Ciceronian fashion to develop a discourse of policy. To do this, I must return to Aristotle, noticing especially the way Obama's speech uses all three Aristotelian appeals and all three types of persuasion that Aristotle theorized in *Rhetoric*. It is perhaps already obvious that Obama strategically uses appeals to logic (*logos*) throughout his speech, and that he joins these appeals to address his audiences' emotions (*pathos*), especially in his extended, action-oriented close. Perhaps it is also already obvious that he yokes these appeals in an effort to establish his own style of presidential authority (*ethos*); he emerges, in the end, not only as a strong and balanced commander in chief, but also as an American deeply sensitive and sympathetic to working-class Americans and citizens of the world whose lives have been fractured not only by Al Qaeda and the Taliban, but also by our own misguided, preemptive invasion of Iraq. However, in an effort to understand Obama's unique use of sophistic dynamism and rhetorical sophistication, I must turn to Aristotle's categories of persuasion.

For Aristotle, persuasive rhetoric is associated with three places and time-frames, and its claims are categorized in relationship to such a typology. The first place is the public forum, and its time-frame is the present. From such a place and time, persuaders make claims of value and participate in ceremonial (or *epideictic*) persuasion focused on praising and blaming people, institutions, actions, etc. The second place is the court of law, and its time-frame is the past. From this place and time, persuaders make claims of fact and participate in forensic persuasion. Of course, this second type of discourse can be associated not only with the court of law, but also with other places in which orators or writers are concerned with establishing any sort of factuality whatsoever. The third place is the legislative assembly, and its time-frame is the future. From this place and time, persuaders make claims of policy and participate in deliberative persuasion. This type of discourse can be associated with a legislative assembly as well as other places where persuaders argue for policy, including interpersonal, academic, and workplace spheres. It is deliberative persuasion that is most important in terms of classifying Obama's West Point Address, for it is a claim of policy that drives his address.

However, another reading of the structure of Obama's speech explains why he swerves away from rhetorical expectations of length and emphasis, especially in his background narration and the extended conclusion. Indeed, in terms of Cicero's default for persuasive arrangement, we can look at the slots for *narratio* and *peroration* as spaces of development in which Obama also uses forensic and ceremonial discourses.

The extended background narration is grounded in forensic discourse, invented as a story concerning past facts. Obama clearly believes that he must establish a kind of authorized story for his policy claim, one that begins with what he believes is a salient opening (our initial involvement in Afghanistan), that comprehends what he considers to be our misstep in Iraq, and ends with his version of what he regards as the deterioration of our original mission. This drive toward a kind of authorizing and forensic narrative is, perhaps, what best explains the unusual length of the second of Cicero's six slots.

In my view, the extended narration is aimed at all of Obama's audiences, but his lengthy, action-oriented close, as an instance of ceremonial rhetoric, or the rhetoric of value, is aimed particularly at the American public. It is as though he speaks directly to Americans, but hopes at the same time that an international audience of onlookers will find in his closing remarks the reemergence of American valuation of balance, diplomacy, and global cooperation. I have discussed at length what is blamed (our inattention to our home economy, rancorous political discourse, and our profligate military spending during the Bush administration), and what is praised (political and diplomatic balance, focus on the problems of working-class Americans, military restraint, and a national sense of unity and common purpose). In fact, Obama marks his close as ceremonial when he says, "We must draw upon the strength of our values by living them at home." He implies that the return he urges is to values that were abandoned during the Bush administration, claiming that the values for which he argues might become, once again, "the moral source of America's authority."

Enacting the link between ceremonial effectiveness and style, Obama uses apostrophe, metaphor, and coordinated (rather than subordinated) syntax as he closes:

> America—we are passing through a time of great trial. And the message that we send in the midst of these storms must be clear: that our cause is just, our resolve unwavering. We will go forward with the confidence that right makes might, and with the commitment to forge an America that is safer, a world that is most secure, and a future that represents not the deepest of fears but the highest of hopes.

It is noteworthy that his apostrophe names not "Americans," but "America," and that even though it is anchored in the pronouns "we" and "our," it inverts the directionality of the binaries Obama associates with the Bush administration (e.g., "*might* makes *right*" becomes "*right* makes *might*"). This evinces concern for the rights and safety of the global community. In the end, Obama exhorts Americans to rediscover America as a kind of newly found land, one in which its own global *ethos* is predicated not on hypocritical military might, but on authentic, international citizenship.

POLICY AND RHETORICAL IMPLICATIONS
OF THE WEST POINT ADDRESS

A careful reading of Obama's West Point Address has convinced me that, despite his controversial policy claim regarding our mission in Afghanistan, the rhetorical complexity of his remarks and their remarkable compression establishes him as a President who *does* do "nuance." Moreover, we can find in this address a return to the values, strategies, and *technes* of sophistic and classical rhetoricians. Like the sophists, Obama's purpose is not to enact policy that is clearly "true" or "correct," but to establish his own *ethos* as a decisive and authoritative commander in chief, and to reestablish our country's *ethos* as an authentic, moral, and cooperative member of the world community. At the heart of his address, we find the primacy of the ancient classical values of balance and moderation. We find the voice of a responsible sophist, clearly concerned with the unification of political factions and with asserting a mediated policy claim that might work to subdue public discourse that is "rancorous" and divisive.

Dan Balz's assessment of the reception and effectiveness of Obama's West Point Address seems correct: Obama did not succeed in convincing our nation as a whole that his policy stance regarding Afghanistan is on the mark.[24] In my own case, as a member of the faction in favor of immediate withdrawal of all troops from Afghanistan, I was disappointed in Obama's proposal of a troop surge, despite his reassurance that there would be a timetable for withdrawal and a thoughtful exit strategy. However, perhaps like many Americans, I was heartened by his exhortation that as a nation we must move toward becoming less belligerent—a nation more interested in cooperating with the global community than flexing military muscle from a position of arrogance, hypocrisy, and ignorance.

From a rhetorical point of view, Obama's address raises many questions that only future time might answer. Will his recuperation of a rhetoric that is sophistic and classical help him shore up his own authority as not only a decisive commander in chief, but also as a compassionate human being keenly attuned to economic and political realities both at home and abroad? Will his address help secure thirty billion dollars of funding in our Congress? Will his moral exhortation succeed in turning our nation toward being—or at least appearing to be—a cooperative member of the world community? Will his remarks succeed in helping to secure the support of our NATO allies and also the peoples of Afghanistan and Pakistan? And might a mediated policy claim, if not fully effective, at least serve to undermine the divisive and rancorous political discourse that threatens the unity of our nation? In the last analysis, Obama's classical address is one that turns from audience to audience, faction to faction, endeavoring to achieve balance and respond to the political constraints and forces in which he found himself at the exact moment of his address. In my estimation, then, Obama's West Point Address, if not immediately effective, will stand for years to come as a brilliant example of deliberative persuasion, one largely guided by sophistic and classical rhetorical impulses and values. It is an address that is decidedly pragmatic, politically and diplomatically constructed, unabashedly mediated, *ethos*-oriented, balanced, and refreshingly nuanced.

CODA

Obama delivered his West Point Address in December, 2009. In July, 2011, he announced his decision to draw down ten thousand troops from Afghanistan (to, in a small way, make good on his West Point policy claim). More time will pass before this essay is published, but perhaps this coda will serve to update political and public responses to Obama's ongoing sophistic rhetoric. Writing for the *Washington Post* shortly after the drawdown speech,[25] Felicia Somnez surveyed the responses of a number of prominent Republican and Democratic elected officials. As might be expected, voices as diverse as John Boehner, Harry Reed, Nancy Pelosi, and John McCain were at odds with each other. Overall, Democrats applauded the drawdown decision, though some wanted to see a more robust and rapid drawdown. The Republican response was mixed, with some voices urging Obama in the future to listen more carefully to his military commanders in the field, some urging continuing vigilance, and others critical of any sort of drawdown at all. Thus, political contention over Obama's policy decisions (and claims) has not abated, even though Obama can now gesture at the death of Osama bin Laden as further justification for the drawdown.

Amanda Terkel, also writing in a July 2011 *Huffington Post* article, focused more on international and public responses. International response is, of course, mixed, but the article emphasized that "Opinion polls show the public is souring on Afghanistan." [11] Thus, there seems to be a divide between political rhetoric and public response to that rhetoric. Nevertheless, Terkel noticed that Obama's ongoing (and stubborn) sophistic rhetoric persists. She quoted his 2011 drawdown assertion: "We must chart a more centered course." One is left to ask, "More centered than *what?*" After all, it was a "centered course" that Obama advocated early on in regard to Afghanistan. No doubt other rhetorical challenges will arise for Obama as the Afghanistan question continues to loom large.

We are left, then, with a view of Obama's recuperation of classical rhetoric at West Point as interesting, intelligent, and articulate. Was the West

Point Address fully effective? In the sense that world events were dramatically influenced by his policy claim, perhaps so. However, as public opinion concerning the war continues to sour, it seems that the original address may be regarded, by posterity, as a rhetorical act that lost force as the war lingered and as economic circumstances undercut political and public support for the war in Afghanistan.

NOTES

1. Dan Baltz. "With Speech, President Makes the Conflict Truly His Own," *Washilngton Post*, December 2, 2009,

<http://articles.washingtonpost.com/2009-12-02/politics/36855655_1_president-obama-afghanistan-conflict-exit-strategy>

2. Ibid.

3. Ibid.

4. . Edith Hamilton and Huntington Cairns, eds., *The Collected Dialogues of Plato* (Princeton, NJ: Princeton Univ. Press, 1971) for the text of Plato's *Protagoras*.

5· George Norlin, trans., *Isocrates*, (Cambridge, MA: Harvard Univ. Press, 1980).

6. See Janet Atwill. *Rhetoric Reclaimed* (Ithaca, NY: Cornell Univ. Press, 1988). Atwill's book offers an impressively comprehensive and readable account of not only Protagoras and Isocrates, but of the other Greek sophists and their lineage.

7. ·Barack, Obama. "Obama Afghanistan Speech: Watch West Point Address," *New York Times*, <http://www.nytimes.com/2012/05/02/world/asia/text-obamas-speech-in-afghanistan.html?pagewanted=all&_r=0I>, May 1, 2012. I used the printed version's page indicators (from page 1 through page 6) as I gesture at specific elements of the address.

8. Readers interested in becoming more familiar with Cicero's writing about rhetoric and persuasion might go to H.M. Hubbell trans., *On Invention* (Cambridge, MA: Harvard Univ. Press, 1968). See also E.W. Sutton and H. Rackham, trans., *On Oratory* (Cambridge, MA: Harvard Univ. Press, 1976).

9. Lane Cooper, trans., *The Rhetoric of Aristotle* (New York: Appleton-Century-Crofts, 1932); George A. Kennedy, trans., *Aristotle on Rhetoric: A Theory of Civic Discourse* (New York: Oxford Univ. Press, 2006). Kennedy's version may seem more accessible and helpful to contemporary readers.

10. Obama, West Point Speech

11. Ibid.

12. Ibid.

13. Ibid.

14. Ibid.

15. Ibid.

16. Ibid.

17. Ibid.

18. Ibid.

19. Ibid.

20. Ibid.

21. Ibid.

22. Richard Leo Enos. *Roman Rhetoric: Revolution and the Greek Influence* (Anderson, SC: Parlor Press, 2008). Enos's book is extremely informative and readable, and I highly recommend it to readers of this essay who wish to find a more comprehensive treatment of Roman rhetoric than my own.

23. Martin Luther King Jr., "A Letter from Birmingham Jail," *Classical Rhetoric for the Modern Student*, ed. Edward P. J. Corbett (New York: Oxford Univ. Press, 1999). This is an authoritative version of King's letter that includes an excellent rhetorical analysis.

25. Balz, "With Speech, President Makes"

25. Felicia Sonmez, "Capitol Hill Reaction to Obama's Afghanistan Address Swift, Varied," *Washington Post*, June 22, 2001, <http://www.washingtonpost.com/blogs/2chambers/post/capitol-hill-reaction-to-obamas-afghanistan-address-swift-varied/2011/06/22/AGWFDWgH_blog.html>; Amanda Terkel, "Obama Announces Afghanistan Troop Withdrawal in Speech to Nation," *Huffington Post*, August 22, 2011, <http://www.huffingtonpost.com/2011/06/22/obama-afghanistan-troop-withdrawal_n_882451.htm>.

Part Two: Obama's Rhetoric Abroad

7 A Few Bad Apples: Barack Obama's Response to the Bush Administration Policy on Torture

Richard Marback

Claiming that Barack Obama is more eloquent than George W. Bush is stating the obvious. Claiming that Obama is less persuasive than Bush is to state something not at all obvious, but for reasons that are not wholly unbelievable. A case could be made for Bush's persuasive powers by recalling that he did succeed in persuading many Americans, the majority of Congress, and enough world leaders to support the invasion of Iraq. A comparative case favoring Bush—one claiming Obama is, despite his obvious eloquence, a less persuasive president—could be made on the grounds that Obama struggled to pass a health care reform bill, even with an historic Democratic majority in both houses of Congress. To be fair, the invasion of Iraq and the reform of health care are perhaps not comparable measures of persuasive ability. One is a matter of foreign policy, the other a matter of domestic policy; each is fraught in its own way. More than this, the circumstances under which Bush was able to mobilize support for his invasion of Iraq created a sense of urgency that facilitated acquiescence and cooperation. The circumstances under which Obama pursued reform of the health care system were overshadowed by other domestic issues, and were overburdened by established health care expectations and interests. To say the rhetorical circumstances favored Obama less than they favored Bush is to state something that is arguable. To say whether and how the differences in circumstance should influence our judgment of the comparative rhetorical skills of Bush and Obama is to invoke issues regarding the articulation of circumstance and skill that are neither obvious nor settled. In what follows, I argue that the appearance of Obama's comparative lack of persuasive skill is the product less of Bush's success with persuasion and more of Obama's inheritance of Bush's aversion to persuasion, an aversion made manifest in the Bush administration's reconfiguration of the resources of presidential rhetoric.

To argue my claim that Obama's rhetorical efficacy depends in some measure on the resources of presidential rhetoric Obama inherited from Bush requires that I first explain what I mean by Bush's retreat from persuasion. At this point, it might already appear that I want to claim that Bush had more persuasive success—that he was more persuasive—at the same time I claim that he disregarded persuasion. Taken together, the two claims do seem inconsistent, and would seem to also excuse Obama by blaming Bush. This is not my point. To acknowledge that Bush did persuade the nation to go to war and to recognize that he eschewed persuasive appeals in his pursuit of war is not inconsistent. It is also not to excuse Obama by blaming Bush. It is instead to bring into question the problem of persuasion in presidential rhetoric.

The presidency is by definition rhetorical, with the most obvious rhetorical feature of the presidency being the constitutional requirement for an address to Congress on the state of the union. The problem of presidential rhetoric, as Jeffrey Tulis has described, is the emergence over the course of the twentieth century of more and more expectations and opportunities for the president to act rhetorically by speaking directly to the people, thereby overstepping the original bounds of executive power and disrupting the democratic functioning of constitutional checks and balances. For Tulis, the problem of presidential rhetoric is not persuasiveness, nor is it eloquence; it is instead a problem of loquaciousness: "The rhetorical presidency is more deleterious than beneficial to American politics because the rhetorical presidency is not just the use of popular leadership, but rather the routine appeal to public opinion. Intended to ameliorate crises, the rhetorical presidency is now creator of crises, or pseudo-crises."[1] Whatever Tulis's appreciation for and understanding of rhetoric, his point is well taken. The degree to which the president foregoes deliberative discourse with Congress in favor of persuasive appeals to the public is the extent to which the president oversteps the bounds of executive power, and in doing so, manufactures crisis. Bush's public declarations after the terrorist attack of 9/11 could very well be argued as a case in point.

Elvin Lim does in fact take Bush as a case in point of the problem with presidential rhetoric, a problem he diagnoses in contrast to Tulis by arguing that the expansion of presidential appeals is less a matter of loquaciousness and more a matter of a lack of eloquence—a lack he characterizes as anti-

intellectualism, a retreat from the "rhetorical leadership and public deliberation" that would "allow the people to govern, keep leaders accountable, and
promote the best public policies."[2] According to Lim, the problem with presidential rhetoric is not that it bypasses Congress, for Congress could surely
respond to an increase in presidential rhetoric with public appeals of its own,
something it surely does. As Lim argues, such appeals have the potential to
enrich debate if they were not themselves also anti-intellectual, reinforcing
rather than restraining a presidential rhetoric of platitudes and pandering.
Here, too, Bush's rhetoric is a case in point. Lim makes this clear in his remarks on a speech Bush gave in 2003 in support of the war in Iraq:

> Bush's words likely sent an electric charge through a large
> portion of his audience. . . . Inspirational language, while it
> might have unifying, epideictic purposes, tends to discour-
> age dialogue and debate. Indeed, inspirational platitudes
> are asserted precisely because they are allegedly so self-evi-
> dent that they need not be argued for.[3]

While Lim is an advocate for rhetoric and wants to enlarge and enrich
its role in government, and while Tulis is suspicious of rhetoric and wants to
keep it restrained, both share a view of the proper role of persuasion as winning assent from those who dissent, and both advocate for a more deliberative model of rhetoric. For Tulis, it is deliberation among the three branches of the Federal government. For Lim, deliberation includes the American
public as well. Lim and Tulis promote deliberative presidential rhetoric and
disparage emotional appeals. Tulis and Lim both want to restrain what Lim
calls the "rhetorical tricks" of "simplistic language, applause-rendering platitudes, partisan slogans, and a heavy reliance on emotional and human appeals."[4] However much we may want to agree or disagree with the entirety
of their arguments, if we can agree with the claim that presidential rhetoric
should be—in some sense, and to some degree—deliberative, then we can
share the conclusion that Bush was, as president, a poor rhetor. Despite what
Lim describes as Bush's ability to rouse an audience, and despite Bush's apparent ability to mobilize and manipulate support for the War on Terror,
Bush was not particularly adept at persuasion because he could not exploit
the deliberative potential of the office. Recalling Tulis, Bush's public appeals
regarding threats to national security allowed him to create crisis and, in
doing so, more easily win support for decisions far less likely to gain congressional approval through deliberation alone.

Then again, Bush had no interest in making use of his deliberative skill.
Prior to being sworn into office for his first term as president, Bush said in
an interview that things were going to be different in Washington and that

he would be uncompromising in his efforts to get things done his way. While Bush's appeal to the tropes of decisive leadership and an end to "politics as usual" may have inspired many Americans, by the end of his second term, many more Americans were appalled by the lengths to which the Bush administration went to pursue its agenda. In particular, controversies surrounding "enhanced interrogations" and memos from the White House Counsel outlining a legal basis for torture blurred the line between legitimate and illegitimate use of state power so that it seems naïve to suggest the problems of the Bush White House can be understood in terms of expanding epideictic rhetoric and the evasion of deliberative rhetoric. The language used by the Bush administration to justify torture can and should be understood as a function of rhetoric, what I characterize as that administration's abandonment of legitimate presidential persuasion. Unlike Tulis and Lim, I characterize the problem of presidential rhetoric in the Bush administration less as loquaciousness or pandering, and more as a preference for coercion. Even though Obama immediately denounced the use of torture in fighting the War on Terror, the Bush administration's retreat from persuasion to coercion created lasting rhetorical problems for the Obama administration, problems I discuss below. Before I get to Obama's problems with rhetoric, it is worth the effort to first discuss Bush's problems with persuasion.

The abandonment of legitimate presidential rhetoric during the Bush administration was, I think, summed up best on April 19th, 2006, during a White House press conference, when Bush announced his support for Secretary of Defense Donald Rumsfeld, who had come under increasing criticism for deepening the prisoner abuse scandal at Abu Ghraib. When asked repeatedly by reporters about his reaction to calls for Rumsfeld's resignation, Bush finally replied, "I'm the decider and I decide what's best."[5]

The expansion of executive power through appeal to the role of "the decider" constrained rhetorical resources and created a rhetorical challenge for the Obama administration, a constraint and challenge best expressed in candidate Obama's remarks issued on October 4th, 2007, the day after initial media reports on White House memos supporting the use of torture. According to candidate Obama, "Torture is how you set back America's standing in the world, not how you strengthen it."[6] The rhetorical challenge created for Obama by the Bush administration's discussion of torture was nothing less than the challenge of rebuilding credibility that had been destroyed. As Obama suggests, the Bush administration "set back America's standing." The challenge posed for the Obama administration, is, again, as Obama suggests: to strengthen America's standing. To strengthen credibility that has been weakened is no easy task. Before discussing Obama's strategies for reaffirming America's standing in the world, it is necessary to first discuss how

I see the setback to America's standing as a casualty of the Bush administration's evasion of rhetoric. In what follows, I focus on the Bush administration's policy on torture. I do so for a number of reasons.

First, during his campaign, and immediately after taking office, President Obama had no choice but to respond to the Bush policy. The challenge was not the decision to reverse the policy. Instead, the challenge was one of responding in a way that reclaimed credibility for the office of the president. To achieve this end, more was required of Obama than a reaffirmation of principled consistency and transparency.

Second, torture, the most severe form of coercion available, is the very opposite of persuasion. Torture makes the power of violence available to the president into a problem of more significance to presidential rhetoric than the problems of platitudes and pandering. As a head of state and the commander in chief of the nation's military forces, the president's exercise of executive power is sovereign. The president may be subject to checks and balances from the legislative and the judicial branches, but the president is also, as Bush so aptly puts it, "the decider." As Carl Schmitt writes about deciding, "Sovereign is he who decides on the exception."[7]. In a memo written on August 1st, 2002, for Attorney General Alberto Gonzales—a memo outlining legal standards for the conduct of enhanced interrogations—the president's executive power to decide on the exception, and to justify the use of torture, is made sacrosanct. The passage is worth quoting at length:

> Even if the interrogation method arguably were to violate Section 2340A [of 18 U.S.C.], the statute would be unconstitutional if it impermissibly encroached on the President's constitutional power to conduct a military campaign. As commander in chief, the President has the constitutional authority to order interrogations of enemy combatants to gain intelligence information concerning the military plans of the enemy. The demands of the commander in chief power are especially pronounced in the middle of a war in which the nation has already suffered a direct attack. . . . Any effort to apply Section 2340A in a manner that interferes with the President's direction of such core war matters as the detention and interrogation of enemy combatants thus would be unconstitutional.[8]

The conclusions drawn in the memo are chilling. I discuss them more fully below. Here it is worth making clear the conceptual nature of this claim to sovereign executive power by recalling Schmitt's argument for the foundational act of deciding on the exception. One who is sovereign "decides whether there is an extreme emergency as well as what must be done to eliminate it. Although he stands outside the normally valid legal system, he nevertheless belongs to it, for it is he who must decide whether the constitution needs to be suspended in its entirety."⁹ Schmitt's point that the sovereign has sole discretion when it comes to deciding the exception recalls Tulis on the dangers of presidential rhetoric, and that its expansion beyond the requirements of deliberation provide resources to manufacture crises.

The idea that the sovereign can decide unconditionally whether there is a crisis and what must be done in response to it leads to the third and final reason for approaching Obama's rhetoric as a response to Bush's expansive use of sovereign, executive power. The use of torture can only be justified through rhetoric. Presidential rhetoric and the coercive use of force are not separable, but are intertwined, a point acknowledged in the White House memos aimed at justifying the retreat from persuasion and the use of coercion. Because argumentation was used to justify torture, Obama's rejection of torture had to do more than merely put an end to enhanced interrogations. Obama's repudiation of torture had to also reclaim persuasion. As I argue below, Obama's skill in rearticulating coercion and persuasion reveals something about the rhetorical nature of his presidential sovereignty.

FROM ABU GHRAIB TO THE ATTORNEY GENERAL'S OFFICE

In April 2004, when images of prisoner abuse at Abu Ghraib first appeared in the media, the Bush administration shared the public's outrage, characterizing the abuses as the actions of "a few bad apples" among the soldiers assigned as guards to the prison. Among the soldiers eventually charged with dereliction of duty and prisoner abuse, the most infamous are Lyndie England and Charles Graner. Over time, details of the personal histories of Graner and England appeared in the media, portraying the couple as disadvantaged and depraved: England because of her impoverished childhood and the depredations of working in a chicken evisceration plant; and Graner because of his zealous sadism as a civilian prison guard.¹⁰ While the moral failings of Graner and England provide some explanation for their actions, both countered that their actions were known to their commanding officers and that they were only following orders.

By June 2004, it became clear to the public that the prisoner abuse at Abu Ghraib was not the isolated actions of a few sadistic individuals. In the 2004 Taguba Report—a report of the investigation conducted by the Army Criminal Investigation Command—Major General Taguba concluded:

> That between October and December 2003, at the Abu
> Ghraib Confinement Facility (BCCF), numerous incidents

of sadistic, blatant, and wanton criminal abuses were in-
flicted on several detainees. This systemic and illegal abuse
of detainees was intentionally perpetrated by several members of the military police guard force (372nd Military Police Company, 320th Military Police Battalion, 800th [11].

Among the numerous instances of systematic abuse the report lists, a few
include the following: "forcibly arranging detainees in various sexually explicit positions for photographing"; "forcing naked male detainees to wear
women's underwear"; "forcing groups of male detainees to masturbate themselves while being photographed and videotaped"; "arranging naked male
detainees in a pile and then jumping on them"; "positioning a naked detainee
on a MRE Box, with a sandbag on his head, and attaching wires to his fin-
gers, toes, and penis to simulate electric torture"; and "placing a dog chain
or strap around a naked detainee's neck and having a female soldier pose for
a picture."[12]

Beyond the "few bad apples" who committed the prisoner abuse, the party
responsible and accountable for the actions became both clearer and cloudier.
As commanding officer at Abu Ghraib, Brigadier General Janis Karpinski
was held accountable for failing to provide adequate oversight and therefore
allowing prisoner abuse. In November 2006, Karpinski reported that she
was not alone in being responsible for prisoner abuse, citing a memo signed
by Secretary of Defense Donald Rumsfeld authorizing civilian contractors to
use harsh or enhanced interrogation techniques. Two years earlier, in June
2004, in response to the prisoner abuse scandal, the White House released
258 pages of documents detailing its position on the necessity for the harsh
treatment and enhanced interrogations of prisoners in the War on Terror.
One memo in particular corroborates Karpinski. In that memo, Rumsfeld
approved "counter-resistance techniques to aid in the interrogation of detainees at Guantanamo Bay."[13] Included among the approved techniques were
subjecting prisoners to mental and physical stress, such as exposing them to
the threat of guard dogs and forcing them to stand for four hours at a time.
Beneath his signature approving the use of these techniques to aid interrogations, Rumsfeld wrote, "I stand 8–10 hours a day. Why is standing limited
to 4 hours?"[14]

For his part, on May 7th, 2004, Rumsfeld said of the events at Abu Ghraib:
"As Secretary of Defense I am accountable for them, and I take full responsibility."[15] While Bush defended Rumsfeld to the end, justifying his decision to
not fire Rumsfeld by explaining, "I'm the decider and I decide what's best,"
Rumsfeld did resign on November 6th, 2006. Regarding the investigation
into the scandal, Rumsfeld explained in May, 2004: "Part of what we believe

in is making sure that when wrongdoing or scandal do occur, that they are not covered up, but they are exposed, they are investigated and the guilty are brought to justice."[16] Several years later, on December 11th, 2008, the Senate Armed Services Committee, chaired by Carl Levine (D-Mich.), released a report concluding that Rumsfeld was indeed directly responsible for the tortures at Abu Ghraib.

It became clear that Rumsfeld did not act alone. He also did not act under the direction of the president. For his part, Bush issued a memo on February 7th, 2002, to Secretary of Defense Rumsfeld, the joint chiefs of staff, and the director of the CIA, and others, in which he reaffirmed "the order previously issued by the Secretary of Defense to the United States Armed Forces requiring that the detainees be treated humanely and to the extent appropriate and consistent with military necessity, in a manner consistent with the principles of Geneva."[17] In the memo, Bush's conclusion that the military should respect the Geneva Convention prohibitions against cruel, degrading, and inhumane treatment of prisoners of war follows his reference to a February 1st, 2002, legal opinion rendered by Attorney General John Ashcroft that the president, as commander in chief, does have "the authority under the Constitution to suspend Geneva," an authority Bush claims in his memo that he chose note to exercise.[18] The letter from Ashcroft concluded that it is legal for the United States to disregard the Geneva Convention in the treatment of Al Qaeda and Taliban prisoners captured in Afghanistan because, at the time of the United States' combat in Afghanistan, the country was a failed state. As a failed state, it could not be a party to a treaty; therefore, the protections of the Geneva Convention did not apply. The letter is relevant because it begins with Ashcroft's request to "comment on the National Security Council's discussion concerning the status of Taliban detainees," a request followed by an observation that "The determination that Al Qaeda and Taliban detainees are not prisoners of war remains firm"[19] From the foregone conclusion of the National Security Council that Al Qaeda and Taliban prisoners were not enemy combatants—and therefore were not protected by the Geneva Convention—the purpose of Ashcroft's memo is clear and worth quoting in full:

> We expect substantial and ongoing legal challenges to follow the Presidential resolution of these issues. These challenges will be resolved more quickly and easily if they are foreclosed from judicial review under the *Clark* case by a Presidential determination that the Geneva Convention III on prisoners of war does not apply based on the failed state theory outlined as Option I above.[20]

In other words, as Bush so aptly put it, he was the decider, and he decided what was best, not only deciding who, among prisoners in the War on Terror, were enemy combatants but also how those prisoners were to be treated. Ashcroft's letter confirms Bush's sovereignty to decide not only whether the Geneva prohibitions apply but also, as became clear in other memos, what does and does not count as torture.

Explaining how and why prisoners at Abu Ghraib were tortured is not simply a matter of documenting accountability to the person responsible as the sovereign decider. The Abu Ghraib prison scandal repeated an unfortunate commonplace relationship between the extreme behavior of subordinates and the apparent sanction of institutional authority, even though it was not always clear just how sanctions and behaviors were articulated.

In *The Lucifer Effect*, Philip Zimbardo draws parallels between the abuse scandal at Abu Ghraib and his now infamous 1971 Stanford prison experiment. In the infamous Stanford Prison Experiment, college students were arbitrarily divided into guards and prisoners, and sequestered together. After less than a week, the experiment was terminated because students assigned to be guards became not only authoritarian but, more disturbingly, sadistic torturers of students assigned to be prisoners. For their part, the prisoners became passive, and some even participated in the abuse of other student prisoners to curry favor from the students assigned to be guards. Drawing parallels from his Stanford Prison Experiment and the Abu Ghraib abuse, Zimbardo concluded that people who are ordinarily good become capable of extraordinary acts of evil when they have been persuaded to dehumanize others.[21] Zimbardo's account of persuasion—and also of rhetoric—is thin at best, and I do not discuss it here. Suffice it to say that he reduced persuasion to three factors: the credibility of the persuader, the social pressure to conform, and the gullibility of those being persuaded. According to this configuration of factors, people such as the student guards at Stanford and the guards at Abu Ghraib torture because of pressure to conform and a readiness to believe those in positions of authority, making the guards more susceptible to persuasion. To avoid acts of evil, Zimbardo suggested, people simply need to be more skeptical and autonomous.

In their 2002 BBC prison study, Alex Haslam and Steve Reicher draw different conclusions from those of Zimbardo. They conclude that people will act aggressively or passively as a matter of identification—itself a process of thinking through individual accountability to others in a valued group. There are two implications for the role of persuasion in acts of torture. On the one hand, as Haslam and Reicher put it, "Successful groups give their members the power to put ideas into practice. . . . Where these beliefs are undemocratic and oppressive, groups can be tyrannical."[22] On the other hand,

"When people cannot realize their own values and beliefs, they are more likely to accept alternatives—however drastic—that provide the prospect of success. In particular, when their group is failing, they are more likely to embrace a strong figure who promises to make things work for them."[23]

What studies of the psychology of abuse contribute to a rhetorical study is a complex picture of agency, authority, persuasion, responsibility, and sovereignty. The initial administration's claim that a few individuals acted outside institutional authorization, joined with the claims that what those individuals did was sanctioned by institutional authorities, forms a claim for the rhetorical construction of agency. For subordinates such as England, the justification for prisoner abuse came from elsewhere, but further up the chain of command, clearly at the level of the Secretary of Defense and higher, responsibility for systemic abuse is joined with the administration's arguments for the executive authority to sanction enhanced interrogations that are claimed to not rise to the level of torture. As argued in the August 1st, 2002, memo quoted above, and discussed below, the president has sovereign authority to decide whether to torture; legal sanctions against torture, or cruel, inhuman, and degrading treatment does not constrain the president's decision one way or the other. Such a claim for sovereignty rests on and aims at abandoning persuasiveness, a sovereign claim to the exception, and is a claim that can be characterized as rhetorical in the worst sense. As David Cole puts it, it is a claim intended to "twist language and law in order to rationalize the unthinkable."[24] To fully appreciate the rhetorical challenges created for Obama through a torture scandal that rationalized the unthinkable, it is necessary to further examine the rhetoric of the Bush administration's claim to the exception.

The search for a justification of torture began with a request from the Central Intelligence Agency for legal advice on limits to detainee interrogation, specifically whether they could utilize enhanced interrogation techniques on high ranking al-Qaeda members captured outside the borders of the United States. White House General Counsel Alberto Gonzalez forwarded the request to the White House Office of Legal Counsel (OLC). The OLC is generally responsible for providing the White House with opinions on questions of constitutionality (Schwarz). The legal question addressed in the memo was whether 18 U.S.C § 2340, outlining obligations to the Convention Against Torture and Other Cruel, Inhuman and Degrading Treatment or Punishment, concerned the definition of torture. The statute defines torture as follows:

(1) "torture" means an act committed by a person acting under the color of law specifically intended to inflict severe physical or mental pain

or suffering (other than pain or suffering incidental to lawful sanctions) upon another person within his custody or physical control;

(2) "severe mental pain or suffering" means the prolonged mental harm caused by or resulting from—

(A) the intentional infliction or threatened infliction of severe physical pain or suffering;

(B) the administration or application, or threatened administration or application, of mind-altering substances or other procedures calculated to disrupt profoundly the senses or the personality;

(C) the threat of imminent death; or

(D) the threat that another person will imminently be subjected to death, severe physical pain or suffering, or the administration or application of mind-altering substances or other procedures calculated to disrupt profoundly the senses or personality

The memo response from the OLC, dated August 1st, 2002, and believed to have been authored by John Yoo, with assistance from David Addington—legal counsel to Dick Cheney—makes the following findings in its interpretation of the law:

We conclude below that Section 2340A proscribes acts inflicting, and that are specifically intended to inflict, severe pain or suffering, whether mental or physical. Those acts must be of an extreme nature to rise to the level of torture within the meaning of Section 2340A and the Convention. We further conclude that certain acts may be cruel, inhuman, or degrading, but still not produce pain and suffering of the requisite intensity to fall within Section 2340A's proscription against torture. We conclude by examining possible defenses that would negate any claim that certain interrogation methods violate the statute.[25]

In his review of the memo, John Dean concludes, "In reading these newly-released memos, along with the previously-released documents relating to the use of torture as an interrogation technique, it is pretty clear who was the bad apple at OLC, it was the lead attorney in pursuing these extreme and baseless OLC positions law professor John Yoo."[26] While it would take me further afield of my discussion of Obama's rhetoric if I were to treat Yoo's justifications of torture in terms of his appeals to presidential sovereignty, I do want to reiterate the point that the arguments made in the August 1st, 2002, memo misalign the persuasive prospects of presidential rhetoric in relation to the coercive force of executive power. The challenge created for Obama by this misalignment was the challenge of re-establishing the persuasive powers of presidential rhetoric.

As a candidate, as president-elect, and as president, Obama was consistent in his rejection of torture. On October 4th, 2007, the day after the media first reported on the Bush administration's policy on torture, Obama released a statement denouncing the Bush policy:

> The secret authorization of brutal interrogations is an outrageous betrayal of our core values, and a grave danger to our security. We must do whatever it takes to track down and capture or kill terrorists, but torture is not a part of the answer—it is a fundamental part of the problem with this administration's approach. Torture is how you create enemies, not how you defeat them. Torture is how you get bad information, not good intelligence. Torture is how you set back America's standing in the world, not how you strengthen it. It's time to tell the world that America rejects torture without exception or equivocation. It's time to stop telling the American people one thing in public while doing something else in the shadows. No more secret authorization of methods like simulated drowning. When I am president America will once again be the country that stands up to these deplorable tactics. When I am president we won't work in secret to avoid honoring our laws and Constitution, we will be straight with the American people and true to our values.[27]

As president-elect, Obama reiterated his position, stating "I was clear throughout this campaign and was clear throughout this transition that under my administration the United States does not torture . . . . We will abide by the Geneva Conventions. We will uphold our highest ideals."[28] On only his second full day in office as president, Obama signed one executive order closing CIA secret prisons, and another executive order requiring all interrogators to follow the non-coercive interrogation techniques of the *Army Field Manual*.

The consistency of his message is undeniable. Obama appeals to the values and ideals (values and ideals we are left to imagine) of decency, honesty, and integrity; these are values and ideals that cannot be sacrificed, but that had been sacrificed. It is one thing, as Obama puts it, to honor the Constitution, to be honest with the American people, and to be true to shared values. It is something else entirely to reinstate somehow respect for the rule of law, to regain the trust of a nation, and to reaffirm shared values that had been discounted. The challenge posed to Obama by the torture memos and by the prisoner abuse scandal was a challenge to recalibrate executive powers, to dial down unchecked sovereignty, and to gain cooperation by reestablishing trust. In rhetorical terms, the challenge of restraining executive authority and privilege is one of reinvigorating the credibility of the sovereign office of the president, and creating the possibility for cooperation and assent. It is the challenge, as Tulis and Lim put it, of affirming the deliberative capacities of the office of the president.

Of course, the president's capacity for deliberation is at least as great as his sovereign authority. As commander in chief of the armed forces, the president does wield a terrifying, coercive power, but having that kind of power at hand never in and of itself justifies its use. It is in fact restraint in using coercive force that can and does bolster a president's rhetorical power. As Alex Bellamy explains, responsible use of military force is a use, the justification of which is both rhetorically constrained and broadly persuasive: "It is not enough simply to persuade ourselves of the justice of what we do. The crucial thing is that we are seen to be behaving justly."[29] To put the point in terms of rhetoric, the challenge of balancing persuasion and coercion in the office of the president is the challenge of persuading others both that the use of force is justified, and that the force justified is used justly.

As I argued above, the Bush administration's justifications for using torture as a weapon in the war on terror were so transparently self-serving that they failed to persuade anyone (outside of those directly involved) of the just use of torture. Here I leave aside the broader debate about the just use of torture to focus instead on President Obama's principled commitment to the Geneva Convention. It was not enough for Obama to sign an executive order banning enhanced interrogations, for such an act is not by itself necessarily enough to persuade anyone of the justice of The War on Terror the Obama administration inherited. Because credibility had been sacrificed by the Bush administration, the Obama administration was put in the position of having to regain credibility for itself in response to demands for establishing accountability for the prior administration's actions. Just how difficult it is for a president to create accountability and regain credibility is captured in Obama's announcement on May 13th, 2009, that he would not release all images of prisoner abuse at Abu Ghraib. In a statement explaining his decision, Obama said, "The publication of these photos would not add any additional benefit to our understanding of what was carried out in the past by a small number of individuals. In fact, the most direct consequence of releasing them, I believe, would be to further inflame anti-American opinion and to put our troops in danger."[30] So firm was he in his conviction to not release the photos that, one month later, Obama was prepared to issue an executive order blocking the release of the photos to the American Civil Liberties Union (ACLU). The ACLU had sued for them under the Freedom of Information Act, a move that appeals, much as Bush had, to the sovereign power of the president to decide the exception.

It is worth attending more closely to the reasons President Obama gave for his decision. Even though it had already become common knowledge by early 2009 that Bush administration lawyers provided legal sanction for torture, and that Secretary of Defense Rumsfeld authorized enhanced inter-rogation techniques, Obama took up the claim that visual evidence of pris-oner abuse represented the actions of a few bad apples; as he puts it, "a small number of individuals," people whose behavior was the exception rather than the rule. It seemed the individuals Obama had in mind were not Yoo and Rumsfeld, but England and Graner. What makes it seem so is the refusal of the Obama administration to appoint special counsel to investigate the abuse scandal and torture memos. Refusal to release the photos, joined with the decision to not investigate further, suggests either that Obama does not consider prisoner abuse and torture to be related (i.e., they are not systemic issues), or Obama recognizes the negative political consequences that would follow from publicly articulating prisoner abuse with the torture memos. Questions of political expediency aside, the persuasiveness of Obama affirm-ing the claim that prisoner abuse was the responsibility of "a few bad apples," and that the behavior of the guards was the exception, rests the public's un-derstanding of the sovereign nature of human agency. It is to say that, despite Bush administration policy, despite conditions at Abu Ghraib, despite even their pasts, England and Graner and the other guards were sovereign, that they could have and should have decided for themselves to take exception to prisoner abuse.

While focusing on individual responsibility for individual acts of injus-tice is appropriate, accountability for the injustice of prisoner abuse does ap-pear to be more systemic and less easily assignable to a few individuals. The abuse of prisoners by a number of guards at Abu Ghraib would seem to point to a breakdown in the chain of command. Restoring confidence after the prisoner abuse at Abu Ghraib, therefore, requires an account that locates responsibility as far as it reaches: through the structural relationships of the "few bad apples" to the policies of the administration and its pursuit of the War on Terror. A number of different groups, among them the ACLU and Democracy Now, have taken this view and accused the Obama administra-tion of obstructing justice by hiding the abuse photos and failing to fully investigate the incidents. As Executive Director of the ACLU Anthony D. Romero remarks,

And when these photos do see the light of day, the outrage will focus not only on the commission of torture by the Bush administration but on the Obama administration's complicity in covering them up. Any outrage related to these photos should be due not to their release but to the very crimes depicted in them. Only by looking squarely in the mirror, acknowledging the crimes of the past and achieving accountability can we move forward and ensure that these atrocities are not repeated. If the Obama administration continues down this path, it will betray not only its promises to the American people, but its commitment to this nation's most fundamental principles.[31]

There is not much doubt in Romero's claim that the Obama administration's decision to not release the photos strains the American values Obama used in claiming the decision to ban torture. In particular, refusing full transparency may, as Romero claims, preclude assigning responsibility systemically instead of exceptionally, only to leave the Obama administration appearing complicit. These are valid policy concerns that can be discussed and evaluated from the perspectives of ethics and politics. They also reveal something about the challenges of presidential rhetoric.

The primary reason Obama gives for blocking the release of the prisoner abuse photos was that circulating them would not add to our understanding of what happened, but fuel outrage further, outrage that could be translated into a disdain for America that could place American troops in greater danger, presumably by providing additional motivation for terrorist attacks on troops in Iraq and Afghanistan. As Romero argues, such reasoning has it backwards, for it is the refusal to release all relevant information and to not hold those responsible publicly accountable that diminishes America's standing abroad. As a matter of rhetoric, these competing claims about perception turn on competing understandings of the nature of deliberation in presidential rhetoric.

The ACLU advocates on the side of Bellamy's observation that the use of force has to appear just, and the appearance of justice resides in complete transparency. Put it in terms of presidential rhetoric, the ACLU's demand for transparency requires the president to overstep the bounds of deliberative rhetoric and appeal directly to the public to make a persuasive case for the justness of the war. While Romero recognizes that outrage may follow from releasing the photos and from investigating prisoner abuse, his view is that such outrage is short term and can be addressed (again, publicly). Addressing the outrage publicly can become a long-term gain in trust because it establishes credibility but also accountability.

The ACLU position more closely aligns with Lim than that of Tulis; it is a position advocating deliberations with Congress and multiple publics, including: the American people, citizens of Iraq, and potential foreign terrorists. Bellamy, Romero, and Obama are aware of these multiple audiences. In the debate about the release of the prisoner abuse photos, it is easy to imagine presidential deliberations with these many and varied audiences would not straightforwardly result in either a gains in the president's credibility or a satisfactory account of responsibility. We can easily imagine each of these audiences requiring something different from the president, and we can also imagine each audience being dissatisfied with the president's appeals, each for their own reasons. An important question here asks how the president is to prioritize deliberations with these audiences. It is not only a question of which deliberations matter more but is also a question of how those deliberations relate to each other. Deliberations with Congress that establish accountability may or may not raise the president's credibility with the American people, and deliberations with the American people that raise the president's credibility may or may not provide the kind of accountability demanded by citizens of Iraq. From these considerations, even the appearance of justice is a rhetorical product that requires more than transparency, and the concession to transparency itself generates a number of problems for presidential deliberation.

On the other hand, Obama's decision to not release the photos and to threaten using an executive order to block their release is a decision to withdraw from public persuasion, a decision that aligns more with Tulis than with Lim, because it is a decision to return presidential rhetoric from persuasion in public to deliberation in government. This is not to deny the need for the president or members of Congress to win the public's trust in their deliberations. Obama certainly demonstrates his understanding that he needs public support to be an effective president. To accept the potential legitimacy of Obama's decision is to recognize that public trust in presidential deliberation does not necessarily require complete transparency. The president can be seen as credible (by at least some publics) and as someone rightly entrusted with sovereign power to issue an executive order without providing reasons that even a majority of any one public finds persuasive. In the case of the prisoner abuse photos, Obama's threatened executive order blocking their release can be seen as an affirmation of sovereign authority paid for in a loss of credibility. That is how the ACLU seems to have seen it. It can also be seen as a legitimate action taken after due deliberation with other government officials. That is how Obama represented it. Whether or not he agrees in principle with accountability and transparency, in this instance, Obama claims the right to decide the exception, an exception claimed on the basis of an anticipated consequence, the consequence being that transparency will do the opposite of persuading others of the justness of the use of force in the War on Terror.

His decision to not release the photos raises the question whether Obama ever considered the War on Terror a just war. He was one of a few senators who voted against the invasion of Iraq, although, as president, he authorized additional troop deployments in Afghanistan. The rhetorical challenge created for the Obama administration by the prisoner abuse scandal and torture memos became most apparent. The Bush administration's arguments for the sovereignty of executive authority rested on perpetuating in public a rhetoric of crisis. Obama's refusal to overextend presidential rhetoric and take up the crisis claims of the Bush administration left a kind of vacuum. Adherence to ideals in making decisions, such as banning torture, interrupts the cycle of the public's appeals to fear and the convoluted legal reasoning that buttressed Bush's claim to executive authority, the claim that he was the decider. Obama's adherence to ideals rejects the rhetorical framework of the sovereign role of the decider, but ideals do not easily substitute for fear. By assuring the public that his is the best decision, it may appear that Obama is himself acting as a sovereign in standing against releasing the prisoner abuse photos. It appears this way not because Obama was in fact taking up the role of the decider but because he appealed less to the public; he had less interest in acquiring authority for his decisions by pandering to public perception. He was less concerned with the overextension of presidential rhetoric, in being the decider, and more concerned with the restraint of presidential rhetoric required for the executive to productively deliberate with Congress. For Bush, the justness of the use of torture in fighting the War on Terror grew out of arguments sanctioning sovereign decision-making: torture was just by virtue of the fact that it could be justified through appeals to fear. For Obama, the justness of a decision does not rest in the possibility of its justification: a decision is just through its adherence to ideals. In the world of politics, where adherence to ideals is tenuous at best, justness is a function of constitutionally appropriate deliberative rhetoric.

Unfortunately, the restrained use of deliberative rhetoric often leaves people unsatisfied. Deliberative rhetoric requires from its audience a sharing of the conviction that what is just can be discovered through just deliberation. In the wake of less restrained rhetoric in particular, the requirements of deliberative rhetoric can not only seem to demand too much, but they can also leave people nonplussed by justifications not grounded in pandering or platitudes.

The impact of the torture scandal on Obama's persuasiveness is felt in his inability to set an agenda for health care legislation. In September 2009, before a joint session of Congress, President Obama appealed to legislators to forego politics and pursue legislation: "The time for bickering is over. The time for games has passed. Now is the season for action. Now is when we must bring the best ideas of both parties together, and show the American people that we can still do what we were sent here to do. Now is the time to deliver on health care." In the middle of the president's speech, Representative Joe Wilson from South Carolina interrupted, shouting "You lie!" This was an outburst that shows, for all his eloquence, that the president was hardly persuasive. Reactions from other members of Congress throughout the speech provided further evidence of partisanship. For instance, when Obama states, "I will not stand by while the special interests use the same old tactics to keep things exactly the way they are," he is applauded loudly by Democrats, but not by Republicans. Republicans also respond coolly to his remark that, "If you misrepresent what's in the plan, we will call you out. And I will not accept the status quo as a solution. Not this time. Not now." This is not to say Obama did not make any efforts to persuade Republicans. He did. In particular, he addressed each political party directly:

> To my progressive friends, I would remind you that for decades, the driving idea behind reform has been to end insurance company abuses and make coverage affordable for those without it. The public option is only a means to that end—and we should remain open to other ideas that accomplish our ultimate goal. And to my Republican friends, I say that rather than making wild claims about a government takeover of health care, we should work together to address any legitimate concerns you may have.[32]

While the appeal itself may not be persuasive because it provides neither reasons nor motivations, Obama does appeal for cooperation:

> I understand how difficult this health care debate has been. I know that many in this country are deeply skeptical that government is looking out for them. I understand that the politically safe move would be to kick the can further down the road—to defer reform one more year, or one more election, or one more term. But that's not what the moment calls for. That's not what we came here to do. We did not come to fear the future. We came here to shape it. I still believe we can act even when it's hard. I still believe we can

replace acrimony with civility, and gridlock with progress. I still believe we can do great things, and that here and now we will meet history's test. Because that is who we are. That is our calling. That is our character."[33]

Obama's turn to a character-based appeal invited those in Congress to rise above their disagreements to work toward passing a health care bill that reflects their collective commitment to the social good of all Americans. Obama appealed further to the character of those in Congress when he invoked a letter he received from the late Senator Ted Kennedy (D-Mass). Obama recalled that Kennedy characterized health care reform as "that great unfinished business of our society."[34] Reading from the letter, Obama expanded his appeal to Congress's character: "He [Kennedy] repeated the truth that health care is decisive for our future prosperity, but he also reminded me that 'it concerns more than material things.' 'What we face,' he wrote, 'is above all a moral issue; at stake are not just the details of policy, but fundamental principles of social justice and the character of our country.'"[35]

In this speech, Obama maintained his integrity, he refused sovereignty, and he appealed to the character of members of Congress and to the character of the country to remain true to his agenda. How much was in the speech on health care reform that persuaded Republicans in Congress to vote for such reform is another question. It is no small task to raise the level of rhetoric from rationalizing the sovereignty of the decider to encouraging the character of everyone. More is required for people to hear such presidential rhetoric than the president merely speaking.

CONCLUSION

When the images of torture at Abu Ghraib were made public, the Bush administration characterized the torture as the actions of "a few bad apples." In the waning days of the Bush administration, it became apparent that the use of torture was sanctioned by a policy decision that was both because of "a few bad apples," and to sanction the actions of those few bad apples." For President Obama, who immediately reversed the Bush administration's policy on torture, the decision to not release images of the sanctioned use of torture was a critical rhetorical moment. It was a moment in which Obama opposed the demand for accountability, and turned it into a need for credibility and stability. This moment is important to rhetoric in that it reveals the limits of rhetorical action and the boundaries of credibility. In denouncing the use of torture, Obama could not claim that torture was either the responsibility of a few bad apples or the fault of an institution. People were responsible, and the institution was at fault. The authority of presidential rhetoric had been undone.

Returning to my suggestion at the beginning of this chapter that Obama is more eloquent, but less persuasive, than Bush, it should be clear I do not mean to suggest Bush was at all persuasive. Instead, invoking the sovereign role of the decider, Bush's pursuit of the War on Terror mismanaged the resources of persuasion made available through the institutionalization of presidential rhetoric. Bush's decisions undid the connection between accountability and responsibility, upon which agency is constructed and through which persuasion is pursued. The implications for understanding Obama's rhetoric are not that Obama is unpersuasive in his deployment of the expansive presidential rhetoric he inherited from his predecessor. The implications are instead that Obama's restraint in his use of presidential rhetoric is a challenge to and challenged by the prior administration's expansive use of presidential rhetoric. Obama's more restrained and more deliberative rhetoric only appears less persuasive because it is less manipulative and less coercive. Obama's rhetoric instantiates persuasion as the product of deliberation between rhetorical agents, rather than of sovereign agents making decisions. Obama's rhetoric, rather than claiming authority and abnegating responsibility, encourages the kinds of identification and participation that are productive in a democracy. Unfortunately, as Obama's health care speech suggests, the success of this kind of rhetoric depends on the character of all those involved in the deliberations.

NOTES:

1. Jeffrey Tulis. *The Rhetorical Presidency.* Princeton, NJ: Princeton UP, 1987, 181.

2. Elvin T. Lim. *The Anti-Intellectual Presidency: The Decline of Presidential Rhetoric from George Washington to George W. Bush.* Oxford: Oxford U P, 2012, 55

3. Ibid.

4. Ibid., 116.

5. See "Bush: 'I'm the Decider' on Rumsfeld," CNN. Com April 18, 2006, http://www.cnn.com/2006/POLITICS/04/18/rumsfeld/

6. See Lynn Sweet, "Sweet blog special: Obama, reacting to NYT report Bush torture techniques, says "betrayal of our core values." *Sun Times* October 4, 2007, http://blogs.suntimes.com/sweet/2007/10/sweet_blog_special_obama_react.html

7. *The Concept of the Political.* Chicago: U of C P, 2007, 5.

8. David Cole, Ed. *The Torture Memos: Rationalizing the Unthinkable.* New York: The New Press, 2009, 80.

9. *Concept of the Political,* 7.

10. Tara McKelvey. *Monstering: Inside America's Policy on Secret Interrogations and Torture in the War on Terror.*

11. "Article 15-16 Investigation of the 800th Military Police Brigade," October 19, 2004, http://www.npr.org/iraq/2004/prison_abuse_report.pdf, 16.

12. Ibid., 17.

13. Donald Rumsfeld, "Memorandum for the Commander, US Southern Command," April 16, 2003,http://texscience.org/reform/torture/rumsfeld-hill-2april03.pdf

14. William J. Haynes, "Counter-Resistance Techniques" Action Memo. November 27, 2002, http://www.gwu.edu/~nsarchiv/NSAEBB/NSAEBB127/02.12.02.pdf, 1.

15. Jim Garamone. "Rumsfeld Accepts Responsibility for Abu Ghraib," May 7, 2004, American Forces Press Service, http://www.defense.gov/news/newsarticle.aspx?id=26511

16. Ibid.

17. Bush memo on "Humane Treatment of Taliban and Al Qaeda Detainees," February http://www.pegc.us/archive/White_House/bush_memo_20020207_ed.pdf

18. John Ashcroft. Letter from U.S. Attorney General John Ashcroft to Pres. George W. Bush on the status of Taliban detainees under the Geneva Convention. 1 February 2002. http://news.findlaw.com/wsj/docs/torture/jash20102ltr.html

19. Ibid.

20. Ibid., 2.

21. Philip G. Zimbardo. *The Lucifer Effect.* New York: Random House, 2008.

22. Stephen Reicher and Alexander Haslam. *Rethinking the Psychology of Tyranny, BBC Prison Study, British Journal of Social Psychology* 45:1, 2006, http://www.holah.co.uk/study/reicherhaslam/

23. Ibid.

24. Cole, *Torture Memos*, 1.

25. John Yoo letter to Albert Gonzales, August 1, 2002, http://www.justice.gov/olc/docs/memo-gonzales-aug1.pdf

26. John Dean. "Beyond the Pale: The Newly Released, Indefensible Office of Legal Counsel Terror Memos," *FindLaw*, March, 6, 2009, http://writ.news.findlaw.com/dean/20090306.html.

27. NBCnews.com, "Obama names intel picks, vows no torture," January, 1 2009, http://www.msnbc.msn.com/id/28574408.

28. Peters, Gerhard, and John T. Woolley, "Obama: Torture and secrecy betray core American values," *The American Presidency Project*, October 4, 2007, http://www.presidency.ucsb.edu/ws/?pid=91016.

29. Alex J. Bellamy, *Fighting Terror: Ethical Dilemmas.* London: Zed Books, 2008, 27.

30. Scott Wilson. "Obama Shifts on Abuse Photos" The Washington Post. 14 May 2009. http://www.washingtonpost.com/wpdyn/content/article/2009/05/13/AR2009051301751.html

31. "Decision Betrays Commitment to Transparency and the Rule of Law." ACLU Press Release, 13 May 2009, http://www.aclu.org/national-security/obama-administration-reverses-promise-release-torture-photos

32. "Obama Health Care Speech to Congress," New York Times, September 9, 2009, http://www.nytimes.com/2009/09/10/us/politics/10obama.text.html?pagewanted=all

33. Ibid.

34. Ted Kennedy quoted in "Obama Health Care"

35. "Obama Heath Care"

8 THE SPECTER OF *NUESTRA AMÉRICA:* BARACK OBAMA, LATIN AMERICA AND THE 2009 SUMMIT OF THE AMERICAS

René Agustin De los Santos

On April 17th, 2009, three months after his inauguration as U.S. President, Barack Obama delivered the opening remarks of the "Fifth Summit of the Americas" Conference, held at Trinidad and Tobago. The speech, his first as president, aimed directly at the hemisphere's leaders and was a highly anticipated event. In his remarks, the president was expected to outline a new vision for how his nation would engage with the Americas. Many questions abounded not only about what the new president would say, but how he would react to what many expected would be a strong anti-American climate at the Summit.[1]

Adding to the complexity of the rhetorical moment were two developments that further threatened Obama's beautillion: the growing, global financial crisis that was beginning to wreak havoc across the Americas and the sudden, shocking resignation of Fidel Castro as Cuba's president on February 18th. The mounting financial crisis had hit the Americas hard, and threatened what had been the fastest economic growth rates in the world. Now those gains were threatened by a downturn that, as Inter-American Development Bank President Luis Alberto Moreno said, "is the hemisphere's first economic crisis not made in Latin America."[2] (qtd. in Whatley).

Just as important was the sudden resignation of Fidel Castro as Cuba's president on February 18th. The political exit of Castro, long considered the gadfly of U.S. and Latin American relations, would come to dominate many of the debates and the news at the Summit. The new political reality of a Cuba *sans* Castro encouraged many leaders at the Summit to speak out against America's influence in the region more forcefully than in years past. Argentinean President Cristina Kirchner, for instance, actively demanded the end of the 1962 U.S. Embargo against Cuba, underscoring the "absurdity that the Embargo today signifies for our sister Republic of Cuba . . . we ask today for its termination."[3] Venezuelan President Hugo Chávez also joined in criticizing American influence, blasting Obama for being a "poor ignoramus" for failing to "read and study a little to understand [the] reality" of the region and promising to veto any declaration as protest for Cuba's exclusion from the summit."[4]

While presidential rhetoric still holds an important oratorical, public, and pathos-driven function, the complexity of this international rhetorical moment demands that we not overlook or downplay how such rhetoric also aims to define political realities in national and international contexts. President Obama's speech, with its proposal of a new "equal partnership" based on "mutual respect and common interests and shared values," especially asks us to rethink the function of the "rhetorical presidency" beyond what is sometimes perceived as its largely ceremonial and negative impact on national rhetorical life.[5]

In this chapter, my aim is to use an analysis of Obama's 2009 Summit speech to reconnect the "institutional" or "definitional" nature of presidential rhetoric with its more pathos-driven or public nature, as outlined by rhetoric scholars such as Jeffrey Tulis and Robert E. Denton, Jr.[6] Using David Zarefsky's work as a launching point, I posit that while the *character* of presidential rhetoric has changed (and there is no denying that the American presidency possesses an increasingly celebrity status), its *institutional function* (i.e., the power of presidential rhetoric to define political reality) has not only survived, but it remains one of its key, yet most neglected or ignored, attributes.[7] In Obama's speech, we find the president attempting to juggle both of these dimensions as he draws upon his ethos as an agent of change. As Obama himself puts it, "As has already been noted, and I think my presence here indicates, the United States has changed over time" in order to define new *identifications* (points of psychological contact) with his Latin American audience based on what he calls an "equal partnership," where there is "no senior partner and junior partner in our relations."[8]

When set against the backdrop of collapsing regional economies and Fidel Castro's sudden resignation, Obama's speech reveals that what a president *does* (i.e., define political reality) and how such *doing* is understood and framed within deeply, often unconsciously, held worldviews with their own rhetorics that function to define reality and give such doing meaning and value. When a president speaks to a national audience, he can often rely on a relatively shared worldview between him and his audience. This is not always the case in international settings, as in this instance. In this case, these twin developments underscore how Obama's summit speech missed how these developments brought to the forefront certain historical memories in his audience that could not simply be overcome by an appeal to shared values like "liberty" and "justice." The issue is not simply that people across the Americas regarded Castro's resignation as a reason for the U.S. to lift an embargo they had always felt was imperialist, or that some leaders did not believe in concepts such as "capitalism" or "free markets." Rather, it was the worldview implicitly guiding Obama's proposal, as well as the material and symbolic conditions of this worldview that added to the anxiety many Latin American leaders expressed in the weeks and months following the Summit.

What the dual realities of Castro's resignation and the faltering global economy thus reveal is that despite Obama's best efforts to draw upon shared sets of identifications—what he calls "bedrock values"—these events divulge how his rhetoric is grounded upon and fundamentally hampered by a world view that had long situated Latin America negatively within a duality of "barbarism-civilization." This duality has operated in the American and European consciousness since at least the mid-nineteenth century, and has historically located Latin America as the "barbaric" other in relation to the more "civilized" Europe and United States. The power of this definitional rhetoric cannot be underestimated. It has grounded the rationale of US and European intervention into Latin America's affairs for decades. This rhetoric, precisely because of its ubiquity and insidiousness, greatly undermines Obama's appeal to "bedrock values." It reinforces the very unequal relationship the president attempted to overcome with his proposal. Ironically, the same economic and political conditions that made it possible for Obama to appeal to shared values were also the conditions that prevented him from fully sharing these values with his audience.

It is precisely because of Obama's location within this "barbarism-civilization" dualism that we are also reminded that it is but one of two major hemispheric rhetorics that have informed how people in the region have historically understood U.S.-Latin American relations. This other rhetoric emanates from *nuestra América* (i.e., Latin America), and was developed out of the realities that shape and have been shaped by Latin America. This other rhetoric situates the battle not between civilization and barbarism, but between European and American cultures. It received its first coherent articulation in the work of the Cuban artist and hero, José Martí (1853–1895).

These subtle, yet key differences between hemispheric rhetorics deserves closer attention, the differences reveal not just how Obama missed some of the rhetorical nuances presented by Castro's resignation and the hemisphere's growing economic troubles, but it also reveals some of the deep tensions that exist between the *character* of the U.S. presidency and the ability of the office to continue defining political reality in the Western hemisphere. The terms "character" and "ethos," one's ability to persuade others of one's commitment to a common good, are often used interchangeably. As I highlight, one limitation and danger of the "barbarism-civilization" rhetoric is that it renders any reality that falls outside of its explanatory and legitimizing power as invisible, irrelevant, and/or doomed to failure. That President Obama neglected to even mention the Mercado Común del Sur (MERCOSUR) in his speech reveals both the limits of this "barbarism-civilization" rhetoric and the ongoing tensions between this rhetoric and the competing worldview offered by *nuestra América*.

To make this argument, this chapter moves in three major sections. First, I provide a brief overview of Jeffrey Tulis's concept of the rhetorical presidency, drawing on David Zarefsky's work as a way of reinserting the "institutional" function (i.e., defining political reality) back into our considerations of this model. Second, I provide readers with an overview of the historic relationship between the United States and Latin America that highlights how the duality of Castro's resignation and the emerging global economic crisis reveals a long-standing tension between competing hemispheric rhetorics that has framed how Americans and Latin Americans have both defined their relationship.

This tension, as it is exemplified in the writings of Latin American writers José Martí and Roberto Fernández Retamar, exists as a rhetorical conflict between competing and ultimately irreconcilable ways of understanding and relating to American hegemony. The importance of highlighting this tension helps us better understand not only Obama's audience but also how Obama's rhetoric failed to fully address the rhetorical requirements of this audience. Third, I return to Obama's Summit speech and engage in a rhetorical analysis that focuses on how he sought to redefine the future of U.S.-Latin American relations. I read his speech in light of the tensions highlighted in the second section. When Obama's speech is read with these tensions in mind, it reveals the complex nature of the rhetorical presidency when articulated in international settings.

The Rhetorical Presidency

To help frame my analysis, I provide a short overview of recent scholarship on presidential rhetoric. In such scholarship, Jeffrey Tulis's notion of the "rhetorical presidency" remains an important concept. To use the influential words of Tulis, "popular or mass rhetoric" is now understood as a "principal

tool of presidential governance" that cannot be ignored or even underestimated.[9] Too often, as David A. Crockett reminds us, "Both fans and critics
of *The Rhetorical Presidency* treat the work as though it were principally concerned with political communication."[10] This literature suggests that rhetorical presidents must garner popular support for their public policies and/or
policy agendas as a prerequisite for successfully implementing these policies
via congressional approval. For Richard Ellis, this transformation reflects
the democratization of the presidency. Conversely, for scholars like Tulis and
Richard Denton, this shift instead often denotes a negative, an erosion of
traditional forms of governance that has even led Stephen J. Harnett and
Jennifer Rose Merceicia to proclaim the death of the rhetorical presidency
and the rise of "post-rhetorical presidency," aimed at "imperial deception,
cheerful dissimulation, and deadly distraction"[11]

Despite the important insights that this scholarship offers, much of this
scholarship operates under a narrow view of "presidential rhetoric" and "effect."[12] On the one hand is the perception that presidential rhetoric operates
under a "limited effects" model that has characterized media research for the
past half century. As Zarefsky reminds us, "Whereas people earlier had been
concerned that mass media were like a hypodermic needle with which audiences were injected with strong doses of propaganda, the empirical research
generally found that mediated messages had little effect at all."[13]

For Zarefsky, these positions offer too narrow an understanding of the
"process of communication and the nature of rhetorical transactions."[14] The
field of rhetorical studies, by and large, Zarefsky argues, offers different ontological assumptions and relies on a more complex view of the rhetorical
transaction. Instead of predictability and control, rhetoric studies emphasizes contingency and choice: "According to this view, the rhetor (speaker
or writer) makes choices, with an audience in mind, about the best way to
achieve his or her goals in the context of a specific situation."[15] Central to
our concerns here is that in this characterization of rhetoric, social reality is
not a "given; it is chosen from a plethora of multiple possibilities and hence
could have always been otherwise. Whatever meanings prevail will depend
on the choices made by political actors as they actively participate in shaping
and giving meaning to their environment and they do so primarily by naming situations within it."[16] Offering alternative meanings (for any number of
reasons) is not always an easy or straightforward proposition, but it is always
possible. For Zarefsky, what presidential rhetoric *does* in the world—and this
is key to our approach—is that "it defines political reality."[17]

Zarefsky's definition helps open a space to understand the complexity
of Obama's Summit speech to fellow American leaders. While naming or
defining a situation is not the same as persuasion, the prominent political

position of the president (and for that matter, any national leader) becomes important in shaping the context in which the public views events or proposals. What this underscores for our purposes is that, even as the modern presidency has become "more" rhetorical, it cannot be reduced to mere "imperial deception, cheerful dissimulation, and deadly distraction."[18] In the specific case of Obama's Summit speech, his presidential rhetoric matters not only because it possessed the potential to persuade his audience; more importantly, his rhetoric matters for how it participated in a larger context of relations, histories, and among other leaders working to define the future of U.S.-Latin American relations.

Regardless of Obama's sentiments towards the region, he, like all American politicians, undertook definitional work under very powerful conditions set by the prevailing rhetorics of the time, with the "barbarism-civilization" dualism being one of the most powerful. This does not mean that Obama's administration (or Obama himself) is dishonest in its/his attempts to radically transform U.S.-Latin American relations, but underscores that we cannot forget that it/he is ultimately an "American" administration/president, and that this reality possesses certain institutional and rhetorical constraints that he himself cannot override or ignore without major consequences.

U.S.-Latin American Relations: An Overview

To represent the rhetorical context of Obama's speech, I turn to a review of U.S.-Latin American relations. One of the greatest symbolic and material constraints upon any U.S. president, including Obama, continues to be the legacy of U.S.-Latin American relations. According to historian Stephen G. Rabe, these relations have largely been defined by a history of "hard" and "soft" intervention by the United States into the affairs of its southern neighbors. Rabe points out:

> Modern U.S. policy toward Latin America can be divided into five distinct periods. From 1895 to 1901, the United States established its supremacy or hegemony in the Western Hemisphere. From 1901 to 1933, under the aegis of the Platt Amendment (1901) and the Roosevelt Corollary to the Monroe Doctrine (1904), the United States repeatedly intervened militarily in the affairs of Mexico and Caribbean and Central American nations. From 1933 to 1945, with its Good Neighbor policy, the United States renounced the right of intervention in Latin America but expected Latin Americans to accept U.S. leadership. After World War II, the United States interpreted its relations with its southern

neighbors through the prism of the Cold War and the U.S. confrontation with the Soviet Union. Since 1989–1991, in the aftermath of the end of the Cold War and the collapse of the Soviet Union, U.S. policy makers have worried less about foreign influences in the Western Hemisphere and focused on issues such as trade, immigration, and the illegal narcotics trade.[19]

How U.S. presidents have rationalized these interventions is worthy of attention. While there is an obvious spectrum, such as the "big stick" militaristic diplomacy of Theodore Roosevelt and FDR's more benevolent "Good Neighbor" policy, the governing impulse driving U.S. intervention since the nineteenth century has aimed at "exercising predominant influence in the region and limiting the freedom of action of Latin American nations."[20] Serving to legitimize such influence and limiting freedom has been a worldview that perceives U.S.-Latin American relations as a struggle between American "civilization" on the one hand, and its "barbaric" southern neighbors on the other. Under this dualism, the United States sees bringing civilization to Latin America's unwashed masses as its "burden." Such efforts have sought to replace Latin America's "savage races" with a more desirable, "civilized" subject, a process that would either be accomplished through direct military intervention or through a plethora of benevolent "development" programs.

Significant for our concerns is how this hemispheric rhetoric also became central to how Latin American political and intellectual elites came to define their own national and pan-Latino identities, in addition to forming their understanding of their northern neighbors.[21] As philosopher Elizabeth Millán-Zaibert points out, "the barbarism-civilization dilemma . . . locked the non-Europeans [i.e., Latin Americans] into a permanent state of barbarism, a position that necessitated the civilizing procedures so eagerly offered by the Europeans."[22] For many Latin American elites, the American continent offers little "originality," a perception that reduces Latin American thought, culture, and history to second-rate or even third-rate copies of French, German, or Anglo societies. Latin America's salvation is thus found not within its own experience, its geography, or its connection to its Iberian past, but through adopting foreign philosophies (e.g., positivism) and economic programs. This eagerness to look outside *nuestra América* is especially evident in the writing of intellectuals like Argentine writer, Domingo Faustino Sarmiento (1811–1888), who saw in Europe and European immigration a blueprint for how Argentina (and by extension, Latin America) could shake off its perpetual "backwardness." For Sarmiento, the struggle for Argentine national character was an epic battle between the "barbarities" of the countryside versus the "civilizing" influence of the (European/Europeanized) city. In this struggle, barbarism was winning; hence Sarmiento's urgency to strongly intervene in his nation's development. As Sarmiento insisted, the solution was to look towards European (specifically, German, Italian, Swiss, and French) immigration as the "principal element of order and morality"[23] that would, over time, disrupt the "predominance of brute force" of a barbaric "authority with no limits," and help inspire and teach Argentineans to be civilized.[24]

From this hemisphere there has also emerged an "other" rhetoric, perhaps best exemplified in the works of Cuban writer José Martí (1853–1895). This "other" rhetoric emerged during the "most aggressive phase" of Theodore Roosevelt's political career, a moment that many Latin Americans saw as a deep threat to the cultural and political voice of Latin America. Almost a decade before the Spanish-American War, Martí warned of the emerging danger posed by the United States: "The hour is near when she [Latin America] will be approached by an enterprising and forceful nation that will demand intimate relations with her, though it does not know her and disdains her."[25] For Martí, Latin America needed to repudiate the "barbarism-civilization" dualism and reorient relations between Latin America and the United States under frameworks developed in and by Latin Americans themselves:

> How can our governors emerge from the universities when there is not a university in America that teaches the most basic element of the art of governing, which is the analysis of all that is unique to the peoples of America? Our youth go out into the world wearing Yankee-or French-colored glasses and aspire to rule by guesswork a country they do not know. Those unacquainted with the rudiments of politics should not be allowed to embark on a career in politics.[26]

This other rhetoric argued for a *nuestra América* ("an our America"), a movement that provided a new orientation point, "a rallying cry to unify the continent in its struggle against the expansive empire of the North."[27] For Martí, the urgent duty of our America (i.e., Latin America) "was to show herself as she is, one in soul and intent, rapidly overcoming the crushing weight of her past and stained only by the fertile blood shed by hands that do battle against ruins and by veins that were punctured by our former masters."[28]

Thus, José Martí helped situate the battle as between European and American cultures not as a battle between civilization and barbarism. Martí opened up a subtle, yet profound conceptual shift that has allowed Latin America to emerge from under the model of "inefficiency," backwardness," and "lack" set up by the rhetoric of the American and European "barbarism-civilization" dualism. What is key here is that the rhetoric of *nuestra América* does not rely upon, and in fact does not need, American and/or European recognition to operate and succeed. Such rhetoric permits Latin America to imagine a world otherwise. This has been especially evident in the meetings of MERCOSUR, the South American trade association established in 1991. In closing the thirtieth summit of MERCOSUR, for instance, Brazilian President Luiz Inacio Lula da Silva directly invokes the spirit of Martí by claiming that "Many still don't realize that we have changed the political profile of *our* America, and we are changing the social profile."[29] Two years later, Raúl Castro drew upon Martí's legacy as he reaffirmed his nation's "supportive spirit to work with [fellow MERCOSUR leaders] towards the unity of these nations that José Martí defined as Our America."[30]

Despite this, many Americans, including Barack Obama—as we shall soon see—remain oblivious or downplay the impact of this other rhetoric, choosing instead to continue operating strictly under the definitional realities and parameters provided by a model of "barbarism-civilization."

"To move forward, we cannot let ourselves be prisoners of past disagreements."

To reveal these tensions, I turn to a focused analysis of Obama's Summit speech. In his speech, tensions between the rhetoric of "barbarism-civilization" and *nuestra América* are evident, especially in how President Obama understands and represents the history of U.S.-Latin American relations to his audience. According to Obama, what has hindered full and equal cooperation in the past has been a plethora of "past disagreements" caused by "stale debates":

> To move forward, we cannot let ourselves be prisoners of past disagreements. I am very grateful that President Ortega—I'm grateful that President Ortega did not blame me for things that happened when I was three months old. Too often, an opportunity to build a fresh partnership of the Americas been undermined by stale debates. And we've heard all these arguments before, these debates that would have us make a false choice between rigid, state-run economies or unbridled and unregulated capitalism; between blame for right-wing paramilitaries or left-wing insurgents; between sticking to inflexible policies with regard to Cuba or denying the full human rights that are owed to the Cuban people.[31]

While President Obama is very careful to distinguish between a "them" (who are just as likely to be American as Latin American) who offer stale debates, and an "us" who are forced to make a "false choice," or take blame for the actions of extremists, he also aims to reinforce the philosophic, economic, and political superiority of his liberal democratic, capitalist model over other competing policies and models.

What operates implicitly here is an argument positing that: (a) while there are other competing models, they are clearly European or American (i.e., not Latin American) in origin and design; and (b) those who are against the American liberal democratic, capitalist model are on the "wrong side" of history. I argue that both of these implicit claims work together to reinforce, and are reinforced by, the rhetoric of the "barbarism-civilization" dualism informing Obama's speech and worldview. Thus, even as Obama does not refer to Latin Americans as barbaric, he nonetheless defines them as needing guidance from their more "civilized" northern neighbor. While Obama operates under what could be called a gentle form of this dualism, its effects are, arguably, just as damaging for Latin America.

In Obama's rhetoric, his definition of "our America" is inherently founded on a view that holds American notions and practices of democracy and economy as the *gold standard*. The validity of this claim is unquestioned, and is offered, like many cases of presidential definitions, as if it "were natural and uncontroversial rather than chosen and contestable."[32] Conversely, and within this rhetoric, Latin America has continually lagged behind, sometimes by adopting erroneous political theories (e.g., Cuba and Venezuela), or through its own innate, violent nature. This claim is also offered matter-of-factly, and one could argue whether these two definitions are right or wrong. The point is, as Zarefesky reminds us, "in defining the situation, [Obama] makes no explicit argument."[33] The historic realities that ground such "facts" are what they are, whether or not people agree with them.

These definitions allow Obama to ground his proposal and the solutions it offers as natural, even obvious: "I'm here to launch a new chapter of engagement that will be sustained throughout my administration."[34] That it is his nation and his administration that will launch this new chapter is telling, for it emerges out of a "barbarism-civilization" rhetoric that presupposes his nation's right and duty to lead. This rhetoric does not ask if the hemisphere wishes to launch a new chapter with the U.S., or ask what this new form of engagement should look like.

Let's explore this point a little further. In relation to Cuba, Obama argues that he is "prepared to have [his] administration engage with the Cuban government on a wide range of issues—from drugs, migration, and economic issues, to human rights, free speech, and democratic reform."[35] As Obama makes clear, it is his nation that will set the parameters and the tone of the engagement. If other issues exist, they are made irrelevant and invisible through Obama's subtle demarcation of what counts as the "wide range of issues" his administration is prepared to discuss.

The nations within the hemisphere itself—comprised of nations with their own, Western-style democracies and economies—are defined as "dull copies" (using Fernández Retamar's term) in comparison to the United States. Unable to combat Latin American phenomena such as "kingpins" and "kidnappings" on their own soil, the United States must come to the rescue:

> Yesterday, President Calderón of Mexico and I renewed our commitment to combat the dangers posed by drug cartels. Today, I want to announce a new initiative to invest $30 million to strengthen cooperation on security in the Caribbean. And I have directed key members of my Cabinet to build and sustain relations with their counterparts in the hemisphere to constantly adjust our tactics, to build upon best practices, and develop new modes of cooperation—because the United States is a friend of every nation and person who seeks a future of security and dignity.[36]

Obama's proposal offers the region a way out of its current dilemmas via the direct guidance of the United States. That this guidance is offered benevolently in order to address mutual hemispheric problems, or as part of an equal partnership, does not diminish how Obama defines *how* each "partner" comes into the new relationship. Outlined in Obama's speech is a clear hierarchy between these supposedly "equal" partners. Obama makes clear that while his nation will propose and act—he outlines four areas where "the United States is committed already to strengthening collective action on behalf of our shared goals"[37]—his audience of fellow American leaders should assent: e.g., "renew the common stake that we have in one another" and "act on behalf of shared goals."[38] While these possibilities are very action-oriented, they nonetheless reinforce and re-posit Latin America as a follower and a dependent player in the region. It is Latin America—not the U.S.—that must rise to the level of equal partnership. It is the U.S.—not Latin America—that holds all the answers and ideas. Latin America may have a more equal place at Obama's table, but it is the United States that still determines how the table is set.

Obama did not stop there. Central to supporting his argument above is positing a major overhaul of how the hemisphere understands its own colonial past and its relationship to the United States. In relation to the colonial past, Obama states, "Every nation has been on its own journey. . . . Our nations were all colonized by empires and achieved our own liberation."[39] By not providing details in support of this claim, Obama implicitly places all American nations *ex aequo* in relation to their colonial pasts and their political liberations. In making this point, Obama indirectly forwards a controversial claim (at least in this hemisphere) as fact. Obama's definition erases all nuances of the historical record, especially the key role that Europe and the United States played and continues to play in intervening in the process of nation-building in Latin America.[40]

This redefinition of the region's colonial past reaffirms the "barbarism-colonialism" model Obama implicitly worked under, for it posited as uncontroversial and unquestioned that his nation's historical prosperity and Latin America's "backwardness" are simply a product of their unfettered and distinct journeys. Moreover, this redefinition clears a path for Obama to offer what he believes must be the future of U.S.-Latin American relations. Key to this future relation is that Latin America must let go of "past disagreements": "And so I think it's important to remind my fellow leaders that it's not just the United States that has to change. All of us have responsibilities to look towards the future."[41] A key component looking "towards the future" is for Latin America to change its attitude towards it northern neighbor: "The United States will be willing to acknowledge past errors where those errors have been made. We will be partners in helping to alleviate poverty. But the American people have to get some positive reinforcement if they are to be engaged in the efforts to lift other countries out of the poverty that they're experiencing."[42]

Like a big brother admonishing his younger siblings, Obama also chides his Latin American colleagues. His nation is offering solutions based on what Obama suggests is an inherent "goodness" that compels them to "lift other countries out of the poverty"; but it is up to Latin America not to derail this plan through negativity.

What that "positive reinforcement" needs to consist of is clear in the next few passages of his speech, where Obama underscores that providing "positive reinforcement" is centered on questions of the past. For Obama, it is clear that *debating* the past—not necessarily the past itself—is the main obstacle to overcome: "I didn't come here to debate the past—I came here to deal with the future."[43] To dwell on the past is to unduly saddle his nation and the region with having to deal with "stale debates" that do not help in preparing and acting in the future: "I believe, as some of our previous speakers have stated, that we must learn from history, but we can't be trapped by it."[44] What the present moment needs is a clear mind towards attaining the solutions that his "new sense of partnership" is extending to the region.

Obama is savvy enough to not completely dismiss the past and its lessons. According to the president, people and nations should "recognize" their past deeds (e.g., "I think it's important to recognize, given historic suspicions, that the United States' policy should not be interference in other countries"), but once they are acknowledged, any recourse to the past by aggrieved parties, especially as a resource to assign blame, is rendered frivolous and without merit: "but that also means that we can't blame the United States for every problem that arises in the hemisphere. That's part of the bargain. That's part of the change that has to take place."[45]

To help cement this argument, Obama directly appeals to his own ethos. While Obama had never set foot in Latin America, his life story is well-known and respected throughout the hemisphere.[46] Rhetorically, Obama's candidacy and election offered him an opportunity to closely inject himself into the historic and ongoing racial dynamics and struggles of the hemisphere: "All of us are extraordinarily excited to have this opportunity to visit this wonderful country–and as somebody who grew up on an island, I can tell you I feel right at home." [47] Moreover, it allows him to posit his relationship to his nation as the example of how the hemisphere should behave towards the United States:

> As has already been noted, and I think my presence here
> indicates, the United States has changed over time. It has
> not always been easy, but it has changed. And so I think it's
> important to remind my fellow leaders that it's not just the
> United States that has to change. All of us have responsibili-
> ties to look towards the future.[48]

Devoid of any nuance and specifics, Obama presents his nation's "change" as something not "easy," but as something nonetheless natural of a civilized nation as it moves through time. While it can be argued that the context of the Summit was not the venue to tease out the complexity of U.S. racial history, Obama's account implies that the major responsibility is primarily "towards the future."

Such a move not only seeks to mark a clear distinction between members of his audience, but it also reveals that this distinction is grounded in the dualist rhetoric of "barbarism-civilization." On the one hand, Obama clearly delineates members of his audience who appear unwilling to "blame the United States for every problem that arises in the hemisphere."[49] This audience, through their applause, is posited on the side of progress and the future. By contrast are members of his audience mired in "stale debates." This other audience, through its insistence on debating America's past errors, promises to stifle or derail any chance of a new partnership. There is no hope for this audience. In case there are any doubts who is in this second group, Obama makes it clear: "I am very grateful that President Ortega—I'm grateful that President Ortega did not blame me for things that happened when I was three months old."[50] Ortega, along with other "Cold War" relics like Castro and their successor, Hugo Chávez of Venezuela, are posited as outside the "right" side of history.

CONCLUSIONS: BEYOND "BARBARISM-CIVILIZATION"

As I have argued, as a rhetoric of definition, Obama's Summit speech offers compelling support for Zarefsky's claims. While his speech will need further support through a variety of other symbolic, material, and institutional acts, his rhetoric nonetheless stands as a powerful statement for how his administration redefines relations with Latin America during his tenure. Given both the office and the nation Obama represents, competing claims will have to address his rhetoric, even if just to point out its limitations and constraints.

How a president defines political reality does not occur in a vacuum, but is implicitly and explicitly grounded in a worldview that helps provide such efforts with meaning and value. This is a point that Zarefsky hints at, but doesn't discuss beyond the concept of "frame shifting." For Zarefsky, a frame shift is "postulating a different frame of reference from the one in which the subject normally is viewed. The effect is that people see the thing in a 'different light' and their attitudes about it therefore change."[51] In Obama's case, it can be argued that his speech engages in a kind of "frame shift," especially in his effort to redefine for his audience what "moving forward" requires of them.

However, the great shadow cast by both Castro's resignation, and by the hemispheric economic downturn, asks us to reconsider such straightforward conclusions. As the context of Obama's speech makes clear, a worldview is but one of many potential worldviews that an audience may have and that a rhetor must contend with. Thus, while a president's words may define *a* reality, there may be a competing worldview that can be argued otherwise. Specifically, these two events remind us that while the rhetoric of "barbarism-civilization" remains an enticing rhetoric for Latin Americans, they have also organized themselves around the rhetoric offered by Martí's *nuestra América*, as evidenced by Castro's long rule, the Andean Community of Nations (CAN), MERCOSUR, the Zapatista Army of National Liberation (EZLN), and the leadership of Hugo Chávez and Evo Morales.

Martí's "other" rhetoric, and its instantiation in the material world (e.g., CAN, MERCOSUR, etc.), helps us understand the intrinsic tensions that Castro's resignation and the hemisphere's economic downturn bring to the surface. Despite current economic ills throughout the region, for instance, countries within the hemisphere have been actively working together to offer another vision of how hemispheric (and global) economies can work. That Obama does not publicly recognize this effort can be explained either as arrogance or as ignorance on the part of the U.S. president. However, when this oversight is understood from a "barbarism-civilization" perspective, I believe other aspects come into focus.

Just like nineteenth-century American and European rhetorics of race and biology were unable to imagine a free Haiti without American or European input, the continued dominance in U.S. and European circles of the rhetoric of "barbarism-civilization" makes imagining a Latin America with MERCOSUR—a trade agreement between Latin American nations that does not always rely upon, and, in fact, does not need America or Europe to succeed—is unimaginable to Americans like Obama.

What Obama does not appear to understand is that for many Latin Americans, agreeing or not agreeing politically with Fidel Castro has never been the issue. His importance for many Latin Americans remains in what he symbolizes. In part, Castro symbolizes the triumph of Martí's rhetoric over American and European aggression throughout the region. More importantly, Castro's resignation also serves as a testament to the continued importance of Martí's vision for Latin America. That is, while Obama sees Castro's resignation as the end of an era, for many Latin Americans, it actually solidifies how another world is possible.

In this sense, Castro's resignation specifically serves to repudiate President Obama's ahistorical vision for the American continent. As Castro's legacy underscores, Martí's rhetoric values historical memory—not for its sense of nostalgia or epideictic (praise or blame) sensibilities, but as a key source of knowledge that would help guide Latin America's political, economic, and social agendas at home and in relation to the "empire of the North".[52] Central to this "other" rhetoric is a community of hemispheric subjects ("the new men of America") who, working together, could find, within the past, practical solutions to questions that plagued the hemisphere. It can be argued that Castro's resignation made clear to many Latin Americans the continued need to repudiate the "barbarism-civilization" dualism offered by Obama in order to reorient relations between Latin America and the United States as a battle situated as *commencing* between equal cultures. This rhetoric is in sharp contrast to the European/American "barbarism-civilization" model, understood in this contest as beginning with superior or "civilized" cultures on top, and inferior or "barbaric" cultures below. Martí's "other" rhetoric is not forwarded as a complete repudiation of America and Europe, but rather in recognition that if Latin America was to survive the "expansive empire of the North," the region had to find a *nuestra América* (a unique Latin American *being* and *doing* in the world) that would allow it to integrate into the world's economies on its own terms.

To conclude, when seen under Zarefsky's description, Obama's speech offers an impressive definitional shift in how the region must understand its history and its relationship with the United States. If ever fully adopted, it would radically transform U.S.-Latin American relations. Nonetheless, despite this conceptual frame shift, his proposal still only makes *sense* within the "barbarism-civilization" dualism that serves to support and rationalize Obama's proposal, even if his proposal is ultimately resisted. In other words, Obama's ability to postulate a different frame of reference, even in the broadest sense, is given meaning and value within a worldview or logic that he unquestionably believes. Partially, he is correct. For two centuries, the dominant "barbarism-civilization" dualism served to establish the conditions under which U.S.-Latin American relational frames make *sense* in the first place. However, despite Obama's stated aims to redefine relations on more equal terms, his rhetoric nonetheless takes for granted the dualism that has Latin America "infected by a hierarchy that [has] condemned segments of humanity to the lower rungs of existence, an existence of dependence and subordination."[53]

Because of this, Obama's rhetoric ultimately comes up short. While it offers a compelling redefinition of U.S.-Latin American relations, it does so without taking up what the legacy of Marti's vision might mean throughout the region, especially in the immediate developments presented by Castro's resignation and the hemisphere's economic downturn. Because of this, Obama is also unable to imagine another reality that may be offered in Marti's rhetoric for the future of U.S.-Latin American relations. That Obama could not have framed his arguments otherwise given his embeddedness within the rhetoric of "barbarism-civilization" is understood; nonetheless, it is precisely this inability to see the world otherwise that reveals deep tensions between the "rhetorical presidency" and its (in)ability to function *institutionally* (i.e., define political reality in Zarefsky's terms) in foreign contexts like Latin America.

NOTES

1. The Summit traces its origins to the First American International Conference of 1890, and first saw the light of day in 1994, "as a proposal from the United States government." Each Summit "has a theme or focus which identifies the priorities for the upcoming years as envisioned by the Government that is the host of the Summit in consultation with the other Member States," and the theme of the Fifth Summit of the Americas, held in Trinidad and Tobago, was "Securing Our Citizens' Future by Promoting Human Prosperity, Energy Security and Environmental Sustainability."

2. Stuart Whately "Summit of The Americas: Obama Seeks New Relations; Chavez Seeks Mischief; Regional Leaders Seek Conviviality." *Huffington Post*. 16 Apr. 2009. Web. 22 June 2012.

3. (translation mine; de Kirchner) de Kirchner, Cristina. "Speech by Cristina Fernández De Kirchner." *http://fifthsummitoftheamericas.org/official_statements%285%29.htm.* governmental. 2009. Web. 3 Sept. 2011.

4. Chávez as quoted in "Chavez: Obama 'A Poor Ignoramus.'" *Huffington Post.* 22 Mar. 2009. Web. 22 June 2012.

5. Jeffrey K. Tulis. *The Rhetorical Presidency.* Princeton U P, 1988. Print.

6. Denton's *On Deaf Ears: The Limits of the Bully Pulpit* (New Haven: Yale University Press, 2003).

7. An often repeated sentiment during the Summit, argued thusly, "The President of the United States is not an individual who you like or dislike; he is an institution."

8. Obama, "Remarks by the President at the Summit of the Americas Opening Ceremony" Summit of the Americas. Trinidad and Tobago. 2009. Speech.

9. Tulis, *The Rhetorical Presidency,* 4.

10. D. A. Crockett, "George W. Bush and the Unrhetorical Rhetorical Presidency." *Rhetoric & Public Affairs* 6.3 (2003), 467. Print.

11. Stephen J. Hartnett and Jennifer. R Merciea. "'A Discovered Dissembler Can Achieve Nothing Great'; Or, Four Theses on the Death of Presidential Rhetoric in an Age of Empire." *Presidential Studies Quarterly* 37.4 (2007), 600. Print.

12. David Zarefsky. "Presidential Rhetoric and the Power of Definition." *Presidential Studies Quarterly* 34.3 (2004): 608. Print.

13. Ibid.

14. Ibid.

15. Ibid., 608-9.

16. Ibid, 611.

17. Ibid.

18. Harnett and Merceicia, 600.

19. S. G. Rabe. "The Johnson Doctrine." *Presidential Studies Quarterly* 36.1 (2006): Print., 49.

20. Rabe, 48.

21. It does bear mentioning that the root of this rhetoric was "imposed by the trauma of the Spanish colonization of America" (Millán-Zaibert 151).

22. Elizabeth Millán-Zaibert. "A Great Vanishing Act? The Latin American Philosophical Tradition and How Ariel and Caliban Helped Save It from Oblivion." *CR: The New Centennial Review* 7.3 (2007): 157. Print.

23. Domingo Faustino Sarmiento. *Facundo: Civilization and Barbarism.* Trans., Kathleen Ross. Berkeley: U of California P, 2003. Print, 248.

24. Ibid., 50.

25. José Martí. "Our America,." *José Martí's Our America.* Web. 4 Apr. 2012.

26. Ibid.

27. Millán-Zaibert, 152.

28. Marti.

29. Lula cited in Patrick J. McDonnell. "Leftist Presidents Take Spotlight at Trade Summit." *Los Angeles Times* 22 July 2006. Web. 22 June 2012, italics mine.

30. Raúl Castro. "Address in the MERCOSUR Summit." *Cuba Debate.* 16 Dec. 2008. Web. 5 June 2012.

31. "Remarks by the President at the Summit of the Americas Opening Ceremony."

32. Zarefsky. "Presidential Rhetoric, 612.

33. Ibid.

34. "Remarks by the President at the Summit of the Americas Opening Ceremony."

35. Ibid.

36. Ibid.

37. Ibid.

38. The four interrelated areas are: coming "together on behalf of our common prosperity"; "Strengthen[ing] the foundation of our prosperity and our security and our environment through a new partnership on energy"; working "together to advance our common security"; and working to ensure "liberty and justice" throughout the region.

39. "Remarks by the President at the Summit of the Americas Opening Ceremony."

40· Partly, of course, the call to Latin America's leaders to "move on" is Obama's attempt to absolve the United States from any moral or legal obligation to the region. By minimizing its history of military, economic, and political interventions to the realm of "historic suspicions," there was no need to provide a full account of its interventions into Cuba (1906-1909; 1917-1933); Nicaragua (1907; 1912-1913; 1981-1990); Mexico (1914–1918); Dominican Republic (1916-1924); and Haiti (1914-1934). While Obama's perspective on history does not encourage complete historical amnesia, it nonetheless defines the past as something the present has no control over, and that the future has no obligation to remember.

41. "Remarks by the President at the Summit of the Americas Opening Ceremony."

42. Ibid.

43. Ibid.

44. Ibid.

45. Ibid.

46. The same could not be said of Obama. According to *Miami Herald* columnist Andres Oppenheimer, "Obama could not even recall the name of a single Latin American leader when he interviewed him for the first time" in 2007 (Juan Carlos Hidalgo), December 11· 2008, *Cato Institute*, http://www.cato.org/publications/commentary/latin-american-agenda-president-obama

47. Remarks by the President at the Summit of the Americas Opening Ceremony."

48. Ibid.

49. Ibid.

50· Ibid.

51. Zarefsky, 613.

52. Millán-Zaibert, 152

53. Ibid., 151.

9 Obama's Cairo Speech: Beyond the Rhetoric and Politics of "Good Muslim, Bad Muslim"

Matthew Abraham

No single speech can eradicate years of mistrust, nor can I answer in the time that I have all the complex questions that brought us to this point. But I am convinced to move forward, we must say openly the things we hold in our hearts and that too often are said only behind closed doors.

And I consider it part of my responsibility as President of the United States to fight against negative stereotypes of Islam wherever they appear.

—President Barack Obama

INTRODUCTION

In his critique of the first one thousand days of President Barak Obama's presidency, and what he calls the "Obama Syndrome," political commentator Tariq Ali notes, "From Palestine through Iraq to Iran, Obama has acted as just another steward of the American empire, pursuing the same aims as his predecessors, with the same means but with a more emollient rhetoric."[1] In an assessment of Obama's June 2009 Cairo speech, and in seeming agreement with Ali's characterization of Obama's presidency, Deepa Kumar writes, "What Obama's speech represents is a repackaging of U.S. imperial aims in liberal terms. It heralds a new rhetorical approach built on the ashes of the now widely discredited cowboy diplomacy of the Bush era."[2] Although Obama positioned himself during the 2008 presidential race as a candidate who would bring sweeping change to America's domestic and foreign policy after the missteps of the Bush administration, many have been disappointed with Obama's inability to fundamentally alter the corrupting influences of corporate greed—from Main Street to Wall Street—and also with the decline of America's image throughout the world as a result of its hard power approach to difficult conflicts.[3] Obama's early and highly anticipated speech to the Muslim world in Cairo, Egypt on June 4th, 2009, represented a supposedly new era of engagement between the United States and nations in the Middle East. Indeed, Obama calls for "a new beginning" in East-West relations.

Obama sought to address many key issues in his Cairo speech: "violent extremism in all its forms"; "the situation between Israelis, Palestinians, and the Arab world"; "the rights and responsibilities of nations on nuclear weapons"; "democracy"; "religious freedom"; "women's rights"; and "economic development and opportunity."[4] Obama sought to seize upon the "We are more alike than we realize" theme, as he referenced several aspects of Muslim culture that are central to the West. The events of 9/11, of course, were used by various neoconservatives as part of a narrative about the clash of civilizations, a narrative that largely backfired since it refused to consider the complexity of the region's people, traditions, and histories. In this speech, Obama's rhetorical task was to create trust and political friendship in the Arab world by locating mutual interests between the East and the West. To accomplish this task, Obama repeatedly noted how neither the West nor the Arab world should be held hostage by the past. Obama was obviously referencing the events of September 11th, 2001, and the U.S.'s military response to those events. Within the Arab world, Osama bin Laden was successful in drawing upon a reservoir of anti-American resentment to justify Al Qaeda's attacks on the World Trade Center and the Pentagon. The Bush administration justified the U.S. bombings of Afghanistan in October of 2001, and the invasion of Iraq in March of 2003, as just responses to the prospect of future terrorism. In his call for a new beginning, Obama invited his audience to re-conceive U.S.-Muslim relations based on a common future instead of a clearly divisive past.

As a political figure, Obama is a study in paradox rooted in his ability to engage in political calculation to avoid division. With respect to his political calculations in forming his positions, and with respect to the turmoil in the Middle East, this paradoxical Obama made himself most evident. Obama's political pragmatism has tempered the very idealism that made him an attractive political candidate in 2008, suggesting that, long ago, Obama understood the demands of concentrated power when it comes to the U.S.'s special relationship with Israel and the Arab states in the Middle East.

As part of his appeal to foreign audiences as the first African American U.S. president, Obama faced an interesting rhetorical predicament: He seemingly possessed sympathy for—and empathy with—the people of the region as a result of his ancestry on his father's side and the time he spent in Indonesia (with the largest Muslim population in the world) as a child, but he had to present his loyalties as being wholly with Americans. Obama did this despite the fact that the U.S. was guilty of supporting state terrorism in the Middle East, and given its reflexive support for Israel in its struggle with the Palestinians, the U.S. aided and tacitly endorsed Israel's occupation. It was in this context, then, that Obama wished to address topics such as confronting extremism in all its forms, the necessity of solving the Israel-Palestine conflict, the importance of addressing nuclear proliferation in the Middle East, creating and maintaining democratic institutions and free elections, upholding religious freedom, protecting women's rights, and fostering economic development and opportunity. These themes are central to addressing the issues of oppression, political instability, questions about the U.S.'s commitments in the region, and the growing sense that Samuel Huntington's thesis of the "clash of civilizations" may have been wildly wrong in approaching various conflicts in the Middle East. It also serves a polarizing but ideologically serviceable role in a particular historical moment that some have called a period of American ascendency. The tragedies of American foreign policy in the Middle East over the last eight years necessitated that Obama separate "Good Muslims" from "Bad Muslims."

In this chapter, I examine how Obama employed a conception of the "Good Muslim, Bad Muslim" in his Cairo speech as part of his rhetorical appeal to the Arab world. I borrow this term, "Good Muslim, Bad Muslim" from Mahmood Mamdami, who, in his book, *Good Muslim, Bad Muslim*, argues that the designation of Arab countries and the citizens within them as either "good" or "bad" since the Cold War has depended upon how these countries have served U.S strategic interests in the Middle East.[5] Obama avoided using the specific terms "Good Muslim" and "Bad Muslim" by speaking of those countries in the Arab world committed to democracy, human rights, and the dignity of all human beings versus those that harbor religious extremists, who deny the authority rule of law, or deny the ability of people to choose a government instead of being coerced into complying with a course of action.

In speaking about "religious extremists," Obama clearly had Al-Qaeda and Osama bin Laden in mind, hoping to make it clear that the United States's war is against radical Islam and not the two billion Muslims throughout the world. Obama made a pitch for the virtues of liberal democracies when he states,

> But I do have an unyielding belief that all people yearn for
> certain things: the ability to speak your mind and have a
> say in how you are governed; confidence in the rule of law;
> and the equal administration of justice; government that
> is transparent and doesn't steal from the people; the free-
> dom to live as you choose. Those are not just American
> ideas, they are human rights, and that is why we will sup-
> port them everywhere."[6]

Within liberal democracies, one has the right to speak one's mind because
free speech is guaranteed under the constitution; one can also be confident
that the rule of law and the administration of justice will be applied equita-
bly, regardless of the color of one's skin or one's religious preference; within
liberal democracies, one can live freely because governments operate transparently without deceiving the people as to their intentions.

Good Muslims and Bad Muslims

Good Muslims are those who serve U.S. interests as loyal proxies, while Bad
Muslims are those who resist modernity, seek to demonize and delegitimize
Israel as a Jewish state, and engage in and support terrorism against the
United States and its allies. In his Cairo Speech, Obama made clear that
the United States wishes to increase cooperation and good will among good
Muslims, and to use good Muslims to control and offset the influence of
bad Muslims, or those seeking to undermine and resist U.S. influence and
dominion in the Middle East. Obama is extremely diplomatic, posturing for
the Muslim world as a friend, while erasing the history of U.S. opposition to
expressions of Arab nationalism and self-determination.

While pointing out the many military mistakes the U.S. has made since
9/11 (Afghanistan, Iraq, Abu Ghraib, etc.), Obama, in an effort to seek a new
beginning between East and West, also acknowledged the distinct problems
presented by religious extremism in the Middle East. In addition, he spent a
great deal of time addressing very specific problems in the region; e.g., lack of
economic development and opportunity, educational opportunity, treatment
of women, and the lack of democratic governments in the region. Obama
called for a new beginning in relations between the United States and the
Arabs. Of course, beginnings presuppose pasts that must be transcended.
In the first paragraph of his speech, Obama mentioned a legacy of colonialism, a clear reference to British and American imperialism. He also noted
the ways in which the forces of globalization and modernity have shaped the
world; these forces are often portrayed as being at odds with religious traditions within the Muslim world.

Obama insisted that the tensions that exist between the U.S. and the Muslim world are "rooted in historical forces that transcend any current policy debate,"[7] a subtle way of avoiding the U.S. invasion of Iraq and the U.S.'s support of Israel's occupation of Palestine. By side-stepping these policy debates, Obama makes an appeal for unity. In the wake of 9/11, he made it clear that those who believe in a common humanity must not allow extremists to undermine cooperation and partnership between people of good will. All of the aforementioned issues create a critical rhetorical situation for Obama as he stood at the podium before his audience at Cairo University. He poetically addressed these issues by appealing to universal themes of life, death, alienation, the fleetingness of time, and the fragility of the human condition when he stated, "All of us share this world for but a brief moment in time. The question is whether we spend that time focused on what pushes us apart, or whether we commit ourselves to an effort–a sustained effort–to find common ground, to focus on the future we seek for our children, and to respect the dignity of all human beings."[8] Indeed, as Obama stated, "So long as our relationship is defined by our differences, we will empower those who sow hatred rather than peace, those who promote conflict rather than the cooperation that can help all of our people achieve justice and prosperity." Obama insists that the United States and Islam need not be in competition, noting that they are both committed to principles of justice, progress, tolerance, and the dignity of all human beings. He stated, "There must be a sustained effort to listen to each other; to learn from each other; to respect one another; and to seek common ground." He poignantly concluded that the interests we share as human beings are far more powerful than the forces that drive us apart."[9]

As the son of Kenyan man who converted to Christianity after being raised in a Muslim family, and a white woman from Kansas, Obama—as the first African American president of the United States—was uniquely positioned to recapture some of the respect and good will the U.S. lost upon declaring the War on Terror during the Bush administration. At the beginning of his speech, Obama claimed that he would work, as president of the United States, to correct harmful stereotypes of Muslims. At the same time, he assured his Cairo audience that the United States does not conform to the stereotype of a self-interested empire, and asked for his audience's help in spreading that message. Obama seemed to tell his audience that he can only do his part to repair the harm done to U.S.-Muslim relations if the audience meets him halfway.

Obama admitted that the United States has made mistakes in its prosecution of the War on Terror, justifying these missteps in the wake of 9/11, as his country sought to separate religious extremists from devout Muslims. In an attempt to heal the rift that religious extremists created on 9/11, Obama appealed to his Cairo audience to transcend religious and national divisions. Obama made clear that the United States has never been at war with Islam, going so far as to insist that Islam has contributed great inventions such as mathematics and calligraphy to civilization. Additionally, he insisted that Islam has always been a part of America, as Muslims play key roles in civic life as doctors, lawyers, teachers, business people, and soldiers. As part of this description, Obama noted that the first Muslim to be elected to the U.S. Congress, Keith Ellison, took his oath of office while placing his hand on the Koran. As Obama puts it, "They [Muslims] have fought in our wars, they have served in our government, they have stood for civil rights, they have started businesses, they have taught at our universities, they've excelled in our sports arenas, they've won Nobel Prizes, built our tallest building, and lit the Olympic Torch."[10] He noted that there were over twelve hundred mosques in the United States. Obama stressed the interdependency between the East and the West by noting their points of identification. As he aptly put it, "That is what it means to share this world in the twenty-first century."[11] We should notice the similarity between Obama's statement and Burke's famous statement on *consubstantiality*: "To identify A with B is to make A consubstantial with B."[12] In other words, a union is created between disparate elements when they identify with a common symbol. Obama stressed the interdependency of our globalized world, what he sees as the unifying aspects of human identity:

> So let there be no doubt: Islam is a part of America. And I believe that America holds within her the truth that regardless of race, religion, or station in life, all of us share common aspirations—to live in peace and security; to get an education and to work with dignity; to love our families, our communities, and our God. These things we share. This is the hope of all humanity.[13]

Obama's rhetorical strategy was to show that the U.S. is not in competition with the Muslim world. To demonstrate this, Obama noted how Islam has been a part of America since the country's founding. He quotes from John Adams, who (in signing the *Treaty of Tripoli*) wrote, "The United States has in itself no character of enmity against the laws, religion or tranquility of Muslims."[14] Obama resolved to show that the world is interdependent and that divisions cannot be drawn between nations and peoples at this historical moment.

By focusing on the tensions between modernity and religious traditions within Islam as contributing to conflict between the U.S. and the Arab world, Obama sought to persuade his Cairo audience that globalization and development will raise the standards of living for everyone. In his Cairo speech, Obama acted as spokesperson for neo-liberalism and its commitment to the flow of capital and the expansion of markets. Obama, seemingly drawing upon the writings of Fareed Zakaria, suggested that the slow rates of economic and technological development in the Arab world can be blamed on Arab culture.[15] If the Arab world will follow the U.S.'s lead on these key themes of economic and technological development, modernity can be harmonized with resisting religious traditions. The United States has been a trailblazer in this respect. As Obama pointed out, "The United States is one of the greatest sources of progress the world has ever known," and that "We are shaped by every culture, drawn from every end of the Earth, and dedicated to a simple concept: *E pluribus unum*–'Out of many, one.'"[16] By stressing the interdependence of regions of the planet, and by noting how events in one part of the word have far-reaching effects on others parts of the world, Obama sought to impress upon his audience the consequences of continuing a clash of civilizations, pitting East against West and Muslims against Christians and Jews. Such a continued divide produces feelings of hopelessness and cynicism.

At the center of the Cairo Speech, and of greater interest to the Cairo audience, was the Israel-Palestine conflict. Obama acknowledged that Israel's occupation of the West Bank and blockade of Gaza are illegal, a continual source of Palestinian suffering, and a source of considerable antagonism in the Arab world, against the demands of the U.S.-Israel special relationship that enables the building of illegal Israeli settlements. Israel is the only country in the Middle East that possesses nuclear weapons, a fact that most denied because of Israel's refusal to sign the Nuclear Non-Proliferation agreement.[17] Of course, the U.S. launched its invasion of Iraq based on the suspicion that Saddam Hussein possessed or had the capability of building nuclear weapons, and is now (along with Israel) placing considerable pressure on Iran to terminate its nuclear program. These circumstances make the U.S. look hypocritical as it seeks to maintain a firm grip on those countries that can manufacture nuclear weapons in the region (Israel, Pakistan, and India) and those that cannot (Iraq and Iran), while continually calling for peace in the Middle East. Clearly, the distinction between those who can possess nuclear weapons and those who cannot are based on U.S. interests. With the exception of Israel, the United States tends to employ the "Good Muslim, Bad Muslim" test to make the distinction. Obama, then, sought to restore through his Cairo Speech a good-faith relationship with the world, a cooperative relationship that he realizes must address past grievances without becoming hostage to them. To these ends, Obama sought to create conditions of possible trust in a region that has little reason to trust U.S. intentions nearly ten years after the terrorist attacks of 9/11.

A Brief History of U.S. Intervention in the Middle East

During his speech, Obama maintained that the U.S. is not interested in building an empire, or in maintaining military bases in the Middle East, but in forging partnerships with Arab countries. To convince his audience of this intention, Obama owned up to the mistakes of previous U.S. administrations. These mistakes included the 1953 coup in Iran that overthrew a democratically elected Mohammad Mosaddegh; the attempted CIA assassination in Beirut of Lebanese cleric Sheikh Fadlallah on March 8, 1985, by a truck bomb that killed eighty people; the 1979 Iranian Revolution and hostage crisis; the U.S.'s support of Israel; and the U.S.'s general efforts to suppress pan-Arab nationalist movements such as those represented by Egypt's Nasser in 1967. These events are not easily forgotten, and have to be contextualized and understood as part of a larger historical picture, one where the United States may have temporarily lost sight of its noble intentions, but never deviated from moving toward the larger goal of controlling oil resources in the region.

Obama's acknowledgement of Arab inventions, scientific skills, tolerance, advanced political structures, and institutions was meant to offset the stereotypes that are often presented as fact about the Arab world; that it is uncivilized and resistant to science, the development of democratic institutions, and social progress. These stereotypes must be dispensed with before Obama can meet his audience on firmer ground about divisive and immediate political issues, such as the Israel-Palestine conflict. Obama's back and forth rhetorical strategy, moving between establishing the greatness of the Arab and Islamic past, dissociating it from Islamic extremism, and tying this to the exigencies of the present, was a conscious strategy. He appealed to an audience psychology that wishes to trust Obama the person, but has little reason to trust him in his role as President of the United States. Obama seemed to understand this tension as he draws upon his biography: "Part of this conviction [about the greatness of Islam] is rooted in my own experience. I am a Christian, but my father came from a Kenyan family that includes generations of Muslims. As a boy, I spent several years in Indonesia and heard the call of the azan at the break of dawn and the fall of dusk."[18] This aspect of his personal story, Obama directly connected to his Cairo audience, insisting that he understood what it means to live as a Muslim, to endure the difficulties of a living a Muslim's life, and perhaps most importantly, the particular religious commitments devout Muslims observe (e.g., *zakat,* "religious giving"). No previous U.S. president has demonstrated this level of understanding and compassion for Muslims in the Middle East.

Obama's multicultural upbringing in Indonesia and Hawaii created the conditions for his capacity to connect with people in various regions of the world, such as the Middle East. Several of Obama's relatives are Muslim, although he is not.[19] Of course, this aspect of his background has become fodder for conservative critics. For example, in his *The Roots of Obama's Rage,* Dinesh D'Souza argues that Obama is driven by his rage against colonialism, spurred on by the memory of his father ("Luo tribesman of the 1950s"), who died in Kenya in a car accident. D'Souza claims that Obama is haunted by the ghost of his father, a fierce anti-colonialist who resented Western power and influence in Africa, although he himself was educated in the West.[20] D'Souza paints a complex psychological portrait of Obama, arguing that he is not the suave, cool individual on the outside that the public sees, but is instead a fierce anti-colonialist ideologue inspired by Franz Fanon's writings, and trying to live up to his father's disappointments and failed expectations. D'Souza goes on to argue that this psychological portrait of Obama provides a far more accurate indicator of Obama's disposition on key domestic and foreign policy issues than his policy speeches. Although D'Souza does not directly address Obama's stance on the Israel-Palestine conflict, we can infer that Obama, as an "anti-colonialist" (to use D'Souza's characterization), is privately cheers for the Palestinians because they are an oppressed people resisting Israeli occupation, regardless of what Obama states in public.[21]

Obama's election to the presidency signaled that the country had expressed a desire to change on several fronts. Beyond changing the occupant of the Oval Office, the country sought to repair the country's image throughout the rest of the world, particularly the Middle East. The U.S. had elected its first African American president, an indication that U.S. citizens had left identity politics behind, and that they possessed a readiness to engage different cultures beyond their historic comfort level. To prove this, Obama drew upon his own interesting biography. As Obama said, "Now, much has been made of the fact that an African American with the name Barack Hussein Obama could be elected President. But my personal story is not so unique."[22] Obama wished to show that his story could be anyone's story in the Land of Opportunity. However, Obama's journey to this moment at Cairo University in June of 2009 can be seen as topping off a lifetime of efforts to understand racial politics and division in the United States as well as the vast, persuasive potential that could be untapped by successfully navigating the shoals of the racial divide.

Growing up, Obama learned the hard-won lessons that came with facing white resistance to discussions about race and racial justice. He quickly learned that whites could not be directly confronted with evidence, no matter how convincing or compelling, that they were somehow responsible for the failure of blacks in social, political, and economic spheres. What is the direct relationship between the history of the struggle for racial equality in the United States and the struggles for democracy, economic development, freedom, women's rights, etc. in the Arab world? Both took place in the shadow of colonialism, are parts of the story about modernization, and are enmeshed in the rise of globalization. Obama hits all three of these themes in his speech.

Obama positioned himself as if to suggest that he is better able than previous U.S. presidents to help the divisions within the Arab world by virtue of who he is and also because of the political conditions that led to his election to the presidency. Obama pointed out that his election itself is evidence of how committed and tolerant the United States is with respect to judging racial/ethnic/religious difference. He attempted to quell those concerned that the U.S. is committed to Islamophobia as a normal part of American life, seemingly incapable of appreciating individuals for who they are by pointing out the many visible signs of cooperation between Muslim Americans and Christian and Jewish Americans. By insisting that the way forward in diplomatic relations between the West and the Middle East depends on good-faith negotiations on both sides, Obama drew a symmetry where none exists: the U.S. has been responsible for illegal invasions of countries such as Iraq and Afghanistan on the basis of flimsy pretexts, in addition to inflicting massive violence against the indigenous populations during those invasions. Using a "On the one hand, on the other hand" logic, Obama deftly wove a nicely constructed tapestry that leaves American exceptionalism and military power unacknowledged, as if U.S. culpability for the numerous deaths because of the war in Iraq could be erased by not mentioning them. He got right to the point when he stated, "So America will defend itself, respectful of the sovereignty of nations and the rule of law. And we will do so in partnership with Muslim communities which are also threatened. The sooner the extremists are isolated and unwelcome in Muslim communities, the sooner we will all be safer."[23] Although he called for a partnership between the U.S. and the Arab world, Obama made it clear that the U.S. will continue to serve its interests. Despite this stance, Obama seeks to help his audience see past stereotypes.

GETTING PAST STEREOTYPES

Stereotypes hold people back in terms of responding to the complexities of individuals and their circumstances in a world of contingency, change, and difference. It is far too easy to reach for the easy categorization than do the hard work of explaining how each individual is situated in the world. It is these stereotypes that Obama sought to disable as he spoke in Cairo, asking his audiences to move past the caricatures that reduce discussions about the Middle East to misleading sound bites that erase not only what different cultural groups hold in common, but also the diversity of their experiences. The assumption that we must engage in the politics of division by subscribing to the "Clash of Civilizations" thesis made popular by Huntington obscures the fact that lines of solidarity are created within the human community outside of the common racial, religious, and gender classifications.[24]

Obama forced his Cairo audience to reflect not only on the creation of community, but also on how identities sometimes work to divide communities on the basis of flimsy premises, with the result that we fall victim to illusions about those we assume are our enemies.[25] The politics and rhetoric of demonization are created too easily, allowing for the facile separation between "us" and "them" that is consistent with the demands of the current propaganda need. By recognizing the destructiveness of identity politics, Obama sought to create points of identification between people throughout the world despite the intractable conflicts in the Middle East. Obama uses this speech to demonstrate that more brings Muslims and Westerners together than what pulls them apart. Furthermore, he emphasized the importance of listening, mutual respect, and identifying common ground. Obama spent several years in Indonesia, the home of the most Muslims in the world. Drawing on his time as a community activist in Chicago, a city with a large Muslim community, Obama suggested that he knew Muslim religious traditions. More importantly, he established that he was comfortable speaking to and dealing with Islam and Muslims—a far cry from previous U.S. presidents.

Through his election to the presidency, Obama introduces new communicative modalities and competencies, enabling historically marginalized groups to present their grievances within the public sphere, through Obama's life story. This is extremely significant. It is this promise invested in his presidency that Obama has exploited rhetorically in various speeches, including the Cairo Speech. Through his election, Obama hoped to lend an ear to suffering voices in the Muslim world that had been previously ignored under the Bush administration. Though not a Muslim, he has obviously been accused of being one—as if being a Muslim would have somehow made him ineligible to be president. Although the U.S. declares that it is not at war with Islam, the parameters of Islamophobia in the U.S suggest otherwise. Obama's election, it might be claimed, is confirmation that those marginalized voices—Muslims in America and in the Arab World—can no longer be misrepresented by extremists. As he noted in his speech, "And throughout history, Islam has demonstrated through words and deeds the possibilities of religious tolerance and racial equality."[26] Obama sought to show his Arab audience that he, as the President of the United States, intends to represent Islam as a tolerant religion.

Obama emphasized that the U.S. was born out of revolution against an empire, the British Empire, and does not easily conform to the stereotype of a self-interested empire: "We were founded upon the ideal that all are created equal, and we have shed blood and struggled for centuries to give meaning to those words—within our borders, and around the world." He continued:

> For human history has often been a record of nations and tribes subjugating one another to serve their own interests. Yet in this new age, such attitudes are self-defeating. Given our interdependencies, any world order that elevates one nation or group of people over another will inevitably fail. So, whatever we think of the past, we must not be prisoners of it. Our problem must be dealt with through partnership; progress must be shared.[28]

In the first paragraph of the Cairo speech, Obama mentioned the colonial legacy that has shaped modern relations between the West and the Middle East, the very relations that form the basis of present Arab resentments. This legacy "denied rights and opportunities to many Muslims." While recognizing this historical background, Obama identified the centrality of the forces associated with globalization and modernity that shaped the current predicament—forces that are often portrayed as being in conflict with the religious and cultural traditions of the Arab world. For Obama, this is the "[h]armony between tradition and progress." Furthermore, he poignantly noted, "All of us share this world for but a brief moment in time," pushing his audience to recognize that "It's easier to start wars than to end them. It's easier to blame others than to look inward. It's easier to see what is different about someone than to find the things we share. But we should choose the right path, not just the easy path."[29]

These attempts to encourage his audience to look beyond the mistakes in the War on Terror and its occupations of Iraq and Afghanistan, however, sound hollow. By blaming the current tensions between the U.S. and Arab countries on "violent extremists," Obama avoided directly addressing how U.S. imperialism and the wars in Afghanistan and Iraq—as well as strong signals that the U.S. would like to invade Iran because of its burgeoning nuclear weapons capability—have affected the region. However, Obama made clear, "As the Holy Koran tells us, 'Be conscious of God and speak always the truth.' That is what I will try to do today—to speak the truth as best I can, humbled by the task before us, and firm in my belief that the interests we share as human beings are far more powerful than the forces that drive us apart."[30]

OBAMA AND THE ISRAEL-PALESTINE CONFLICT

While fully aware that U.S. support for Israel's settlement project poses a serious problem for building and maintaining good will toward the U.S. in the Middle East, Obama was forced to walk a very narrow tightrope, balancing the need to be protective of Israel—and to refrain from being overly critical—in his public statements. This is consistent with the behavior of past U.S. presidents, who acknowledge legitimate grievances in the Arab world, while being highly protective of Israel. These grievances include the U.S.'s support of corrupt regimes throughout the Middle East (Egypt, Saudi Arabia, Syria, etc.), its support for Israel's occupation of the West Bank and the military blockade of Gaza, its support for continued Israeli settlement-building, and its support of Israel's military adventurism in Lebanon, and future possible military action against Iran.

Ever wary of the Israel Lobby's power to shape U.S. foreign policy in the Middle East, and to defeat alternatives to supporting the Israeli right-wing, Obama faced a nearly impossible task: He had to profess undying loyalty to Israel (as every U.S. president must), and all that commitment entails, while also creating the rhetorical ground to slowly revise this support in response to the long-recognized grievances and governmental changes in the Arab world. In other words, Obama had to position himself to back away from Israel's repressive policies toward the Palestinians if and when the time arrives, creating the rhetorical situation to question Israeli hegemony in the Middle East in advance of a regional crisis that could possibly involve the use of nuclear weapons. U.S. support for Israel, as the old saying goes, is the elephant in the room of American politics. Indeed, Obama's May 2011 State Department speech signified a milestone in American politics, as Obama mentioned the international consensus for resolution of the conflict: an Israel withdrawal to the 1967 Green Line and the removal of illegal, "Jews only" settlements in the West bank.[31]

Of course, politicians must genuflect to the Israel Lobby's unspoken power in the hallways of the American political establishment, fully cognizant that criticisms of Israel can be reframed as anti-Semitism if the stakes are high enough, and creating an impossible situation for those seeking to pursue alternative policies in the Middle East.[32] At the beginning of his remarks about the Israel-Palestine conflict, Obama made clear that the U.S.'s bond with Israel is unbreakable: "America's strong bonds with Israel are well known. This bond is unbreakable. It is based upon cultural and historical ties, and the recognition that the aspiration for a Jewish homeland is rooted in a tragic history that cannot be denied."[33] Reflexive congressional and senate support for Israel's punishing treatment of Palestinians in the territories is a seemingly permanent part of the American political landscape. Although criticisms of Israel exist at the margins of America political life, the establishment speaks with one voice when it comes to supporting Israel.[34]

We are told that Israel is the only democracy in the Middle East; yet, the very conditions of possibility for the state (as the state of the Jewish people) is that the majority must always remain Jewish, even if this means expelling the growing Arab Palestinian population that constitutes just over twenty percent of Israel's total population. Israel is a democracy to the degree that it is a democracy committed to the preservation of a Jewish majority. As Obama has openly cited the international consensus for resolving the conflict, specifically the 1967 borders that are recognized as the legitimate basis for bringing all hostilities to an end, he has come under increased criticism from U.S. supporters of Israel, such as from Alan Dershowitz and others. While it is easy for Obama to criticize Islamic extremism, as Obama frequently does, criticizing Zionist extremism is taboo; it is an unspeakable "crime" that no U.S. president can afford to commit and expect to politically survive. For Obama to acknowledge publicly what was long ago acknowledged privately—that Israel has long been in violation of international law—is considered by Israel's U.S. defenders to be tantamount to heresy.

Far too often, commentators attempt to draw symmetries between Israeli and Palestinian power; inevitably, these symmetries are drawn because of a desire to assign equal blame in the conflict, leaving out any analysis of Israel's disproportionate counter-violence to Palestinian terrorism. Obama falls into this trap in the Cairo Speech, suggesting that blame for the continuation of the conflict can be equally apportioned between Israelis and Palestinians. This tendency is extremely unhelpful, and obfuscates many important issues in an attempt to appease audience psychologies—in this case, the bases of Israeli power. While recognizing the legitimacy of Palestinian suffering, Obama insisted upon protecting Israel's right to exist as a Jewish state, even if protecting that right entails denying, and demanding as a prerequisite for recognition at the negotiating table, that Palestinians give up their right to return to their previous homes. In other words, a starting point for negotiations is that Palestinians renounce any and all claims to historical Palestine or a recognition of their dispossession, as they are required to accept Israel's "right to exist" as a state committed to preserving a Jewish majority.

Obama's calls for an end to Palestinian terrorism ring hollow in this context, particularly since the balance of power is overwhelmingly in Israel's favor. Similarly, the ledger sheet of violence shows that Palestinians die at the hands of Israel's military machine at far greater rates than Israelis do at the hands of suicide bombers, Hamas, Fatah, etc. However, Obama simply cannot avoid addressing the international consensus on the resolution of the Israel-Palestine conflict, leading him to openly acknowledge U.N. 242 and the illegality of Israeli settlements. This is a major step for a U.S. president. Israel's open flouting of previous agreements to cease settlement construction at Camp David, as described by Carter in his *Palestine: Peace Not Apartheid*, suggests that it is not interested in peace, except as a rhetorical device to advance its own strategic interests in the region.[35]

Building a Relationship

Ever since he announced his candidacy for the presidency of the United States in February 2007, Barack Obama has had to prove who he "really" is, while simultaneously working to prove—in the midst of what have often been wild mischaracterizations about his birth and person—what he is not. Whether proving that he is a native-born American citizen, that he is not a Muslim (the implications of which, if it were true, are unclear), or that he does not hold the same beliefs as Bill Ayers or Jeremiah Wright, Obama has been forced to remove doubts about his birth place, his genealogy, his political loyalties and affiliations, and his religion.[36] This sort of skepticism about the background of someone elected president of the United States is unprecedented, emerging within a discursive environment plagued by racism and Islamophobia. This discursive environment plays a key role in mainstream media representations of Obama's Middle East policy, and have also been plagued by caricatures and misleading propaganda about how Obama's religious and ethnic identity informs his perspectives and sympathies toward the Arab world, particularly in the context of the Israel-Palestine conflict.[37]

Aaron Klein, in *The Manchurian President*, claims that "Future historians will have to grapple with the fantastic phenomenon of the U.S. news media's having, as a class, almost completely abdicated their traditional responsibility when it came to investigating the background of the 'unknown politician' running for the country's highest office."[38] My analysis of Obama's 2009 Cairo's Speech reveals how Obama sought to achieve a balancing act of sorts in this rhetorical situation, assuring his Arab audience that the U.S.'s intentions toward the Arab world are not malevolent, despite the War on Terror launched by his predecessor, George W. Bush.

Barack Obama has used a rhetoric of commonality to great effectiveness in the course of advancing arguments in support of his domestic and international political agendas. Through this rhetoric, Obama reminds us that despite our divisions, we hold our humanity in common; it is this common humanity that is the source of strength, possessing the potential to surmount division and conflict. As he stated in his Cairo Speech, progress, respect for the dignity of human life, and a belief in co-existence should guide those seeking to defeat the religious extremists. He reminded his Cairo audience that, "whoever kills an innocent is as—it is as if he has killed all mankind . . . whoever saves a person, it is as if he has saved all mankind."[39] Obama was, of course, talking about Muslim extremists such as Osama bin Laden and his associates. Although these extremists may successfully tap into a reservoir of legitimate grievances within the Arab world against the U.S., Obama—as president—had to defend the country and its citizens against terrorist attacks, but he also had to assure the Muslim world that he would combat damaging stereotypes about Islam.

Despite his own personal differences from a perceived American norm, Obama employed a rhetoric of commonality to rebut those who question his origins and loyalties to the U.S. and its interests. A combination of Islamophobia and racism has produced an insurmountable challenge for Barack Obama's presidency. Obama has had to prove his loyalty to the United States and its interests because of his racial/cultural difference from the white norm, despite a conventional educational background and an enviable multicultural upbringing. However, this elite education and exotic background have in fact made Obama an object of suspicion. In other words, the country's multicultural impulse only extends so far. In this sense, Obama must continually prove his political bona fides even though he won the 2008 election. His use of the words "partnership," "moderation," "mutual interests," "progress," and "reconciliation" suggested that he was interested in working past differences through negotiation and compromise.

By demonstrating through his behavior and measured words that he was not a Muslim, a closet terrorist, a radical, or a "chip-on-his-shoulder" black civil rights activist, Obama had to run away from political instincts that are perhaps grounded in concerns about justice and equity. His desire to transform the world is tempered by a moderation that is grounded in the recognition that reality does not accord with his political vision. While much has been written about Obama's psychological appeal to white voters, little is known about how Obama's positions on Israel allowed him to engage in a political transformation that would catapult him into the White House. His connections to American Jewish activists deeply committed to Israel and its survival, particularly to figures like Abner Mikva, Newton Minnow, Marilyn Katz, Bettylu Salzman, Rabbi Arnold Wolf, Saul Alinsky and Harry Pritzker, explain Obama's reticence in directly engaging Israel on its settlement policy in the West Bank.

While recognizing how detrimental the U.S. invasions of Afghanistan and Iraq have been to the U.S.'s image in the world, Obama was clear that he, as the U.S. commander in chief, must address the geopolitical conditions that led to the tragedy in Manhattan on September 11th, 2001. Of course, these conditions are ones that can, at least to a degree, be attributed to U.S. Middle East policy, particularly U.S. support of Israel's occupation of and settlement-building in the West Bank and its evisceration of Gaza. Indeed, Osama Bin Laden claimed as much, insisting that Israel's oppression of the Palestinians is the single biggest example of how the West dominates the Arab world.

Despite his condemnation of Palestinian terrorism in his Cairo Speech, Obama recognized that Israel's continued building of settlements (and the U.S.'s seeming tolerance and support of these actions) only fuels perceptions throughout the Arab world that the U.S. stands in opposition to the Palestinian people's national aspirations. As he forthrightly acknowledged, "America will not turn our backs on the legitimate Palestinian aspiration for dignity, opportunity, and a state of their own."[17] While Obama condemns acts of violence by groups such as Al Qaeda, Hezbollah, and Hamas, he also recognized that this violence, whether directed at the United States or at Israel, cannot be so easily dismissed as senseless. At the same time, however, he cannot justify or provide the appropriate historical context for this violence, even in front of his Arab audience. In the course of moving toward a rapprochement with his audience in Cairo, Obama subsequently alienated a few hard-line American supporters of Israel by pointing out Israeli wrong-doing, and appeared to place Jewish and Palestinian suffering on the same plane.[40]

> [I]t is also undeniable that the Palestinian people—Muslims and Christians—have suffered in pursuit of a homeland. For more than 60 years they've endured the pain of dislocation. Many wait in refugee camps in the West Bank, Gaza, and neighboring lands for a life of peace and security that they have never been able to lead. They endure the daily humiliations—large and small—that come with occupation. So let there be no doubt: The situation for the Palestinian people is intolerable. And America will not turn our backs on the legitimate Palestinian aspiration for dignity, opportunity, and a state of their own.[41]

The political constraints around this speech were enormous, especially given the domestic constituencies at home that he had to please. The political

198 / Matthew Abraham

strength of American Jews who support Israel constitutes a major bloc of support within the Democratic Party, a bloc of voters Obama could not afford to alienate, even if his remarks referenced past agreements between Israel and the Palestine, and each party's commitments under international law.

Obama received extensive criticism from American Jewish groups supportive of Israel. Some hard-liners insisted that Obama showed true hostility toward Israel through his speech. According to Lanny Davis, "Some American Jews do not like the fact that Obama's speech publicly called out Prime Minister Benjamin Netanyahu for refusing to support a two-state solution and a freeze on all settlements." As Davis notes:

> [M]any American Jews and Israelis feel strongly that Obama should better understand that such public scolding of Israel, which breaks with the bipartisan tradition of previous administrations, will only strengthen the hard-liners within Israeli (and Arab) politics, and thus, weaken Netanyahu's ability to make peace, given his already fragile coalition government dependence on right-wing parties.[42]

Obama specifically spoke out on the issue of illegal Israeli settlements on the West Bank: "This construction [of settlements] violates previous agreements and undermines efforts to achieve peace. It is time for these settlements to stop."[43] The Anti-Defamation League noted: "We are disappointed that the President found the need to balance the suffering of the Jewish people in a genocide to the suffering of the Palestinian people resulting from Arab wars."[44] Additionally, the ADL was concerned that Obama created "the impression of equating the Holocaust with Palestinian suffering." In creating an inventory of the positive themes in Obama's Cairo Speech, Abe Foxman, head of the ADL, wrote:

> If this [the concept of a balanced U.S. approach to the conflict] is directed toward saying that each side has to make concessions, as the president indicated in his speech, that's realism and that's a legitimate appeal to the Muslim world. If, however, as also was part of the president's speech, an impression is left that Palestinian suffering is comparable to the Holocaust, or that Israel has simply been responsible for Palestinian suffering, ignoring Israel's peace offers and Palestinian rejectionism, that's unhelpful pandering which ignores the moral difference between the sides and is a poor basis for a U.S. role as a interlocutor.[45]

Furthermore, Charles Krauthammer maintained that Obama had done more to delegitimize Israel in the three minutes he talked about the Israel-Palestine conflict in the Cairo Speech than any other U.S. president.[46] It seems many Zionists were disappointed in Obama for his unequivocal pronouncement that just as one must admit that the Jewish people have the right to a state of their own, the Palestinians, who have suffered for so long, also deserve a homeland. It is this recognition of Palestinian suffering and the call for a Palestinian state that made so many defensive.

Conclusion

Barack Obama's biography, *Dreams of My Father*, provides some insight into the philosophy and strategy behind Obama's June 2009 Cairo Speech. In the context of one of the most important of his speeches to the Arab world, Obama drew upon the life lessons that he obtained while growing up as an interracial child in Indonesia and in the United States. Obama used his multiracial, multicultural identity, and his election as the first African American president of the United States, to argue for the wisdom of seeking common ground, seeing past stereotypes, and working toward international cooperation. As Mohammed Zaki reminds us, "Both the Western and Islamic civilizations have very strong bonds, which have been cemented over centuries, and which have benefitted mankind." Furthermore, according to Zaki, "It is for us to harness the good that exists and to chart a path of friendship for the ultimate goal of peace, prosperity and progress of mankind."[47] Despite the progress he has shown in re-engaging leaders in the Muslim world in comparison to past U.S. presidents, Obama still relied upon drawing a clear distinction between Good Muslims and Bad Muslims, reflecting his commitment to maintaining the U.S.'s stronghold in the Middle East.

NOTES

1. Tariq Ali, *The Obama Syndrome: Surrender at Home, War Abroad.* (London: Verso, 2010), 56–57.

2. Deepa Kumar. "Obama's Cairo Speech: A Rhetorical Shift in US Imperialism," *Dissident Voice* http://dissidentvoice.org/2009/06/obama%E2%80%99s-cairo-speech-a-rhetorical-shift-in-us-imperialism/ (accessed on August 5, 2012).

3. See Jeffrey St. Clair and Joshua Frank's *Hopeless: Barack Obama and the Politics of Illusion.* (London: AK Press, 2012.)

4. Barack Obama, "A New Beginning," June 6, 2009, http://www.whitehouse.gov/the-press-office/remarks-president-cairo-university-6-04-09.

5. Mahmood Mamdami. *Good Muslim, Bad Muslim: America, the Cold War, and the Roots of Terror.* (New York: Pantheon Books, 2004).

6. Obama, "A New Beginning"

7. Ibid.

8. Ibid.

9. Ibid.

10. Ibid.

11. Ibid.

12. Burke, Kenneth, *A Grammar of Motives.*

13. Obama, "A New Beginning"

14. Ibid.

15. See Zakaria's *From Wealth to Power: The Unusual Origins of America's World Role* (Princeton: Princeton U P, 1999); *The Post-American World* (New York: W.W. Norton Company, 2007), and *The Future of Freedom: Illiberal Democracy at Home and Abroad* (New York: W.W. Norton Company, 2009).

16. Obama, "A New Beginning"

17. See Seymour Hersh's *The Sampson Option* (New York: Vintage Books, 1993); Michael Karpin's *The Bomb in the Basement: How Israel Went Nuclear and What That Means for the Word* (New York: Simon and Schuster, 2007); Avner Cohen's *Israel and the Bomb* (New York: Columbia U P, 2004); and Yoel Cohen's *The Whistleblower from Dimona: Israel, Vanunu, and the Bomb* (London: Holmes and Meier Publishers, 2003).

18. Obama, "A New Beginning"

19. See Grant Farred's "The Ethics of Colin Powell" in Manning Marable and Kristen Clarke's *Barack Obama and African American Empowerment* (New York: Palgrave-Macmillan, 2009).

20. Dinesh D'Souza *The Roots of Obama's Rage.* (Washington: Regnery Press, 2010).

21. According to D'Souza:

> The most powerful country in the world is being governed according to the dreams of a Luo tribesman of the 1950s—a polygamist who abandoned his wives, drank himself into stupors, and bounded around on two iron legs (after his real legs had to be amputated because of a car crash), raging against the world for denying him the realization of his anti-colonial ambitions. This philandering, inebriated African socialist is now setting the nation's agenda through the reincarnation of his dreams in his son. The son is the one who is making it happen, but he is, as he candidly admits, only living out his father's dream. The invisible father provides the inspiration, and the son dutifully gets the job done. America today is being governed by a ghost (198).

22. Obama, "A New Beginning"

23. Ibid.

24. Samuel Huntington. The *Clash of Civilizations and the Remaking of World Order.* (New York: Simon and Schuster, 2011).

25. See Amartya Sen's *Identity and Violence: The Illusion of Destiny.* (New York: W.W. Norton and Co., 2007).

26. Obama, "A New Beginning"

27. Ibid.

28. Ibid.

29. Ibid.

30. Ibid.

31. See Obama's "A Moment of Opportunity" speech at State Department.

32. See Findley's *They Dare to Speak: People and Institutions Confront the Israel Lobby* (Chicago: Chicago Review Press, 2003); Peter Grose's Israel *in the Mind of America* (New York: Schocken Books, 1984); Edward Tivnan's *The Lobby Jewish Political Power and American Foreign Policy* (New York: Simon and Schuster, 1987.)

33. Obama, "A New Beginning"

34. See Walt and Mearsheimer's *The Israel Lobby and U.S. Middle East Policy* (London: Farrar and Strauss, 2008).

35. *Palestine: Peace Not Apartheid* (New York: Simon and Schuster, 2006)

36. See Sean Hannity's six-part series on "Obama and Friends: A History of Radicalism," http://www.youtube.com/watch?v=kyXJKzUxDlY&feature=related.

37. The insinuations been made about the implications of Obama's relationship with Professor Rashid Khalidi and Edward W. Said, Professor of Middle East Studies, have verged on the bizarre. See Andrew McCarthy's "L.A. Times Suppresses Obama's Khalidi Bash Tape," http://www.nationalreview.com/articles/226104/i-1-times-i-suppresses-obamas-khalidi-bash-tape/andrew-c-mccarthy.

38. *The Manchurian President: Barack Obama's Ties to Communists, Socialists, and Other Anti-American Extremists* (Washington: WND Books, 2010).

39. Obama, "A New Beginning"

40. A surprising defender of Obama's views on the Israel-Palestine conflict is Harvard Law Professor Alan Dershowitz. See Dershowitz's "Obama Has Undeserved Bad Rap on Israel," http://www.israelnationalnews.com/News/news.aspx/140066. Ironically, Dershowitz reversed course with his "Obama Explains—Makes It Worse," http://www.huffingtonpost.com/alan-dershowitz/obama-explains-and-makes-_b_867004.html; and "President Obama Has Right Goals on Israel-Palestine Peace, but Wrong Strategy," http://www.huffingtonpost.com/alan-dershowitz/obamas-failing-grade-in-t_b_870443.html. As Dershowitz notes in "Obama Explain": "Central to Israel's continued existence as the nation-state of the Jewish people is the Palestinian recognition that there can be no so-called 'right of return' to Israel, and that the Palestinian leadership and people must acknowledge that Israel will continue to exist as the nation-state of the Jewish people within secure and recognized boundaries."

41. Obama, "A New Beginning"

42. See Lanny Davis's "Many American Jews Unnerved by Obama's Cairo Speech," http://www.nhinsider.com/press-releases/2009/6/12/newsmax-lanny-davis-jews-unnerved-by-obama-speech.html.

43. Obama, "A New Beginning"

44. See "Obama's Speech to Muslim World Is 'Groundbreaking' But Misses Opportunities On The Israeli-Palestinian Pitfalls of Engagement," http://www.adl.org/ADL_Opinions/International_Affairs/20090610-Op-ed+JW.htm.

45. Ibid.
46. http://www.youtube.com/watch?v=3uKrt2yy3OU, *YouTube*, June 8, 2009
47. *America's Global Challenges: The Obama Era*. (New York: Palgrave, 2011), 44.

WORKS CITED

Anti-Defamation League. "Obama's Speech To Muslim World Is 'Groundbreaking' But Misses Opportunities On The Israeli-Palestinian Pitfalls of Engagement" at: http://www.adl.org/ADL_Opinions/International_Affairs/20090610-Op-ed+JW.htm

Ali, Tariq. *The Obama Syndrome: Surrender at Home, War Abroad*. London: Verso, 2010.

Burke, Kenneth. *A Grammar of Motives*. Berkeley: University of California Press, 1969.

Cohen, Avner. *Israel and the Bomb*. New York: Columbia U P, 2004.

Cohen, Yoel. *The Whistleblower from Dimona: Israel, Vanunu, and the Bomb*. London: Holmes and Meier Publishers, 2003.

Davis, Lanny. "Many American Jews Unnerved by Obama's Cairo Speech" at http://www.nhinsider.com/press-releases/2009/6/12/newsmax-lanny-davis-jews-unnerved-by-obama-speech.html

D'Souza, Dinesh. *The Roots of Obama's Rage*. Washington: Regnery Press, 2010

Findley, Peter. *They Dare to Speak: People and Institutions Confront the Israel Lobby*. Chicago: Chicago Review Press, 2003.

Grose, Peter. *Israel in the Mind of America*. New York: Schocken Books, 1984.

Hersh, Seymour. *The Sampson Option*. New York: Vintage Books, 1993.

Karpin, Michael. *The Bomb in the Basement: How Israel Went Nuclear and What That Means for the Word*. New York: Simon and Schuster, 2007.

Klein, Aaron. *The Manchurian President: Barack Obama's Ties to Communists, Socialists, and Other Anti-American Extremists*. Washington: WND Books, 2010.

Kumar, Deepa. "Obama's Cairo Speech: A Rhetorical Shift in US Imperialism," Dissident Voice http://dissidentvoice.org/2009/06/obama%E2%80%99s-cairo-speech-a-rhetorical-shift-in-us-imperialism/ (accessed on August 5, 2012).

Mamdami, Mahmood. *Good Muslim, Bad Muslim: America, the Cold War, and the Roots of Terror*. New York: Pantheon Books, 2004.

Marable, Manning and Kristen Clarke. *Barack Obama and African American Empowerment*. New York: Palgrave-Macmillan, 2009.

Obama, Barack. *Dreams of My Father: A Story of Race and Inheritance*. New York: Crown Publishing, 2007.

—. Cairo Speech ("A New Beginning"). 4 June, 2009. http://www.whitehouse.gov/the-press-office/remarks-president-cairo-university-6-04-09.

—. "A Moment of Opportunity" (May 19th, 2011). http://www.guardian.co.uk/world/2011/may/19/barack-obama-speech-middle-east

Sen, Amartya. *Identity and Violence: The Illusion of Destiny*. New York: W.W. Norton and Co., 2007.

St. Clair, Jeffrey Joshua Frank's *Hopeless: Barack Obama and the Politics of Illusion*. London: AK Press, 2012.

Tivnan, Edward. *The Lobby: Jewish Political Power and American Foreign Policy*. New York: Simon and Schuster, 1987.

Walt and Mearsheimer's *The Israel Lobby and U.S. Middle East Policy*. London: Farrar and Strauss, 2008.

Zakaria, Fareed. *From Wealth to Power: The Unusual Origins of America's World Role*. Princeton: Princeton U P, 1999.

—. *The Future of Freedom: Illiberal Democracy at Home and Abroad*. New York: W.W. Norton Company, 2007. W.W. Norton and Company, 2007.

—. *The Post-American World*. New York: W.W. Norton Company, 2007. W.W. Norton and Company, 2009.

Zaki, Mohammed M. *American Global Challenges: The Obama Era*. New York: Palgrave, 2011.

10 REFLECTIONS ON *THE MAKING OF BARACK OBAMA*

David A. Frank

B arack Obama appeared in a moment of history bereft of eloquence and in need of an uplifting voice. His literate and informed public speeches during the 2008 campaign placed the more plainspoken and clear reasoning of his predecessor, George W. Bush, and his 2008 opponent, John McCain, in stark relief. Obama was re-elected in 2012. George Packer, in a contribution to *The New Yorker*, surveyed Obama's rhetoric during his first term as president and concluded, "Obama has given . . . few truly great Presidential speeches." Although Packard praises Obama as "the best writer-President since Lincoln, it's not because of an extraordinary gift for language—it's because of his breadth of experience and depth of thought."[1] Packer claims, "Obama is too complex, too nuanced, too elusive, and too careful, for words that stick."[2] Packer implies that complex, nuanced, and careful thought may not survive their translation into great presidential speeches.

Harvard historian James Kloppenberg, in his book *Reading Obama: Dreams, Hopes, and the American Political Tradition*, argues that Obama is a "philosopher president" who has read, understood, and internalized the writings of John Rawls, Eugene Weber, Fredric Nietzsche, Thoreau, Emerson, Langston Hughes, Ralph Ellison, and others.[3] Witness how Kloppenberg frames rhetoric in his book. Rhetoric, according to Kloppenberg, is a synonym for "unyielding partisanship" that combines to displace "reasoned deliberation;" rhetoric, in his estimation, is "charming but empty."[4] Unlike Kloppenberg, Packer recognizes "great political speechmaking depends on turns of phrase joined to profound ideas that answer the pressures of a historical moment." Obama poses a significant challenge to rhetorical critics, as the poetry of his campaign speeches often trumped in quality and effectiveness the prose of his presidential addresses. In his best public speeches, Obama effectively intertwines poetry and prose, expressing his powerful intellect in symbols that can be understood and acted on by his audience.

The Making of Barack Obama is dedicated to the proposition that Obama is a rhetorician *par excellence*. The editors of this book have assembled an impressive set of essays explaining how Obama has sought his persuasive ends, a different agenda than Kloppenberg. In Kloppenberg, Obama's situated audiences do not affect his reading or how he adapts his ideas to people. The essays in this book, both individually and collectively, are tethered to the goal of analyzing key speeches of candidate and then President Barack Obama. *The Making of Barack Obama: The Politics of Persuasion* offers thoughtful insight on Obama's powers of persuasion, providing useful explanations of his command of language and symbols as he uses them to persuade audiences to action. In what follows, I distill what rhetorical critics can learn from this book. In short, *The Making of Barack Obama* deepens the line of thought highlighted by Packer, offering the rhetorical complement to Kloppenberg's more philosophically oriented *Reading Obama*, and also provides a rhetorical history challenging Packer's assertions.

The book provides a history that allows rhetorical critics to consider the trajectory of Obama's rhetoric. The first two chapters offer proof for the adage that politicians campaign in poetry and govern in prose. Obama's campaign rhetoric is aspirational; one function of campaign rhetoric is that it is designed to excite with upward inflected and uplifting myths. Jue demonstrates that the "Yes We Can" slogan serves as a foundational, symbolic anchor, helping to constitute the identity of his audiences, and allowing him to represent their interests and visions in his campaign. The slogan does not declare *what* his audience is or can do. Rather, the slogan counters the cynicism that appeared in the wake of the Bush administration to motivate his audience to join him. With this slogan, Obama outlines a vision of agency and optimism. Obama embellishes the "Yes We Can" slogan with a second, "We are the ones we've been waiting for," borrowed from a civil rights song. The slogan gives his audience agency; it refutes and inoculates against the claim that change must come from outside, from a great leader. McCain, as Jue demonstrates, uses the "I" rather than "we" to set forth his vision of agency.

Obama's campaign rhetoric, with the "Yes We Can" slogan, served a cathartic purpose. The slogan suggests the problems his audience faces will yield to solutions, justifying optimism and a buoyant outlook. Obama appropriates Reagan's optimism, urging Americans to believe they could rise to the crises they faced. He has certainly not adopted Reagan's understanding of government, foreign affairs, or any other substantive public policy advocated by "The Great Communicator." Jue helps us understand how the "Yes We Can" slogan allows Obama to conflate his persona with that of his audience, achieving a sense of what Burke terms as "consubstantiation." Campaign slogans often do not survive after election.

Rowland, in the most thorough study of the claim I have read that Obama's presidential rhetoric has been ineffective and flaccid, provides, in his chapter, striking insight into the constraints faced by Obama after his January 2009 inaugural. Rowland considers what scholarly studies of the rhetorical presidency often fail to fully consider: the very real obstacles to persuasion faced by a president. Krugman, Dowd, and other critics who damn Obama's failure to persuade, or who believe the rhetoric does not help presidents (like George Edwards), do not account for the audiences who may be beyond the pale of persuasion. The audience, rather than the speaker, fossilized attitudes, or rhetoric, may be the culprits. The key point Rowland makes—one that should be the prism through which rhetorical criticism takes place—is that the success or failure of Obama's rhetoric must take into account the constraints he faces.

Jasso and Wachs track the appointments of Catholics to key positions in the Obama administration. Their analysis, with many intriguing rhetorical implications, is that the appointments provide the elements of "a compelling narrative that tells the story of a developing relationship between the President, Catholic voters and official voices of the Catholic Church." They note an initial pattern appointing Catholics to important posts, representing the dissident wing, followed by appointments acceptable to conservative Catholics.

Jasso and Wachs offer several explanations of this trajectory. I believe the most plausible one, based on Obama's rhetorical signature, is that the "later appointees were indeed different in their adherence to Catholic doctrine, not as a product of discovery, but rather out of a shrewd political calculation that allowed him to 'come to a realization' of what genuine dialogue meant only after his most important policy posts were already filled by dissident Catholic voices." My belief is justified by Medhurst's important analysis of the approach taken by Obama toward Protestant Evangelicals during the 2008 election.[5] Rather than avoiding or "writing off" evangelicals, Obama, who self-identifies as a progressive Christian, reached out to Evangelicals, winning more votes from the group than previous democratic presidential nominees. He selected an Evangelical to offer the initial prayer, and a progressive Christian to deliver the benediction at his inaugural. His appointment of both progressive and conservative Catholics is consistent with a theological consilience he seems to embrace.

Steven Salaita, in a footnote of his contribution, notes that Republican Colin Powell, a former member of the Bush administration, offered a moral and powerful answer to the "criticism" Obama was a Muslim: "Well, he's not a Muslim. He's a Christian. He's always been a Christian. But the right answer is, Well, what if he is? Is there something wrong with being a Muslim in America? Is there something wrong with some seven year old Muslim-American kid believing that he could be president?" In response to this "charge," Obama responded by declaring he is a practicing Christian. Salaita is right to criticize Obama and his campaign for failing to adopt the approach taken by Powell.

In his 2008 "More Perfect Union" speech and his inaugural address, Obama elegantly outlines how it was both possible and desirable for Americans to acknowledge the coexistence of different ethnic and racial identities. By "refuting" the "charge" he is a Muslim by simply stating that he is a practicing Christian, as Salaita argues in his essay, Obama grants, with his silence, a pejorative interpretation of Islam. Salaita rightly argues that expressions of orientalist and Islamaphobia should be rooted out. Obama, and those who defended him by reflexively claiming he is a Christian without affirming, as Colin Powell did, Islam, betray the cosmopolitan values Obama rightly celebrates in his campaign speeches and inaugural address.

Obama's "A More Perfect Union" speech has received significant attention from rhetorical critics. Smith adds his voice to the conversation with a thoughtful meditation on the address by highlighting the speech's strengths and weaknesses. Among the numerous strengths, Smith notes that the speech encourages Americans to begin a discussion about race, that Americans would need to collaborate to attack racism, and that the speech affects an "air of neutral culpability."

I appreciate Smith's effort to tease out the complicated threads of the speech, refusing to meld them to a simplistic judgment of praise or blame. Drawing on his experience as a diversity officer and the chairman of a diversity committee, Smith enters the rhetorical situation faced by Obama, allowing him to empathize with Obama's rhetorical aspirations. Smith calls on the work of Barber and the notion of "strong democracy" to identify citizens not as great leaders, but as the agents of change. "This is a speech," writes Smith, "that both explains the racial condition in America and invokes the American citizenry to stand together to do something about it." Drawing on Rowland and Jones's excellent analysis of the same speech, Smith, in a nicely written conclusion, suggests that Obama "sets the stage for American citizens—black and white—to be a collective savior through dialogue and understanding." Smith tempers his consideration of Obama's aspirations with some deserved skepticism.

Richard Marback, in his contribution on Obama's response to the Bush administration's policy on torture, unearths an anxiety faced by scholars of rhetoric. Jeffrey Tulis and George Edwards have challenged the notion of the "rhetorical presidency" on two levels. Tulis, Marback notes, sees great danger in a president's appeal to popular opinion. When successful, such appeals, argues Tulis, sacrifice deliberative discourse on the altar of public persuasion, shortcutting rational decision-making. Edwards takes a different tact, claiming that presidential rhetoric does not persuade or move audiences to action. Marback's study of Obama's rhetoric on the issue of torture revolves around a series of paradoxes. George Bush, Marback claims, had greater persuasive success than Obama, but was less eloquent. Bush was better able to persuade than Obama because Bush "disregarded persuasion." Here, Marback has introduced some truly novel ideas.

George W. Bush, Marback observes, reduces the powers of the president to that of an absolute sovereign in a statement made during conference press conference on April 19th, 2001: "I'm the decider and I decide what's best." In his analysis of an August 2002 legal memo, Maraback writes, "the president's executive power to decide the exception and justify the use of torture was made sacrosanct." Marback reveals how, with this policy, Bush "undid the connections between accountability and responsibility upon which agency is constructed and through which persuasion is pursued." In contrast, Obama banned the use of torture and views "persuasion as the product of rhetorical agents deliberating rather than sovereign agents deciding" by banning torture. In his contribution, Marback turns both Tulis and Edwards on their theoretical heads, constituting an important contribution of this chapter, one deserving of development and elaboration.

In his contribution, Michael Kleine examines Obama's December 1st, 2009 West Point Address. In the speech, Obama outlines his administration's approach to the war in Afghanistan. Kleine rightly identifies the many audiences of the address, including the military, congress, the American public, NATO, Pakistan, Afghanistan, and others. Perelman and Olbrechts-Tyteca call this a "composite audience," noting that these audiences call forth addresses based on pluralism.[6] Obama faced a rhetorical situation with a host of incompatibilities; the American public wanted disengagement, if not a policy of withdrawal, but Obama maintained a commitment to American exceptionalism. Obama's generals, who he inherited from the Bush administration, pushed for an escalation. In his address, Obama approaches this incompatibility by offering both an escalation and a targeted withdrawal.

To explain how Obama attempted to resolve such works, Kleine draws from the insights of ancient rhetoricians. With these insights, he describes the organization and lines of argument Obama uses to achieve his rhetorical purpose. The rhetorical techniques Obama employs in his West Point address are nicely illuminated by the rhetorical theories of Aristotle, Isocrates, and Cicero. In assessing the effectiveness of the speech, Kleine is careful to offer qualified judgments. While the address uses a "recuperation of classical rhetoric," it is far from clear that Obama effectively resolved the incompatibilities he faced with an initial escalation followed by a phased withdrawal.

Obama's April 17th, 2009, address to the Fifth Summit of the Americas Conference, held at Trinidad and Tobago, rehearses themes introduced in his March 25th, 2008, Philadelphia speech and foreshadows lines of argument developed in the June 4th, 2009, speech in Cairo. De los Santos, in his thoughtful analysis of Obama's first speech to the leaders of the Americas, joins Smith in seeing both promise and peril in Obama's rhetoric. "Obama's speech," de los Santos concludes, "does offer an impressive definitional shift for how the region must understand its history and its relation with the United States. If ever fully adopted, it would radically transform U.S.-Latin American relations." The peril Obama faces, as de los Santos explains, is the foundational, colonial assumption held by the U.S. that Latin America is barbaric and the U.S. is civilized. Obama, de los Santos argues, does not escape the gravitational pull of this duality with the language of cosmopolitanism found in the text of the address.

Obama's address, de los Santos notes, operates "within the 'barbarism-civilization' dualism." Although Obama calls for an engagement of equals and for a "new beginning," the implicit ruling frame of the "barbarism-civilization" duality dictates that the U.S. will determine the nature of the engagement and the structure of the "new beginning." De los Santos, drawing from Marti and the MERCORSUR trade agreement, offers an alternative vision of a Latin America that does "not need America or Europe to succeed—unimaginable to Americans like Obama." While I am not persuaded this vision is beyond the imaginative capacities of Obama, de los Santos offers Obama and the U.S. a touchstone that might be used to repudiate the "barbarism-civilization" dualism, replacing it with authentic engagement between two equal, autonomous, and overlapping cultures and economies.

Matthew Abraham interrogates Obama's Cairo speech, finding at its core a neo-liberal frame dividing the Muslim world into the good and the bad. The Good Muslim serves "U.S. interests as loyal proxies," while the Bad Muslim resists "modernity, seeks to demonize and delegitimize Israel as a Jewish state, and engages in and supports terrorism against the United States and its allies." Like the other contributors to the book, Abraham acknowledges and lauds Obama's efforts to achieve communion, but fears they mask an ideology unfriendly to the Arab world. He notes Obama's implicit defense of Israel.

Here, Abraham notes that Obama is on tenuous rhetorical ground. Abraham rightly notes how Obama renders the Palestinian and Israeli trauma narratives essentially equivalent. In so doing, Obama angered some Jews who heard him place the Holocaust on the same plane as the Palestinian tragedy, the Nakba. Abraham teases out the implications Obama leaves that Palestinians have as much power as Israelis, an empirical fact defied by the Jewish state's powerful military that is sponsored by the United States. Abraham could build a claim that the Cairo speech did not succeed with his Israeli audience, pointing to the refutation offered by Prime Minister Netanyahu the following week in his Bar-Ilan speech. Netanyahu argued that Obama failed to recognize the Jewish historical claim on the land. Most experts on foreign policy suggest Obama's major foreign policy flop has been the Israeli-Palestinian conflict. Abraham, in his consideration of Obama's Cairo speech, suggests that the speech, in mis-framing the Israeli-Palestinian conflict, explains why Obama's Israeli-Palestinian policy failed.

What, then, do the editors and authors offer the reader of *The Making of Barack Obama*? First, the authors encourage us to give Obama and his audience(s) agency. Rowland is correct in identifying the constraints Obama faced. At the same time, Obama's public addresses are, on occasion, flawed—some deeply so. Obama's campaign rhetoric, aspirational to its core, is often reduced to a "stump" speech with repeated slogans like "Yes We Can," certain themes reused, and a basic narrative refined and honed. The presidency, an institution vested with very real power, must respond to a host of real and variegated crises. No stump speech or simplistic slogan can frame the Israeli-Palestinian conflict or defend the Affordable Care Act. Obama's presidential rhetoric has been, as a result, uneven.

Considering the powerful constraints Rowland sets forth, some of Obama's speeches in the first term were flawed, and there are several plausible explanations. First, the rhetorical exigencies of the presidency require agile speechwriters who face rhetorical situations with severely restricted time limits to construct speeches. For example, Obama's Nobel speech remained in process while the presidential plane landed in Oslo. Similarly, an iteration of his "New Beginnings" speech at Cairo was composed in Saudi Arabia on the eve of the address. Second, Obama's speechwriters are young, often political science or international studies majors, who may help turn a phrase, but they don't appear to have sufficiently challenged texts or their boss to reach higher rhetorical planes. Obama appoints older, experienced, cabinet members to State, the Department of Defense, and other key posts. Third, a handful of Obama's speeches have failed because his reasoning has not met the exigency. Two of his most praised speeches, the "A New Beginning" speech in Cairo and his Tucson Memorial speech, I would argue flounder on weak conceptual platforms.[7] Fourth, and most important, presidents must develop a rhetoric for a composite audience, consisting of individuals and groups adhering to multiple and sometimes incompatible values. Presidents do not have the luxury of deploying theories of the world and persuasion detached from situated audiences.

The authors of the chapters in this book invite a deeper exploration into Obama as a transitional president, his use of reasoning, and the role of the contemporary rhetorical critic. Rhetorical critics, and I place myself among them, often draw on theories created in incubators full of rarified air—they are disconnected from the reality of the composite audience. While it is, perhaps, cathartic to hold Obama and other presidents to the highest standards of criticism and find them guilty of betraying the distilled, and often prophetic and demanding, theories of Edward Said, Michel Foucault, Jacques Derrida, Jürgen Habermas, and a host of others, such criticism often does not offer insights into how presidents are to persuade a composite audience.

More concretely, presidents like Obama and those who campaign for the presidency, must be anchored to the realities of white, working-class voters in Ohio and in other swing states. These voters are proud Americans. Some of these voters harbor xenophobic or racist attitudes. A minority supports Obama. To maintain this support, Obama cannot rehearse the themes sounded in the work of Noam Chomsky or other critical theorists. Consider Karl Rove's statement in a *Wall Street Journal* editorial. In the aftermath of Obama's international debut as president, Rove claimed that Obama had engaged in an "international confession tour. In less than 100 days, he has apologized on three continents for what he views as the sins of America and his predecessors."[8] The speeches Smith, de los Santos, and Abraham hear celebrating archetypal U.S. dualisms of "civilization and barbarism" and "Good Muslim and the Bad Muslin," are the speeches others hear as evidence that he is the "Apologizer in Chief." How, then, does a president like Obama, who must account for a composite audience enveloping individuals and groups holding seemingly incompatible views, engage in the persuasive act?

Obama's promise, to me, is his apparently sincere aspiration to reconcile opposites in search of unity. He uses rhetoric to fulfill this promise. The contributors to *The Making of Barack Obama* identify the opposites and antimonies in his discourse. To his credit, Obama has sought to use his speeches to reconcile opposites. He places this impulse on display in his 2004 speech before the Democratic National Convention, in his 2008 race speech, and in many of his addresses as president. Obama's inaugural address, a quite explicit effort to build from cosmopolitan values, establishes the rhetorical blueprint of his presidency.[9] Obama believes it possible to be both black and white, an American and a citizen of the globe, and that one can commit to local and universal values.

That Obama has not always or often been successful in affecting a reconciliation of opposites has led some to condemn the attempt. A plausibly better approach than the one used by Obama would be to use the essays by Salaita, Smith, de los Santos, and Abraham as models of criticism that pairs the promise of Obama's outlook with the perils it faces when introduced to situated audiences. When these chapters are joined with Kleine's effort to illuminate Obama's efforts to reconcile opposites in his West Point speech, it strikes me that rhetorical critics need to develop post-classical and post-postmodern theories to explain how opposites can be reconciled through rhetoric. Classical theories tend to favor a vision of truth as unitary, whereas postmodern approaches emphasize the indeterminacy of truth. Obama's rhetoric falls somewhere in between.

Rhetorical scholars can use Roland's powerful insights on constraints to place Obama's rhetoric, and that of the presidency, in its context. Jasso and Wachs offer an exemplary study of Obama's discourse as he has faced the constraints he encounters appointing Catholics to his administration. By using a diachronic rather than a synchronic approach, they demonstrate that Obama has sought to reconcile opposites over a period of time rather than relying on one particular address. Rhetorical scholars can also appreciate and draw from Marback's essay on rhetorical paradox, that effectiveness is not the only criterion that ought to be used to judge discourse. Marback is correct linking persuasion to "rhetorical agents deliberating," as opposed to the dictates of an imperial president, even though the latter may be more "persuasive." Finally, we return to the first chapter, Jue's analysis of the "Yes We Can" slogan, to identify Obama's rhetorical DNA that draws from the optimism of Reagan—the principles of prophetic theology and a modestly progressive theory of the economy. Ultimately, I leave the book inspired to think through how presidents deal with the challenge of reconciling opposites and the rhetorical problem of the composite audience.

Readers of *The Making of Barack Obama* will leave it with a deeper appreciation of Obama's rhetoric and how it has made him. Arriving at an important moment in the unfolding of the Obama phenomenon, this book captures how a diverse collection of rhetorical scholars explain and judge Obama's rhetoric. These explanations and judgments offer touchstones for rhetorical scholars who will draw from them in subsequent studies of presidential rhetoric. The book also offers the general audience insights into Obama's successes and failures as a rhetorician. That the book ably addresses a truly composite audience is a testament to its success.

NOTES

1. George Packer, "Can Obama Speak to History in His Second Inaugural?," *New Yorker* (2013), http://www.newyorker.com/online/blogs/comment/2013/01/can-obama-speak-to-history-in-his-second-inaugural.html.

2. Ibid.

3. James T. Kloppenberg, *Reading Obama: Dreams, Hope, and the American Political Tradition* (Princeton, N.J.: Princeton University Press, 2011).

4. Ibid., xxxv, 4.

5. Martin J. Medhurst, "Barack Obama and the Politics of Faith," The Obama Phenomenon Conference, Texas A&M University, March 4–7, 2009.

6. Chaïm Perelman and Lucie Olbrechts-Tyteca, *The New Rhetoric: A Treatise on Argumentation* (Notre Dame: [Ind.] University of Notre Dame Press, 1969), 21.

7. David A. Frank, "At the Limits of Trauma: Barack Obama's Tucson Memorial Speech, 12 January 2011," *Rhetoric & Public Affairs* 16: Forthcoming.

8. Karl Rove, "The President's Apology Tour," *Wall Street Journal*, 23 April 2012, A15.

9. David A. Frank, "Obama's Rhetorical Signature: Cosmopolitan Civil Religion in the Presidential Inaugural Address, January 20, 2009," *Rhetoric & Public Affairs* 14 (2011): 605–30.

GLOSSARY

Abu Ghraib: A prison facility in Baghdad that was the site, beginning in 2004, of human rights abuses committed by soldiers of the United States Army against Iraqi detainees.

accountability: Responsibility for particular actions, whether performed by oneself or by one's subordinates. A person who has accountability is someone who is held by others as in the position of answering for the consequences that follow from some action or actions. The person held accountable need not be the agent of the actions. In organizations with hierarchical structures, superiors are in the position of answering for actions taken by their subordinates. Such accountability can take a variety of forms. Hierarchical organization can displace accountability by making superiors more answerable for an action than subordinates. It can also redistribute accountability by making superiors and subordinates equally answerable. Superiors and subordinates can also, by virtue of their different locations within a hierarchical structure, be held to differing standards of accountability.

agency: The capacity to decide to take action and, in deciding to take an action, to become an agent of an act. Agency involves awareness of actions and the possibilities of their consequences.

Arrangement: Classical rhetoricians in both ancient Greece and in Rome had long been interested in the "canon" of arrangement (or organization). This canon, the second among four other process-based canons (invention, style, memory, and delivery), was perhaps most comprehensively articulated by the lawyer, statesman, and rhetorician Cicero, who died as the Roman Republic began giving way to the Roman Empire. Many contemporary rhetoricians attribute a "six-part structure" to him. Each part of the structure can be seen as a spatial or auditory slot that needs to be filled in relationship to the progression of the persuasive discourse at hand—especially with the psychology of the audience being addressed or evoked.

Below are the six parts (all of which show up clearly in Obama's "West Point Address"). First, the Latin name for the part (or slot) is given. Then the English name, plus an essential question that each part needs to address. Richard Enos points out that a part named the "*digressio*," or digression, needs to be included; such digression might not be essential to the advancement of the persuasion.

1. *Exordium* (Problem): What problem, contradiction, issue, or dispute will the claim address?

2. *Narratio* (Background): What, briefly, is the history of the problem, contradiction, issue, dispute?

3. *Dispositio* (Claim): What, exactly, is being claimed? How will the following arguments be laid out?

4. *Confirmatio* (Arguments, including mainly data, but also, perhaps, the warrant): What arguments can be brought to bear on supporting the claim?

5. *Refutatio* (Refutation): What counter arguments might be posed? How might they be addressed?

6. *Peroration* (Action Close): What are the implications of accepting the claim? What should be done if the claim is accepted?

It is important to realize that the above arrangement structure is a kind of default, and that the parts can be rearranged to some degree. Furthermore, an individual part can be eliminated or diminished if rhetorically justified. Thus, it is possible to begin a persuasive discourse with the *Narratio* (or a compelling story), and then go on to use the other parts. In Martin Luther King's "Letter from Birmingham Jail," King relies hardly at all on the development of his own decontextualized arguments. Most of the text is advanced through refutation of the argumentative points raised by his putative audience.

Appointment: The presidential selection of an individual to fill a position; e.g., in the cabinet, judiciary, diplomatic corps, etc. Each appointment is accompanied by a press release, and often by pre-appointment speculation and post-appointment reactions. As such, appointments are viewed as symbolic acts of dialogue with the constituency to which it most appeals.

Bad Muslim: "Bad Muslims" believe in religious extremism, radical Arab nationalism, martyrdom, and even suicidal violence for the promotion of their political aims. "Bad Muslims" refuse to submit to the U.S.'s quest for dominance in the Middle East. Such Bad Muslims include Osama bin Laden, Ayatollah Khomeini, Saddam Hussein, Gamal Adbel Nasser, and Muammar Gaddafi. These "Bad Muslims," some of whom are not Muslims, have interfered with or resisted U.S. military aims in the Middle East through the support of terrorism.

Catholic: An adjective that denotes a specific religious identity; i.e., members of the Roman Catholic Church. While the term remains constant, both its substance and its use were hotly debated before and after the 2008 election. This book includes an essay that traces the rhetorical content of those debates (about what it means to be Catholic) as they apply to the president's political appointments.

Catholic group: An organization that is identified as Catholic and comprised of individuals who self-identify as members of the Roman Catholic Church—including laity and religious—yet do not speak on behalf of the Church itself.

Catholic hierarchy: Those officially holding offices within the Roman Catholic Church, especially those recognized as having the authority to speak with the voice of the Church, such as Bishops and Cardinals.

Catholic politician: A politician that self-identifies as a member of the Roman Catholic Church.

Ceremonial rhetoric: This type of rhetoric might be associated with public addresses oriented to the present, those addresses making claims of praise or blame. Contemporary applications of this kind of rhetoric might include funeral orations or written elegies, public-relations testimonials, advertising, reviews of movies or books, etc. The claims have to do with *value*. An example of such a claim might be: "Ulysses is the most important novel of the twentieth century."

coercion: To force or manipulate someone to do, say, think, or believe something that person would not otherwise do, say, think, or believe. Coercion need not be overt. Covert coercion can take such forms as peer pressure and administrative organization—both constrain people's choices. Coercion is not necessarily always wrong or immoral. The coercive power of the state, for instance, can preserve the rule of law. The coercive power of the state can also be used to undermine the rule of law.

coherence: Logical consistency in an argument. Coherence is endangered when false syllogisms and logical fallacies, especially faulty connections of cause and effect, enter one's argument. Often, speakers purposely use such fallacies as modes of persuasion, assuming that an audience is not savvy enough to pick up on a sudden lack of coherence in the speech. Attention to coherence is a large aspect of rhetorical analysis.

consilience: The construction of a theory or discipline out of aspects of other theories or disciplines. Interdisciplinary departments within academia are results of consilience. Such an act recognizes the intersections of various standpoints and outlooks. Agents of consilience recognize the strength and practicality in combining certain aspects of pre-existing theories and practices into a new paradigm.

constituency: A symbolic collection of voters identified by certain shared qualities.

definition: In rhetorical theory, definition is a topic of invention—a commonplace mode of organizing an argument—that focuses on the larger group to which a particular subject or thought may belong. The point is to show how this subject or thought is similar to other subjects or thoughts within the group. For example, if Obama can define himself by showing how he is similar to others in the group designated as "American," he can construct a persona more favorable to voters.

deliberative rhetoric: This type of rhetoric has to do with the future. It is this kind of rhetoric that predominates in legislative assemblies. With it we associate a claim of *policy*, or a proposition having to do with what should be done. Again, the legislative assembly serves as a kind of metaphor, and contemporary texts and speeches such as the recommendation report, the proposal, a family discussion in which a vacation plan is suggested, etc., can be classified under this category. For example: "We should begin to initiate air strikes in Syria."

discourse: Ideology is reflected in a mode of rhetoric, demeanor, behavior, concern, and even attire. James Gee, in *Social Linguistics and Literacies: Ideology in Discourses* ventures to call discourse an "identity kit" of sorts, "which comes complete with the appropriate costume and instructions on how to act, talk, and often write, so as to take on a particular social role that others will recognize" (142). Each belief system has a discourse, although many discourses can overlap. Knowing the constituent parts of a particular discourse can endear one to those who embrace that discourse, thus fortifying one's ethos.

division: Division can be defined as the lack of identification. The human experience is inherently individual (as a result of our physical bodies); thus, it is divisive in nature. It is rhetoric's goal to shift an audience from division to identification.

eloquence: A demonstration of fluency in presentation. To be eloquent is to be capable of an accomplished or polished style. Eloquence can be either appropriate and welcome, or inappropriate and off-putting. As a result, eloquence in and of itself is no guarantee of persuasiveness.

enhanced interrogation: A neologism for torture. Since the Geneva Convention outlaws the abuse, mistreatment, and torture of prisoners of war, the notion of enhanced interrogations was developed within the Bush White House to provide legal justification for such techniques as water boarding.

Ethos: The credibility or appeal of a speaker or writer. One often establishes ethos by placing oneself in a favorable discourse—a set of rhetorical moves, behaviors, interests—to which an audience can relate. In *Rhetoric*, Aristotle stresses that such credibility should be contained in the speech, itself, and not the prior reputation of the speaker (1.2.2). Thus, speakers must create a favorable persona within a particular speech act without relying on past successes. This understanding of ethos can release a speaker from the grip of past transgressions when speaking.

Executive Privilege: The power claimed by the president of the United States to suppress or withhold information. It is not a power explicitly granted to the president by the Constitution. It is instead a power that has emerged over time. Claims of executive privilege rest on appeals to protect national security interests.

forensic rhetoric: This type of rhetoric has to do with the past, and can be associated with courtroom persuasion (though the courtroom becomes a kind of metaphor, as do the other two "places" of persuasion). In forensic rhetoric, a claim of *fact* is advanced (e.g., "John Doe committed first-degree murder when he killed Joe Wilson."). We can use the taxonomic category to think about a number of persuasive addresses and texts. Academic or scientific writing tends to be forensic, and we can look to Martin Luther King's "Letter from Birmingham Jail" as a great example of forensic argumentation. (It is as though King is on trial!)

Geneva Convention: An international agreement establishing rules for protecting the basic rights of civilians, non-combatants, prisoners, and the wounded during times of war. The fact that the War on Terror is not a war fought between nation states has allowed some to argue that the rules of the Geneva Convention do not apply.

Good Muslim: Although Obama does not use the phrase "good Muslim" in his Cairo Speech, he references them by talking about the millions of Muslims throughout the world who believe in and practice religious tolerance, follow the rule of law, promote the rights of women, and believe in economic development and prosperity.

hard power: The use of military power, coercion, and threats to force a weaker nation to bend to the will of a stronger nation. The Bush administration adopted this approach to foreign affairs between 2001 and 2008. Hard power includes military force, sanctions, and severing diplomatic ties with nations refusing to comply with U.S. wishes in a particular region. The phrases "hard power" and "soft power" were made famous by political analyst Joseph Nye, who is the author of a several books on soft power.

identification: Identification occurs when two individual entities are united by common ideas, attitudes, property, or beliefs. When these entities are united by these commonalities, they come to identify with each other. Language brings these commonalities to light.

Islamophobia: Literally, "a fear of Islam," Islamophobia condemns Islam as condoning a culture of terrorism and martyrdom, an ideology that achieved some widespread circulation after 9/11. Within this ideological construction, all Arabs are perceived to be Muslims, even though many Arabs are Christians or secular. An extension of this ideological view necessitates viewing Arab men and women with suspicion, as potential terrorists or supporters of terror against the United States and its allies, and provides a rationale for racial profiling and possible internment. In his book *Islamophobia: The Ideological Campaign Against Muslims*, Stephen Sheehi conducts a careful and nuanced analysis of how Islamophobia promotes a particular political configuration conducive to the aims of U.S. Empire after 9/11, demonstrating that this configuration enabled the United States to launch wars for oil and territorial domination in the Middle East—effectively erasing the cultural differences between millions of people in the name of fighting the "War on Terror." Deepa Kumar conducts a similar analysis in her *Islamophobia and the Politics of Empire*.

Kairos: The rhetorical situation in which one speaks. *Kairos*—consisting of subject matter, audience, and speaker—determines what rhetorical strategies should and should not be utilized. Aristotle's definition of rhetoric as "the ability, in each particular case, to see the available means of persuasion," i mplies the concept of *kairos*; "the particular case" has both constraints and opportunities for one's use of rhetoric. Aristotle, *On Rhetoric: A Theory of Civic Discourse*, Trans. George A. Kennedy (New York: Oxford University Press, 1991), 36.

Menexenus: One of Plato's dialogues. It consists mainly of a funeral oration reminiscent of the famous one given by Pericles, the first democratic leader of Athens.

nomination: A step within the appointment process. Though not all people nominated are appointed, the nomination itself contains symbolic meaning. Consequently, failed nominations are also viewed as worthy of rhetorical analysis.

non-negotiable: An issue that is identified as definitive for a certain constituency and that cannot be compromised.

persuasion: The ability to gain someone's ascent. People who are persuaded acknowledge their willingness to ascent. Willing ascent is not necessarily the result of a process of logical reasoning. People are motivated to ascent to things by a range of attitudes, beliefs, dispositions, feelings, preferences, and values that can go largely unexamined.

political constraints: Typically, constraints placed on a politician by other members of Congress. Political constraints include an incredible rise in partisanship, creating a situation in which the president's opponents make it their top priority to defeat any policy initiative proposed by the administration, including policies that conservatives have long supported. Additional political constraints include: the sizable group who label the president as, in some sense, illegitimate; a group that often vowed to "take back" their country; the fact that it is much easier to demonize a policy than explain it; the gerrymandering of House districts that created a situation in which most members of the House of Representative were in safe seats; and the inflow of campaign spending produced by the Citizens United Supreme Court decision.

post-racial: An adjective denoting an eradication of racism and bigotry in the current period in American history. Many decided the election of an African American president would usher in a post-racial era. However, most people see this idea as naïve and wildly inaccurate.

racial reconciliation: The attempt to overcome racism through partnerships across racial and socio-economic lines. According to the William Winter Institute of Racial Reconciliation, this term has three parts: (1)

recognition of the system and institutional nature of racism; (2) support of authentic dialogue between formerly divided groups; and (3) promotion of restorative justice—justice that emphasizes healing and reparation over retribution—as an essential goal of anti-racist efforts.

responsibility: Responsibility is an attribution of culpability for an action and its consequences. People are said to act responsibly when they measure their actions against a consideration of the consequences of their actions. People who do not act responsibly can still be said to have responsibility for the consequences of their actions. It is largely in instances when actions have negative consequences that we are concerned about assigning responsibility. In cases when actions have negative consequences or in cases when people have not carefully weighed the consequences of their actions that we often determine responsibility by asking whether the people involved could have—or, in many cases, should have—acted differently.

rhetoric: According to Aristotle, rhetoric is "the ability, in each particular case, to see the available means of persuasion." Put simply, it is the way one uses language, in speech or in writing, to best persuade one's audience. Rhetoric, then, involves a knowledge of one's subject matter as well as an understanding of one's audience—what that audience knows, understands, respects, likes, and dislikes. Aristotle, *On Rhetoric: A Theory of Civic Discourse*, Trans. George A. Kennedy (New York: Oxford University Press, 1991), 36.

rhetorical presidency: A phrase made famous by Jeffrey Tulis's book *The Rhetorical Presidency* (Princeton, NJ: Princeton Univ. Press, 1987). The concept of the "rhetorical presidency" seeks to establish the rhetorical power of the president to reach out to constituencies within the public to solidify executive power against the other branches of government, especially Congress. The president is positioned to make direct appeals to the public when his domestic or foreign policy agendas meet resistance within the House or Senate. As Tulis writes, "Today, it is taken for granted that presidents have a duty constantly to defend themselves publicly, to promote policy initiatives nationwide, and to inspirit the population" (4).

rhetorical situation: This phrase was made famous in Lloyd Bitzer's famous article, "The Rhetorical Situation." A rhetorical situation, according to Bitzer, consists of an exigence, an audience, and constraints. Exigence is "an imperfection marked by urgency," some event in the world to which a rhetor is responding. Obama's Cairo speech, for example, sought to repair the U.S.'s damaged relations with Muslims throughout the world, particularly the Arab world. An audience may consist of an immediate audience, such as the audience in Cairo attending Obama's speech, or a global audience, consisting of those watching the speech on television or on the Internet at a later time. Constraints consist of material and attitudinal constraints, such as the fact that Obama addressed the Muslim world after the hard power interventions of the Bush administration in the Middle East after 9/11, as well as the more mundane constraints such as the audience's limited attention span. Richard Vatz and Barbara Biesecker have demonstrated the limitations in Bitzer's thesis, noting how the rhetor demonstrates agency in the process of framing the rhetorical situation, questioning the idea that the rhetorical situation is natural and evident. See Lloyd Bitzer's "The Rhetorical Situation," Philosophy & Rhetoric 1:1 (1968): 1-14.

soft power: Encouraging or persuading a weaker nation to follow a course of action set out for it by a stronger nation as result of the weaker nation's desire to emulate the stronger nation's example. Obama sought to use soft power in reaching out to various regions of the world, particularly the nations of the Middle East. As a renunciation of the hard power approach of the Bush administration, Obama's soft power approach has relied upon a rhetoric of partnership and cooperation to regain a loss of prestige and standing in the world. The phrases "hard power" and "soft power" were made famous by political analyst, Joseph Nye, who is the author of a several books on soft power.

sovereignty: Following Carl Schmitt, sovereignty is the capacity to decide to act without concern for precedent. To be sovereign is to be able to decide in any specific instance whether precedent should be followed or whether it should be ignored. Whether following precedent or ignoring it, the sovereign's decision remains sacrosanct.

special relationship: The United States and Israel are said to share "a special relationship." This describes the military, economic, and diplomatic support the United States provides unconditionally to Israel. Israel's avoidance of international law, particularly UN Resolutions 242 and 181, can continue because of the key role the United States plays in providing Israel diplomatic immunity within the United Nations. As a member of the UN's Security Council, the United States' negative vote is tantamount to a veto against any resolution in support of the Palestinians. The support that flows as a result of the special relationship is considered controversial in the Arab world because of: Israel's unrivalled military superiority—viewed as inflicting massive harm upon Arab populations. The 1982 Israel-Lebanon War and 2006 Israel-Hezbollah serve as two visible examples. John Mearsheimer and Stephen Walt's *The Israel Lobby* discus the U.S.-Israel special relationship in some detail.

systemic constraints: These include public lack of knowledge and interest in complex domestic policies, the failure of the media to cover policy in detail, and the need for sixty votes to enact any policy in the United States Senate.

torture: *Torture* is the intentional physical and/or psychological degradation of another. Torture is unequivocally banned by the Geneva Convention.

trauma: an emotional response to a trying and hurtful event that. If untreated, trauma can lead to mental, physical, and relational disorders.

CONTRIBUTORS

Matthew Abraham is Associate Professor of English at the University of Arizona in Tucson. He has published articles in *JAC: An Interdisciplinary Journal of Rhetoric, Culture, and Politics*, *College Composition and Communication*, *Cultural Critique*, *Arab Studies Quarterly*, and *South Atlantic Quarterly*. He is currently completing a book project entitled *Out of Bounds: Academic Freedom and the Question of Palestine*.

René Agustín De los Santos has research interests in the study of Latin American rhetorics, with a specialized emphasis on Mexican rhetoric from the late nineteenth century to the contemporary era. He currently lives in Chicago.

David Frank is Dean of the Honors College at the University of Oregon. He is the author of numerous articles on rhetorical theory and public address. He is co-author, with Robin Rowland, of *Sharing Land/Conflicting Identity: Trajectories of Israeli and Palestinian Symbol Use* (East Lansing, MI: Michigan State University Press, 2002).

John J. Jasso is a doctoral candidate in the Department of Communication, and a Master's student in the Department of Philosophy at the University of Pittsburgh. His research focuses on the confluence of rhetoric, philosophy, and theology in the ancient and medieval periods, with an eye towards practical application. He is especially interested in constructing neo-medieval theories of rhetoric for the purpose of critiquing contemporary popular and political culture.

Courtney Jue Sloey wrote the essay "'Yes We Can!': Identification and the Invitation to Collective Identity in Barack Obama's Campaign Rhetoric" to present at the Rhetoric Society of America in 2010. Courtney received her Bachelor of Arts in English Literature at Westmont College, and her Master of Arts in Rhetoric and Writing Studies at San Diego State University. Her research interests center around the intersections of rhetoric, politics, and religion. She currently resides in Los Angeles with her husband, and is working for a government agency in Public Information.

Michael Kleine is a professor in the Department of Rhetoric and Writing at the University of Arkansas at Little Rock, where he teaches courses in first-year writing, persuasive writing, composition theory, rhetorical history and theory, and language theory. His published articles have appeared in *Rhetoric Review, Rhetoric Society Quarterly, Technical Communication Quarterly, Communication and Religion, Journal of Business and Technical Communication, JAC: A Journal of Composition Theory, Journal of Medical Humanities, Journal of Teaching Writing, The Writing Instructor, ex tempore* (a music-theory journal), *Journal of Psychological Type, Centrum,* and *Composition Forum.* He has published book chapters in *The Philosophy of Discourse* and *(Re)Visioning Composition Textbooks.* He has published poetry on Italian art and literature in *Poem* and *The Formalist.* In 2006, he published, with Parlor Press, *Searching for Latini,* a book-length study of Brunetto Latini, the teacher of Dante.

Richard Marback is a Professor of English at Wayne State University, where he teaches courses in the theory and history of rhetoric. His most recent book is *Managing Vulnerability: South Africa's Struggle for a Democratic Rhetoric* (Columbia, SC: Univ. of South Carolina Press, 2012). He is currently working on a book-length project on the place of empathy in public persuasion.

Robert C. (Robin) Rowland is a Professor in and Director of Graduate Studies of Communication Studies at the University of Kansas, where he teaches rhetoric and argumentation. He has written more than seventy-five articles, book chapters, and proceedings essays, and has had research appear *QJS, Rhetoric and Public Affairs, Communication Theory, Philosophy and Rhetoric, Communication Monograsph,* and numerous other journals. He has published three books, including *Shared Land/Conflicting Identity: Symbolic Trajectories of Israeli and Palestinian Symbol Use* (with David Frank, East Lansing, MI: Michigan State Univ. Press, 2002), winning a national award for rhetorical criticism, the Kohrs-Campbell Prize. His most recent book is *Reagan at Westminster: Foreshadowing the End of the Cold War* (with John Jones, College Station, TX: Texas A & M Univ. Press, 2010). Based on this book and roughly a dozen refereed articles on the rhetoric of President Reagan, he was asked to present the keynote in a panel on Reagan's rhetoric jointly hosted by USC and the Reagan Presidential Library as part of the Reagan Centennial celebrations. In 2011, the National Communication Association honored his research in rhetoric with the Douglas W. Ehninger Distinguished Rhetorical Scholar Award.

Erec Smith is an Assistant Professor of English and Writing at York College of Pennsylvania. Smith has published on the connections of rhetoric and Buddhist philosophy. As a rhetorician and former diversity officer, Smith sees fecundity in the rhetorical analysis of diversity and identity constructions. He is currently exploring and publishing in Fat Studies and the effects of being labeled and self-identifying as "fat." Smith is an editor for *College Composition and Communication*, and sits on the executive board of Spells Writing Lab, a community writing center based in Philadelphia.

Anthony M. Wachs is an Assistant Professor and the Director of Forensics in the Department of Languages, Literature, and Communication Studies at Northern State University. He completed his doctoral studies in rhetoric from Duquesne University, with an emphasis in the rhetoric of technology. His research agenda is focused on the intersection of Catholic humanism and media ecology. In particular, he analyzes how technologies and media influence human culture and lived experience.

INDEX

CPSIA information can be obtained at www.ICGtesting.com
Printed in the USA
LVOW12s1508280913

354572LV00003B/15/P